Empowered Equines

Jessica Gonzalez

Foreword by Shawna Karrasch

Dedication

I dedicate this book and my whole life to a group of special horses who have guided me down this path. Every equine who has entered my life has shaped me into who I am today, teaching me the lessons and techniques I try to share in this book. Our equine rescue program can only save so many individuals, so I hope the ideas and concepts shared here will carry on to help so many more equines stay in wonderful homes and reduce the need for rescues.

Table of Contents

Acknowledgments

Running a horse rescue is no easy task, especially when you're also trying to introduce a new concept to the whole horse world. It takes a farm full of passionate and empathetic people supporting the program as a whole. I can't thank my farm family enough for all the time, dedication, love and hard work they put in everyday. Our rescue program couldn't run without the caring support of my wonderful husband, Alberto. While horses were new to him, he has fallen in love with each special equine and welcomes every one of them into our family. He supports me in my ever-growing life-dreams in every way he can. He shares his wife and home with an eclectic herd of animals and a crew of kids and teens who volunteer here. You'll see many of these awesome volunteers pictured here in the book. I'd like to mention two in particular - Emerson and Larkin Michniewicz. These two sisters have devoted all their free time to caring for, loving on, and training the animals here at Empowered Equines Rescue. Emerson has found her life's calling here, and she is devoted to making a beautiful change in the horse world. She's been a huge support to me in listening to every rough draft of every page of this book! Through the education of these volunteers, students, and kids our program is able to make a much larger difference in the world of horses as a whole. We can only rescue so many horses, but if we can educate our youth we can really make a great change.

I also want to say a special "Thank You" to all my friends on the Empowered Equestrians group. I created this on-line community to provide mutual support for all the people alone in the horse world trying to transition to positive reinforcement. This group has grown beyond my wildest dreams and I've met some of my most special friends here. Here is where I met Shawna Karrasch, who was the first to introduce me to positive reinforcement. She helped me through my troubles and showed me all that could really be done with kindness and empathy. I want to thank Shawna, so much, for our continued friendship through all these years and the beautiful foreword Shawna has written. Here I met my friend Mary Richards, a zoological manager from Disney's Animal Kingdom, who helped plan the horse-related parts of my wedding and also edited this whole book for me. Thanks Mary! I also have to thank my wonderful friend, Janneke Koekhoven, the artist behind Fed Up Fred, a great horse comic promoting positive reinforcement. She created many special illustrations just for this book.

FOREWORD

When I first met Jessica on a forum chat. It was many years ago as she was trying to overcome a challenging behavior issue with one of her horses. Positive reinforcement as a training method for horses, was still relatively unknown. She took my advice and ran with it! Over the decades, I have had the privilege of watching this new concept grow into a ground swell movement in the horse world. There have been lots of people emerging as trainers and teachers in this new realm of the equine learning. However, no one has impressed me as much as Jessica. Over the years as we have grown closer, I have watched her soak up every bit of information from every source that she can. Jessica started a remarkably successful and active Facebook group called Empowered Equestrians. This has been a successful conduit for many newcomers to the world of positive reinforcement over the year. She continues to take all of the information and share it in a balanced and comprehensive way. This book is a collaboration of the things that she has learned, both from academic sources, like books, lectures, workshops and clinics but also from her real life experiences. You will learn the basics of behavior, science of applied learning theory, the neuroscience that is a part of every thing's emotional make-up as well as exercises to help you understand and the big picture and how it relates to your equine partners. Jessica is objective, humble, positive and tireless with her pursuit to improve the emotional lives of horses. I can honestly say, this book is a priceless addition in the world of equine behavior. As one truly begins to understand how they think and learn, it forever changes the way you look at horses. I already consider this book to be a cherished part of my collection and highly recommend it for both beginner and experienced alike.

~Shawna Karrasch

Author of "You Can Train Your Horse to do Anything", a former marine mammal trainer. Shawna took these positive reinforcement techniques and introduced them to the equestrian world. She started her business, On Target Training and currently she is resident trainer at Terra Nova, a large positive reinforcement training facility.

A few years ago I was pretty desperate. I had seen so much aversive training and saw my horse grow more depressed and pessimistic every day. He was considered lazy and many of my instructors who had taken over when I failed to get him moving or yielding, had started to get violent towards him. If that was considered necessary to succeed with him, I didn't want anything to do with success anymore. I turned to clicker training, but as Deejay was very anxious about food I needed help. The lack of clicker trainers in my surroundings in real life forced me to try to teach myself, but this turned pretty ugly pretty fast. The search was finally fruitful when I joined the Empowered Equestrians (Facebook Group) and Jessica took me under her wing. She was my first real positive reinforcement mentor. She inspired me with her creativity and optimism, and taught me how to look out for Deejay's feelings *and* mine at the same time. Through the years Deejay and I have become pretty clicker savvy and we're more on the same page than ever. Not only did he inspire me to go force free, but he also inspired me to contribute to the "equine revolution" as much as I can. With Fed Up Fred I try to bust myths and hopefully make people laugh as well as think. I love how Freddy influences everyone in a different way. Some people suddenly have a huge eureka moment where others will dig their heels deeper in the sand. But most people can share a laugh about it despite the discussions and I think humour is definitely Fred's strength. Jessica is now my dear friend and I'm honored that I can be part of this book through Fred. I still learn from her "express yourself!" Attitude without feeling the need to impress others or live up to their standards. The only one you have to impress is your horse and yourself.

~Janneke Koekhoven
Illustrator, vlogger, and professional positive reinforcement horse trainer. Artist of Fed Up Fred and organizer of the positive reinforcement library, hippocrit.tv.

Introduction

If we gave our horses the right to say "no", would they? How can we encourage them to want to say "yes"? Horses have been partners with humans for many centuries; they've worked our farms, provided us with transportation, competed for money and ribbons, entertained us, and even fought beside us in war. Horses and humans have been knit together through history, so tradition runs deep in our veins. They have served us well through the centuries. In our modern age, we no longer need horses to fill the roles of days' past. But that doesn't mean we no longer need horses! The time has come for the tides to change. Our partnership is reaching a new level beyond our wildest dreams.

We've seen relationships between humans and horses in books, movies and in our dreams that engulf our hearts with hope and joy; relationships of mutual love, trust, and pleasure. Many of us have dismissed this sort of relationship as a sort of childhood fairy tale that can't be achieved in real life. We were told from a young age horses need a firm hand, you mustn't be too soft, and never, never let them win - but when did we start fighting?

Fairy tales turn to heart ache when the bond is sacrificed in exchange for high powered trainers and competitive goals. A bond is built on a relationship of mutual trust, communication, and compassion. We think we can find this through lessons, trainers, competitions, or different styles of riding, but that's not where it is. The relationship, the childhood fantasy, is with the horse. Nothing more, nothing so complicated. It doesn't need confirmation with show ribbons or blind obedience from your horse. It requires a level of empathy and understanding often forgotten or overlooked in the modern horse world. So what is the path for this relationship, this communication?

Like any healthy relationship, it begins with a good understanding of your partner as a species and as an individual. What are their physical and emotional needs? While not all of us are able to study equine anatomy and physiology there are some basics we should understand. For the rest we have the support of professionals like veterinarians and farriers. Ensuring a healthy emotional life for our horses can be difficult. The horse can be exceptionally stoic, and those who weren't born that way frequently lose touch with their voices when they go unheard for long enough. It's important we stop and analyze our horse's complete lifestyle and ensure all their physical and emotional needs are being met. A healthy horse will lead to a healthy relationship between you both.

With this understanding we also need to learn to communicate clearly - this is where learning theory and behavioral science come into play. We'll want to delve into this to understand how our actions influence our horse's behaviors, emotions, and our relationships with them. We'll dig a little more deeply into equine emotion from a scientific perspective. Which emotions do horses feel and how do these emotions affect their daily lives? While we necessarily put a strong focus on the science behind learning we will also consider the ethical aspects of how we train. And while we want our training to be productive, we also want it to be as kind as possible. I find the two usually go hand in hand. With all the best training and management arrangements, there is still the chance of running into a few bumps in the road. We'll go over some typical techniques for overcoming problems and mis-communications. With a solid understanding of our horses, how they learn, and how we fit into their lives, we can learn to build that relationship we've always dreamed of, the one we always knew was out there waiting. We can develop true, two-way communication to build a mutually empowering relationship.

For those of you who don't know me, my name is Jessica Gonzalez. From the first moment my eyes met a horse's I knew I had found my passion. They were more than a hobby, more than a love, more than an obsession – they were my everything. I wanted to ride them, hug them, groom them, learn every ounce of information I could get my hands on about them. I went about the beginning of my horse life the typical way, taking riding lessons. I rode every discipline for several years each, learning the differences and details about each until I reached competitive levels, and then I moved on to a new style. While I enjoyed every minute at the barn, something was missing. I was continually in search of something bigger, something better, something kinder. I worked at many different local farms, some lesson programs, and other farms where I could work to ride. I learned a great deal from these experiences, but nothing was satiating that need.

When I was 14 years old I found an opportunity to volunteer at an equine rescue not far from where I lived. This was the closest I'd come to what I was looking for. I surrounded myself with old, broken horses who taught me all about life, love, and loss. Here I didn't focus much on training, riding, or competing, but rather on learning about the horses themselves. I continued volunteering there for over ten years (and I am still involved) and four of my horses were adopted from there. I carried on my equine career no matter where my life took me. While I was in college I found a job driving carriage horses in downtown Boston. This was the closest I could get to horses in the city, but the dark side of the industry took its toll on me. When I finally left that job I bought the horse I worked with, using all the money I had saved that he had earned for me in that time. He bought his own freedom. I then moved on to teach therapeutic horseback riding lessons. Many of my favorite lessons in that capacity were those that I taught on the ground, because the students worked eye to eye with the horses. The horse was not just a tool for their therapy, but a companion and friend to encourage them. This was among the most rewarding things I had ever done in my life. I'd worked so long watching humans heal horses – it was a beautiful sight to watch horses heal humans.

While I loved my therapy job, my life moved on for other reasons. I went on to work in other show and lesson barns, managing the horse husbandry side and teaching lessons. While I always loved being with the horses, things always felt wrong. There was too much force, too much intensity, too many horses who didn't want to be caught from the field.

In the background of all these jobs, I was undergoing a transformation. I was learning and discovering the very thing I'd been seeking all that time.

*We are only just **beginning** to understand the **power** of love*
Because we are just **beginning** to understand the **weakness** of **force** and aggression
-B.F. Skinner

I got my very own rescue horse to work with my own way. I wanted to do everything just right, but I had so much to learn. I began to intensively study horse training. I studied all the styles, methods, and professional programs. It quickly became clear to me that horses worked for us because they must through force, because we make their lives difficult if they are not compliant. This was a devastating realization for me. All the methods came down to the same bottom line; we will hurt, frighten, annoy, work or otherwise cause them distress if they do not comply. It didn't matter what fancy words they used, or what romanticized rationale they offered, the basic premise was the same. What I'd always experienced was becoming clear to me, horses only worked for us due to force and fear. I just didn't know or trust any other way until my horse pushed me to look further.

It was at this point in my journey that I discovered Clicker Training. The situation I found myself in with my horse convinced me that I had nothing left to lose by trying this radical approach. I'm glad I did. My horses became open to me in a way beyond my wildest dreams. I was finally able to have two way communication with my horses! I devoted myself fully to positive reinforcement training. I went to clinics, events, and demos, I read every book that even mentioned the subject. I devoured everything I could find about using positive reinforcement with horses, exotic animals, marine mammals; I even read extensively on the topics of ethology, biology, anatomy, and neuroscience! Then came the real test - I started trying it with my horses; as things evolved and I learned more it became so obvious to me that this was what I had been looking for all my life. I shared my learnings with the kids at the rescue. In turn, they started teaching their favorite ponies cute tricks and fun games. The rescue became alive with activity and everyone felt the change in the air. I got to learn on my growing herd of rescue horses as well as the rotating herd at the larger rescue, as I continued my education by teaching people and their horses locally.

About this time, I founded an on-line group called Empowered Equestrians, which was designed to be a safe place for people to learn about clicker training horses. The group has grown and blossomed, with learners and practitioners from around the world. The group has gotten so large, we needed to subdivide it in order to have focused discussions for people getting started, for younger members of the group, for various countries, for people interested in studying emotions of the horse, or people looking to read and discuss books on the topic. This group has provided me a window into the future, seeing all the great changes for horses happening globally.

Since then, I have moved onto my own farm, where we have a growing number of rescued horses, donkeys, sheep, and assorted other small animals. Our rescue is constantly growing and we are truly becoming a big part of our local community. We also have had great support from our on-line community of Empowered Equestrians on Facebook and Instagram. We have a group of dedicated young volunteers learning how to work with animals in a fun and positive way.

Our Future

Now that I have found this wonderful form of communication, I hope to spread the word about it as best I can, to anyone interested. I offer lessons, clinics, and demonstrations whenever and wherever I can. However, I do have a bigger goal in mind. We have founded Empowered Equines as a 501(c)3 non-profit business. We are building our rescue, rehabilitate, re-home program to help even more horses in need. The program will also include a therapeutic aspect for survivors of trauma. The students will help rehabilitate the rescue horses through an organized curriculum, based on positive reinforcement training. With the help of psychologists, therapists, and positive reinforcement horse trainers, the students will learn and heal themselves, while helping horses undergoing similar difficulties. We will also work to spread education about ethical animal handling and training to the general public, creating more access to ethical homes for horses.

Meet Our Herd

Revel, a Belgian draft gelding, is as huge in body as he is in my heart. He and I have known each other for years. I watched as he suffered a life of labor, used until his body could give no more. When his owners could no longer squeeze another penny out of him, they sold him to me. It took time, love and a lot of help from the vets and farriers, he regained his weight and body condition. With the weight he gained back, his heart and soul were restored. He is 19 hands tall and every inch of him is filled with love and play! Since coming home with us, he has learned about positive reinforcement training and how awesome it can be to love a human. He is a favorite of all the teenage girls who volunteer here, and he kindly allows them to climb all over him as they play together.

Will O' Wisp (Wispy for short), a Clydesdale mare, came to us recently and has come along very quickly behaviorally. Emotionally she was quite a bit slower in progressing. She was very introverted and reluctant to engage with people but has begun to open and has learned to use her voice. That voice is kind and gentle (but strong) and is so nice to 'hear'. While we've worked on typical skills for agility and riding, we've put a particular focus on teaching her methods of communication - this gives her the ability to have more control over her own life. Wisp has become so much more confident, friendly, and expressive.

About a year after Wispy joined our family we heard that her 'sister', who came from the same home, was now in need of a soft place to land. While similar in appearance, **Fable** (also a Clydesdale mare) couldn't be more different in personality from her sister! She confidently states her opinions and will tell us exactly how she feels. When she first arrived, she could hardly stand to be touched. While she 'behaved' well, she was extremely uncomfortable in her own skin. We put our strongest effort into showing her that life was new and safe here, and that her opinions would be heard and acknowledged. We wanted her to understand that there would never be a need to yell. With patience and understanding Fable has come a long way towards trusting us as she relearns old skills in new ways.

Gummy Bear is the playful nickname for our sweetest horse, a Percheron x Standardbred cross gelding. This precious member of our herd came to us rather suddenly. I woke up to a text message from my number one volunteer, with a picture of a sickly horse - he was at a holding lot on his way to slaughter. I barely looked at the picture before I dialed the number. He had to come home with us. He arrived a week later, and we saw what was truly in store for us all; he was massive and beautiful - and broken. He had been raised and used by the Amish, and at 15 was considered useless. When his body could no longer bear the burden of the labor his owners needed him for, they removed his shoes, cut off his tail (to sell for extensions), and sold him to slaughter. He has a degenerative disease (DSLD) that causes his connective tissue to be unable to repair themselves after damage. Most horses with this disease are kept in limited to no work most of their life - but work he did, until his body fell apart. His skin is soft and thin, showing every inch of the harness that rubbed into his body. His suspensory ligaments have deteriorated, dropping his pasterns almost completely to the ground. His back is roached, not due to poor conformation,

but due to compensating for the pain in his hind end. His desire to live was gone but we were determined to give him as much quality time as we could. He promptly received a vast array of treatments and procedures from veterinarians, chiropractors, dentists, herbalists, farriers, and so on. Over the first few months his wounds healed, his scars faded and his eyes brightened. Soon he was out playing with Wispy in the field; it was obvious that his joy for life had returned. Though his days with us will likely be limited due to his medical condition, every day he has left will be full of love.

Tank, a Canadian Draft mare, was my first horse and an unwitting guide on my journey to positive reinforcement. She came home with me as an alternative to being sent to auction, but it immediately became clear how consumed she was by fear. She imprisoned herself in her stall and could not come out; she was simply terrified of the world. Tank's fear pushed me to learn far beyond where I'd ever looked before. With adjustments to her lifestyle and a lot of slow, patient work we began to tear down the emotional walls she had built. As she emerged from her self-induced imprisonment, she blossomed into a magnificent girl, full of life and joy. Our primary focus was to teach her about the world; one step, one object, one event at a time. We taught her how to be curious, to investigate her environment, to control it, rather than be controlled by it. She has made a huge emotional turn around, and fear is just in her memory now. She has become our wise-woman, training all the newest students.

Viking was our magical unicorn who was never meant to be. He was born by the accidental breeding of a Shetland pony and Gypsy Vanner. He rapidly outgrew his pony dam and bounced from home to home, primarily due to his challenging behavioral issues. After a very poor upbringing his outbursts became so dangerous he couldn't be safely handled. Soon after arriving at our rescue we determined that much of his extreme behavior was caused by a neurological condition (Wobbler Syndrome). He wasn't aware of the space he was in and he had little control over his body -this frustrated him to no end. With the help of his special human friend, Emerson, a teenage girl who devoted herself to his daily physical therapy and training his

emotional control to help him learn to cope with his regular husbandry needs. Sadly, his neurological disorder worsened as he grew, and there was little we could do to help him. As difficult as it was, the kindest thing we could offer him was a peaceful release from his disease, so we said our painful farewells to our little magic boy.

After about a year living with the gaping hole Viking left in our hearts, an ad of a pony for sale appeared on the internet that caught my breath. It was her. Viking's mother, there was no doubt about it. We knew Viking's mother was a black Shetland pony named **Marshmallow**, and here was a black Shetland pony, named Marshmallow! It couldn't have been just a coincidence. After confirming her identity with her previous owner, we brought her home the very next day! She came into our lives like a tiny, fluffy, ball of fire. She is so opinionated, so honest, and so much fun. It turns out she bounced home to home most of her life, just as Viking did, being bred and popping out babies almost everywhere she went. She was a frequent visitor at the local slaughter auction, with a baby at her side each time, and each time getting bailed out just in the nick of time. After we treated her Lyme disease, mites, and thyroid problem, Marshmallow has become a wonderful little friend for all the young girls who volunteer here. She is game for whatever fun they have to offer her!

Punk'n, our little mix breed pony, is our little rocker boy! He came to us as an aggression case, angry and full of piss and vinegar. Luckily for him our youngest student (8 years old!) fell madly in love with him. With the use of positive reinforcement training, protected contact, and a lot of work on impulse control, this tiny team made massive strides in their relationship and communication. Punk is still wild and full of himself, but the rage has faded and given way to a desire to play. He progressed extremely quickly, learning every behavior in the book, but was always in a rush. He was always ready for the last step before he was halfway through the first. They put most of their focus on channeling his energy, teaching him healthy outlets for his play, and how to bring himself back to calm after excitement. This partnership knows no bounds; the two of them do agility, riding, trail (rides and hikes), tricks, and even mid-evening snuggles in the snow.

Sunflower and her baby **Nymph** (miniature donkey Jenny and filly)! They came from a terrible hoarding situation in Texas, young and untouched. This pair made a rapid turnaround with just a little patience and some of their favorite goodies. Nymph is extremely inquisitive and bold, quick to tackle new things, and always up for an adventure. Sunflower is slow and thoughtful; she carefully analyzes each situation and watches how Nymph handles it before deciding if it's worth a try. They are both as sweet and loving as can be, and always ready for snuggles, nose kisses and ear rubs.

Sugar Plum, a miniature horse mare, was our dear, sweet, tiny friend. She was the smallest in stature in the barn, but she made the biggest impact on us all. She came to us old and broken in the early days of our rescue. She was foundered at some point and had very few teeth left (and the ones that were left were malloccluded). She was as kind and gentle as a pony could be, but she was so, so tired. She had no try, no effort left to give, and it took every ounce of strength she had just to keep going. With adequate health care and a lot of love she truly began to open to us. She became quite vocal

when she thought it was time for her soup (a necessity because of her awful dental situation). We worked to keep her mind active with lots of brain games and problem-solving puzzles. She knew many vocabulary words and a few colors. She had the difficult job of training the younger volunteers at the rescue; while she had to tolerate a lot of their inconsistencies and extreme displays of affection, she also got plenty of extra goodies in exchange as they learned. We said a heartbreaking goodbye due to a choke we couldn't resolve, just a few short months after Viking.

Butterfly, another miniature mare, came to us at the same time as Sugar Plum. She was born in a terrible hoarding situation, but luckily, she was rescued in her early years. She spent most of her life at an animal sanctuary and sadly progressively went blind (due to a genetic disease). I met her at that sanctuary when I was only 14 years old, and we've been buddies ever since. When I grew up and was able to build my own farm and rescue, she and her best friend Sugar Plum came home with me. It was important that they not be separated; due to her blindness, Butterfly depended heavily on Sugar Plum. Separating them would have been nothing short of cruel. She has learned all the basic husbandry behaviors, but we put most of our focus on empowering her to be confident in her environment. Using scented objects and bell targets we've been able to help her learn how to navigate her world. She struggled with the passing of her friend Sugar Plum, but we made sure she had other companions; two rescued sheep who have proven to be loyal friends to her. They are soft when she bumps into them and so noisy she always knows where they are. While she previously clung to her friends for security she is slowly learning to be curious and bold on her own.

Twinkles, an Icelandic sheep, is the world's smartest ovid! OK, that might just be my opinion. She was born and raised to be slaughtered for food, but her likeness to my precious Tank caught my eye (maybe explain how you watched her from your window? That's a great story). She had to come live with us! Of course, she was shy and nervous... for all of one day, and then she realized how awesome people could be. Twinkles has taught me all about sheep - particularly how very intelligent they are. She has learned a number of cues, goes for hikes, and rocks the agility course as well as any border collie (OK maybe just another of my personal opinions). The loss of Sugar Plum hit Twinkles hard; she cried out loud for weeks looking for her. A few months after Sugar Plum's passing we contacted the farm where Twinkles was born to inquire about a sheep companion for her. The farmers told us they had a lamb who was unusually small and couldn't be used for meat - and thus, **Faun** joined our family! Faun and Twinkles became fast friends, though Twinkles isn't thrilled about sharing the attention. They're so much more fun and full of love than I ever imagined sheep could be.

PART 1:
EQUINE ETHOLOGY

In this chapter we'll discuss the foundations of what it means to be a horse. By studying ethology, we can learn to be better observers and interpreters of equine behavior. You can utilize this knowledge to best fulfill your horse's needs, both emotionally and physically.

Evolving Science

As we delve into the world of equines we have several areas to learn about to fully understand the horse as a whole, not just from a training perspective. We'll cover a number of scientific areas that enable us to provide our animals with the best, most informed care. We'll study ethology, anatomy, neuroscience of emotions, and behavioral science. These are a lot of fields of science to learn about and absorb, and it can seem overwhelming at times. The wealth of knowledge available to us is astounding. At the same time, this level of discovery and understanding allows us to reach more new understandings than ever before. With this information, we can approach our daily handling, care, and training from a factual point of view. This enables us to read between the lines when listening to a trainer and find the truth under the romanticized language. While science can often seem cold and devoid of feeling, it allows us to see our options from an analytical point of view and choose the most ethical course of action. There is a great deal of 'pseudo-science' in the horse world in particular, due to the industry's long and complicated history. Many traditions, folklore, and justifications of cruel techniques form the roots of the common myths we see in the horse world. My goal is to strip away the romantic lingo, find the facts behind these myths, challenge them with science, and find more ethical alternatives.

One key aspect to remember about science, regardless of the type or source, is that it is always evolving. The accepted science today may sound prehistoric tomorrow. Every new theory, new discovery, new link, new correlation and new understanding leads to more questions and more possibilities. Our ability to meet the needs of our horses gets ever stronger as science opens doors into their physical and emotional well-being. So we, as caretakers, need to be open and flexible enough to change as our education grows and as science explores deeper. It's important we don't get stuck in old beliefs or opinions, as new information challenges or adds to it, especially when these new realizations can benefit our horses. Keep yourself open to new information.

Now That You've Met Our Horses, Let's Meet Yours!

Equus ferus caballus. They are a romantic fantasy animal come to life with the most beautiful face that shows thousands of years of shared history and thousands more to come. Their regal body and strong back have carried us for so long, through war and peace. Their long, strong legs have taken humans new places, places too far to go on our own, places we have built our homes and lives. That being said, they are unique and complete beings in themselves; they are intelligent, social creatures with intricate social structures. They're all individuals, some bold and adventurous, naturally curious – while others are more cautious, gentle, and thoughtful. In a herd, they work well together, taking advantage of each other's natural strengths. Their lives in nature can be beautiful and fulfilling, but it can also be challenging, dangerous, and short. Their lives with humans through the ages has also been far from ideal; they have worked as laborers, soldiers, and vehicles for countless generations. Now, however, with technological and scientific advancements, the lives of horses in domestication are ready to take a turn for the better. We can look at the ideal lifestyle that nature can offer them, remove the dangers and challenges, and replace it with pleasurable enrichment and an incredible interspecies partnership. We finally have something wonderful to offer in return.

Each horse is uniquely individual, a combination of their breeding and their life experiences. Their genetic makeup predisposes them to have different levels of strength, stamina, athletic ability, conformation and temperament. Their daily care, training, and experiences can also influence these, which is why it's vital that we know our horses - but continue to adapt our approach to bring them to a healthy balance for themselves. We'll start by looking at the ethology of horses and how it should affect our regular care and keeping.

Horses are as different in personality, physical and emotional needs as they are in appearance! These three epitomize this. The tiny, cautious, blind Butterfly with her friend and protector Punk, a bold, over-confident pony friend, both compared to our playful giant, Revel. They are each cared for, handled and approached very differently based on their individual needs.

Ethology: the science of animal behavior and social organization from a biological perspective.

Ethology

For now, let's look at horses as a species. How do we analyze such a diverse group as a whole? Ideally, we examine how nature designed them and how well it works (or doesn't). We can then transfer this information to domestication and see how things have adapted or could be improved. We do this by watching and analyzing their behavior. This study is called Ethology, an objective and honest observation of animal behavior in a specific scenario. As we watch horses in nature or in our backyard, we can sit passively and record the behaviors we see and watch with an unbiased perspective. With this we can form a simple list and categorization of the behaviors for further study and understanding. This master list is called a "Species Ethogram". We can then reorganize and divide up the list of their behaviors to test hypotheses or provide clarity to a specific scenario, called an "Experimental Ethogram". When we list these behaviors we can describe them as either "exclusive" (where each behavior is listed individually-usually in a species ethogram) and "exhaustive" (where the behaviors can be lumped into categories for quicker and easier observations and assessments in an experimental ethogram).

Renowned ethologist Niko Tinbergen utilized the principles of ethology to understand each behavior more completely. His goal was to determine four aspects of every behavior:

- Function
- Causation
- Development
- Evolutionary history

Examining these four aspects helps us to understand the behaviors of our horses thoroughly before we begin to attempt to influence them. The function of the behavior is about how the behavior influences the individual's chances of survival or reproduction. Understanding the function can help us understand why the behavior is performed. The causation looks at which stimuli elicits the response and how the response has been influenced by recent learning. This is one of the most important considerations as equine trainers (which antecedents generally elicit which behaviors) in helping us understand how to inspire the behaviors we like and in turn how to reduce unwanted behaviors. Development focuses on how behavior changes with age and how early experiences influence their future behaviors. Understanding appropriate development needs of a species can help us nurture the young, and help us identify and understand the fallout when the developmental needs haven't been met. Weaning too early is a common example of developmental needs not being met; this can lead to the beginning of food-related anxiety. Evolutionary history takes a broader perspective in examining behavior. We look at how the behavior compares with similar species and how it may have developed through the generations. These four ways of looking at behavior often work together to fully describe and understand behaviors, so we know where they came from, how and why they work, as well as when they're expressed inappropriately. This is absolutely necessary for us to wrap our minds around as we begin to influence our horses' behaviors and develop a mutually beneficial and healthy relationship.

WORKSHEET

Observational Skills Part 1

Let's practice our ability to see horse behavior objectively. We can begin by describing what we see analytically. Try to describe the image as if you were explaining it to a sculptor over the phone. Detail shapes, colors, textures, and all aspects of the horse as seen in the images below - then practice with your own images. Take care to observe without interpretation - this can be more difficult than it sounds!

From here we can label the behaviors observed and make conjectures about the function, causation, development, and evolutionary history of those behaviors. We'll start with a simple cartoon horse, then a few photos to help us practice, then feel free to practice with photos, videos, or in-person viewing on your own!

Observations black pony, laying on right side, each leg stretched straight out, upper foreleg stretched forward, upper hind leg rested on top of lower hind leg. Belly is fluffy and round, obvious line across body from elbow to stifle where the pony has been clipped. Head is resting on the ground, thick forelock covering forehead and ear on the ground, visible eye mostly closed, ears softly drooped and turned backwards, nose elongated, top lips dropping down toward ground, facial muscles loose.

Label Rest recumbent (laying down)

Function REM sleep, allows them to recover and have energy throughout the day. Allows their body to rest and heal.

Causation Time of day, safe environment, feeling tired

Development Instinctive behavior

Evolutionary history Sleeping in short bursts and only while they feel safe keeps them safer from predators

Observations_____
_____
_____
_____
_____

Label _____

Function_____

Causation_____

Development _____

Evolutionary history _____
_____

Observations _____
_____
_____
_____

Label _____

Function_____

Causation_____

Development _____

Evolutionary history _____
_____

Observations_____
_____
_____
_____
_____
Label _____
Function_____
Causation_____
Development _____
Evolutionary history _____
_____

Observations _____
_____
_____
_____
Label _____
Function_____
Causation_____
Development _____
Evolutionary history _____
_____

Observations_____
_____
_____
_____
_____
Label _____
Function_____
Causation_____
Development _____
Evolutionary history _____
_____

Observations _____
_____
_____
_____
Label _____
Function_____
Causation_____
Development _____
Evolutionary history _____
_____

Practice using
your own photos

Know Your Species, Know Your Individual

Before we begin working on altering the behaviors of our learners we really need a good understanding of what their normal is. Starting by learning about the species is vital; we have our ethograms and case studies to learn about this. It's also extremely important that we know our individual. Learn about your horse's preferences and opinions. Learn how they structure their day, how they prioritize things, and who their friends are.

Do you know your horse's favorite food? You may be surprised. Do they prefer salty or sweet? Who's their favorite friend? Do they have priority access to anything in their environment? Or do they struggle to meet their needs? Is there anything that concerns them; sights, sounds, smells in the air? Do they prefer privacy or socializing? Do they like shelter or open areas? Are they playful or quiet?

Spending time observing our horses as individuals is crucial for our relationship and future training. Take the time to sit with your horses and get to know them. We can then take this information and compare with other horses and wider species ethograms. We can use this information to discover if our horse is healthy, both physically and emotionally. Knowing how they compare with the species norm can really help us to notice when something is going wrong. We can also use this information to determine which would be the best ways to approach training or options for reinforcement. We can learn which direction to focus our training and which situations to reinforce more or less heavily.

Spending time sitting with and observing your herd, seeing how they interact and prioritize their life can teach us a great deal about their daily norms.

Ethograms

When designing an ethogram we'll choose a subject (or many) to observe and a context in which we will be studying them. We may study stallions during courtship and mating, or mares while rearing their foals, or our own backyard herd at feeding times. If we are trying to test a hypothesis we may want a large and varied study group, while if we're looking to study our individual subject we may want to study them alone and compare their ethogram to a general species ethogram. This is commonly done to determine what behaviors are normal for the group as a whole. We can use this to assess whether our horses are happy and healthy by if they are expressing themselves in a normal manner. We could even pick a specific body part to study (facial expressions being the most common).

When we write the ethogram we'll list the behaviors we see and define them analytically - without assumptions or adding emotional context. For example, we might say the horse 'rolled', which is defined as "dropping from a standing to sternal position, then rotating one or more times". We wouldn't add "he enjoyed a nice roll" or "he looked like he was in pain", rather we analyze the behavior for just what we see (not what we think they feel). This helps us examine behaviors as tangible, definable acts, as opposed to using common labels or constructs to define our horse's behavior. Constructs can lead to emotional or biased interpretations of a behavior which can result in improper ways of addressing it.

We'll start with our initial observations, studying the animals in the context we desire, making notes and sketches (or photos). With these initial observations, we'll be able to list all the behaviors we may see in a longer study. Once we've identified and listed the unbiased behaviors we've watched, we can begin to categorize them. We'll divide them up as appropriate for our ethogram; there can be a lot of categories! Some common examples of categories include:

Ingestion: eating, drinking, foraging, grazing
Elimination: urination male, urination female, defecation
Locomotion: stand alert, walk, trot, canter, gallop, jump, swim
Rest: rest standing, sleep standing, rest recumbent, sleep recumbent, stretch
Grooming: roll, shake, auto-groom, mutual groom, swish insects, stamp
Comfort Seeking: back to weather, back to windbreak, huddle, sunning, stand
Investigation: sniff, mouth, lick, paw, flehmen, licking
Socializing: affiliative interactions, agonistic behaviors, vocalizations, parental
Mating: masturbation, mounting, mount attempt, erection
Play: locomotor play, object play, paw, object toss, rear, kick threat, bite threat
Appeasement: licking, empty chewing, averting gaze, turning head away, yawning, slow blink
Anomalous or Aberrant: self mutilation, crib-biting/wind-sucking, weaving

These are some basic categories and behaviors - there are hundreds more behaviors that can be grouped any way appropriate to your ethogram. Understanding how to categorize your ethogram can help you determine how your horses budget their time or how well they are thriving in their lifestyle. From here, we'll continue our observations, substantially longer, quantifying the behaviors we're seeing in duration or distance.

At this point, we have a basic ethogram summarizing the behaviors we're studying, but we may want to take it a step further. We may want to make an assumption, an hypothesis about the topic at hand. Is the aggression during feeding time stereotypical or resource guarding? Are these behaviors symptoms of pain? Do horses spend most of their day eating? How much do horses move in domestication vs. nature? We'll state our hypothesis in the form of a guess, for example "horses move more in nature than in domestication". At this point we'll likely focus only on locomotive behaviors and "everything else", putting in a substantial amount more observation time and maybe add more groups and variants to our study.

With a list of how much time was spent on locomotive behaviors during the day and how much distance was covered, we'll be able to compare our study groups (a few domestic groups in various set ups and a few groups in a natural setting). From here we can have a reasonable proof for or against our hypothesis.

Foraging: The act of looking or searching for food or provisions.
Grazing: To feed on growing grasses and herbage.
Auto-groom: Grooming of an animal by itself.
Allogroom: Grooming performed by one animal upon another animal of the same species.
Affiliative: relating to the formation of social and emotional bonds with others or to the desire to create such bonds.
Agonistic: any social behavior related to fighting. The term has broader meaning than aggressive behavior because it includes threats, displays, retreats, placation, and conciliation.
Appeasement: pacifying behaviors, to suppress aggressive behavior that might happen
Anomalous: deviating from the common order, form, or rule; irregular; abnormal
Aberrant: something that does not follow the correct or expected course or something that is not typical or normal.

WORKSHEET
Write an Ethogram!

Pull up a chair, grab a watch, a camera and a notebook! It's time to write your own ethogram. Find some time to watch your horse(s), varying the time of day you observe to get the full picture. Begin listing the behaviors you see and the time the horse spent on these behaviors. Define these behaviors pre-determined definitions from another ethogram (this sentence is confusing to me, maybe reword it?). Then organize the behaviors you observed into appropriate categories of your choosing. In other ethograms you can focus on different variables aside from time. You may choose to examine facial expressions, arousal, anomalous behavior, and then compare these by time, distance, type, or frequency of behaviors displayed, or anything else you're interested in learning more about.

Category	Behavior	Description	Time %
Ingestion 55%	Grazing	Horse bites and ingests grasses and other food stuffs close to the ground (scattered hay)	42.00%
	Browsing	Consuming woody plants and trees	4.50%
	Herb bar	Exploring and consuming herbs grown in garden	1.50%
	Mineral/salt licks	Licking salt or mineral block	0.50%
	Food puzzle	Interacting with food providing object, consuming food worked out	4.50%
	Hard feed	Consuming processed feed from feeder	0.50%
	Drinking	Consuming water from bucket or natural water source	1.50%
Rest 20%	Standing rest	Head lowered, eyes close, may rest a hind foot	15.00%
	Lying laterally	Lying down flat out on one side	2.50%
	Lying Sternal	Lying down upright	2.50%
Social 10%	Mutual grooming	Two horses lick, chew, nibble on each other, usually on each other's withers	2.50%
	Scent-investigation	Smelling, nose-to-nose sniffing, flehmen's	0.60%
	Vocalization	Nickering, whinnying, squealing, neighing, calling	0.60%
	Play chase	Locomotive, running together, mock herding behavior	1.00%
	Play fight	Bucking, rearing, bite-threat, strike-threat, kicking threat, mock agnostic behaviors	0.70%
	Resource guard	Agnostic behaviors displayed to defend a resource	1.90%
	Agnostic	Lunge, bite, kick, strike, pin ears, threaten and fighting	1.00%
	Appeasement	Moving away, yawning, empty chewing, lateral ears, snapping/clacking, looking away/showing neck, lowering head, licking and chewing, displaced behaviors	1.70%
Movement 8%	Walk	Four beat, forward moving gait	7.25%
	Trot	Two beat, diagonal pairs, forward moving gait	0.30%
	Canter	3 beat forward moving gait – moving quickly	0.25%
	Gallop	4 beat fastest moving gait	0.10%
	Jump	Leaping over obstacle	0.10%
Self care 7%	Rolling	Lying down and rotating sternal to lateral repeatedly,	1.50%
	Self-groom	Shaking, nibbling, licking, stomping to displace insects	1.50%
	Play (alone)	Running, bucking, object manipulation	1.50%
	Investigation	Looking, smelling, tasting, listening or touching new stimuli	1.00%
	Standing attentive	Standing alert, rigid posture, eyes open	1.00%
	Elimination	Urinate or defecate	0.50%

The Basic Needs of a Horse

Horses in domestication have a unique set of struggles, they are different than any other animal. They have had difficulty finding a category they fit in within human society. They are viewed as pets, livestock, sports equipment, and everything in between. Their lives can vary from near-wild, living in enormous pastures, and rarely, if ever being handled, to completely micro-managed, highly structured lifestyles. They all have their pluses and minuses. So how do we ensure all our horse's needs are met or exceeded?

We can start by looking at the foundation of animal welfare as a whole. What do our horses have a right to as our companions? Animal welfare experts, the Farm Animal Welfare Council in particular, have developed a list of what are deemed to be the most important welfare considerations for animals in captivity, particularly livestock; this list is called the Five Freedoms. These are: freedom from hunger and thirst, freedom from discomfort, freedom from pain, injury or disease, freedom from fear or distress, and freedom to express normal behavior.

Freedom from hunger and thirst: an adequate supply of food and water. Remember horses are trickle feeders, so it is critical that they have access to appropriate forage 24 hours per day.

Freedom from discomfort: Their environment and shelter should provide adequate protection from the elements and a comfortable place to rest but should not restrict natural behaviors.

Freedom from pain, injury or disease: It is vitally important that we educate ourselves about our horses' health, as well as maintain a knowledgeable and accessible support team of professionals for those unfortunate times something does happen. Along with your veterinarian and farrier, there are a number of new equine professionals becoming available, including nutritionists, dentists, chiropractors, massage therapists, body workers and alternative medicine practitioners. Compose your team to prevent and manage any health risks or problems.

Freedom from fear and distress: This involves not only ensuring their home and social life makes them feel safe and comfortable, but also the way we treat and handle our horses. They should never be afraid in our hands.

Freedom to express normal behaviors: Without the freedom to express normal behaviors, the rest of their welfare will fall apart. If they aren't comfortable or don't feel safe in their home and environment they will not be able to perform their natural behaviors, like feeding and self-care. We can create a number of artificial ways to give our horses the ability to express normal behaviors, even in the confines of domestication. Not all of us can design or afford the perfect environment, but we can make accommodations to provide for them - these will be discussed in more detail in the enrichment section (page: 19).

Many people struggle with discussions about the five freedoms, as some things are bound to happen; there are unavoidable situations or even simple accidents. The goal here is not to fight the world or build a box around our horse to protect them from everything. Rather, it is important to be aware of these things at all times. We must pay attention to how we, ourselves, treat our animals and how we can adapt this to best protect our horse's freedoms. This includes how we maintain their housing and lifestyle accommodations, as well as how we train and handle our animals. This can be a more difficult aspect to consider when regarding training. Many methods of training rely on making the horse uncomfortable or fearful until they respond correctly, but this, in itself, is a clear violation of the horse's freedoms. There will be plenty of unavoidable uncomfortable situations in their lives; the environment, social changes, medical procedures, and so on. We don't need to add to it with our training. This can be a more difficult aspect to consider when talking about training. Many methods of training rely on making the horse uncomfortable or fearful until they respond correctly, but this, in itself, is violating the horse's freedoms. There will be plenty of unavoidable uncomfortable situations in their life, the environment, social changes, medical procedures, and so on. We don't need to add to it with our training. We also need to consider the tools we use in our training and how they benefit the horse (if they don't, throw them out), this, of course, includes ensuring proper fit and padding, as needed (for more information on tack go to page: 189).

The basic needs of a horse:
The 6 F's according to Fed up Fred

Forage · Freedom · Friends · SaFety · ComFort · Fun

Recommended Reading:

Ransom, J.I. and Cade, B.S. *Quantifying equid behavior— A research ethogram for free-roaming feral horses*: (2009). U.S. Geological Survey Techniques and Methods 2-A9.

Sue McDonnell PhD *The Equid Ethogram: A Practical Field Guide to Horse Behavior* (2003). Eclipse Press.

Mullard, Jessica & Berger, Jeannine & D. Ellis, Andrea & Dyson, Sue. *Development of an ethogram to describe facial expressions in ridden horses (FEReq).* (2016). Journal of Veterinary Behavior: Clinical Applications and Research.

Leanne Proops, Faith A. Burden, Britta Osthaus. *Social relations in a mixed group of mules, ponies and donkeys reflect differences in equid type.* (2012). Behavioural Processes.

McGreevy PD *Equine Behavior – a guide for veterinarians and equine scientists.* (2004) London: WB Saunders.

Kiley-Worthington, Marthe *Animal language? Vocal communication of some ungulates, canids and felids.* (1984). Acta Zoological Fennica.

WORKSHEET

Equine Welfare Assessment					
	Dangerous	Freedom not met	Freedom Met	Freedom Exceeded	Notes
Freedom from Hunger and Thirst					
Body Condition	Obese/ Emaciated	Fat/ Underweight	Healthy	Nutritional needs met well	
Clean Forage Available					
Clean Water Available					
Freedom from Discomfort					
Skin and Coat Condition					
Thermal Comfort					
Adequate Rest					
Hoof Care					
Ground Quality					
Shelter Quality					
Freedom from Pain, Injury, or Disease					
Physical Wellness					
Tack and Tool Fit and Safety					
Freedom from Fear and Distress					
Stress-Behavior Frequency					
Access to Enrichment					
Freedom to Express Normal Behavior					
Healthy Horse-Horse Socialization					
Healthy Horse-Human Socialization					
Demeanor					

Time Budgets

In order to ensure that we are meeting all of our horse's needs and freedoms, we must first understand what are the appropriate behavioral expressions and time budgets for their species and breeding. Fear not! You don't need to spend endless hours out in the wilds studying horses (as awesome as that opportunity that would be!). Now that we know how ethograms are designed, and what research goes into their development, we can use other previous studies and comparisons to our own studies to make new assumptions and understandings. One major aspect we want to be familiar with as horse owners is about how horses budget their time as a whole.

If horses are given the opportunity, they will spend most of the day feeding. Feeding includes grazing, eating hard feed, browsing, enjoying mineral/salt licks, drinking or eating snow. Horses typically move a lot while eating, so this is important to mimic in captivity as well. We can replicate their natural feeding opportunities in a number of ways. If there isn't much grazing material, we should supplement with hay. Scattering it over large areas or putting it in many small piles can keep the horses moving through their environment. We want the horses to have forage available twenty four hours per day. More than a couple of hours without food going through their system can trigger digestive problems, colic, or ulcers in the long term. Of course, we should also keep their weight in mind. If your horse is an easier keeper, it may be helpful to provide forage in slow feeders. Ideally you should provide as many as possible, in all areas of their environment, to keep them moving. By distributing the daily forage ration among multiple feeders, you can ensure that their food lasts throughout the day. If it doesn't, you may need to increase the difficulty of your slow feeder (double nets or smaller holes). You also want to keep an eye on the social order of the herd and make certain that there are more sources of food than the number of horses in the herd so that no one is prevented access to forage. We can provide their hard feed in a number of enriching ways, which we'll discuss in the enrichment section (page: 19). We can also supplement their grazing with a variety of safe forage. Look up plants/brush/tree types in your area that are safe for horses and bring them clippings to enjoy. Many people even grow "herb bars" for their horses to pick and choose some of their favorite herbs to enjoy. Fresh, clean water should be readily available. If the herd or pasture is large, it's important to have a few locations to get water so everyone has access at all times.

Time budgets are based on healthy horses with free choice over their lives, things may change in real life. This is Sugar Plum, after repeated occurrences of founder, she rests lying down much more than a healthy horse. She is less playful and moves much less. Her time budget will be very different than her friend's

Our horses also spend a great deal of their day at rest. Horses sleep in short bouts, frequently throughout the day. They'll rest, standing often with a hind leg resting, and sometimes they will huddle together for protection from the weather or bugs. When they're ready for full REM sleep they'll lie down and snooze. We can assist this by making sure there are comfortable places to rest, shady areas, or warm shelters with nice bedding. In this

Recommended Reading:
Lee E. Boyd, Denise A. Carbonaro, Katherine A. Houpt *The 24-hour time budget of Przewalski horses* (1998). Applied Animal Behavior Science.

Haifa Benhajali, Marie-Annick Richard-Yris, Marine Leroux, Mohammed Ezzaouia, Faouzia Charfi, Martine Hausberger *A note on the time budget and social behaviour of densely housed horses: A case study in Arab breeding mares*(2008). Applied Animal Behavior Science.

Kiley-Worthington, Marthe *Time-budgets and social interactions in horses: The effect of different environments.* (1984). Applied Animal Behaviour Science.

case as well we want to carefully observe the social structure to make sure no one is being bullied or isolated and not being allowed to rest. A bad night's sleep or a few days of not being able to rest due to bullies in the herd can make for a very grumpy horse! Horses are absolutely majestic when they get moving! Unfortunately, they don't do it nearly as much as we would like. Movement is vital to a horse's health (as with most of us!) so it's an important part of their life we want to encourage. In nature, horses move while feeding. They can move long distances seeking out better food or water sources, move while socializing, and move in self-defense. A well balanced social unit will keep your horse pretty active, but you can supplement this in a number of ways, particularly if the herd is small or inactive.

Providing substantial space between feeding locations encourages your horses to keep moving and exploring. You can add a variety of enrichment objects that also encourage movement. You can add a number of environmental obstacles for your horse to negotiate, for example logs, substrate, or hills. Varying the terrain can keep your horses fit and engaged. There are also many designs that can be applied, even for small acreage, for encouraging movement within the paddock. Additionally, we can supplement their need for motion through our training. Keeping your exercise varied, utilizing flat work, obstacles, various terrains and trails are all great ways to keep your horse mentally engaged through physical exercise. If you're supplementing their exercise with training, remember that horses aren't designed for long, intense exercise, but rather short bursts, or slow and gentle. An hour of intense exercise can be detrimental to their health without proper fitness or dietary preparation. It's more effective to work for a few minutes, a few times a day.

Horses spend a small portion of their day fulfilling their own emotional needs as well, whether it be self-care, grooming, rolling, or playing. They take the time to enjoy themselves and defend themselves. When we see horses stop and look attentively in the distance, they may just be curious or feel threatened. They may scurry off, return to what they were doing, or approach what they were focused on for a better look. Providing interesting stimuli around the area can keep horses alert and curious, but be careful that the stimuli doesn't frighten your horse. It should be enriching, not scary (for more enrichment options go to page: 19). You also want to keep an eye on their physical maintenance - are they eliminating in healthy ways? (Watch for liquids that should be solids and pay attention to color, know your horse's normal routine to know when things are off). A depressed or unhealthy horse may spend less time on these behaviors. This is a big warning sign to watch out for. If your horse isn't taking time out of their day to make themselves comfortable, consult your veterinarian.

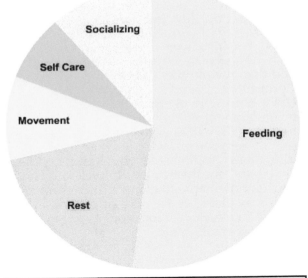

I put together this pie chart based on the ethogram I developed observing my own horses with the time budget averaged between my 8 horses. Time budgets can vary heavily based on the horse's age, gender, lifestyle, whether they're confined to stalls or have indoor/outdoor choice, whether they have access to all of the options at each time, how their social structure is set up...The options are many and varied. Each individual's time budget will be different and change frequently depending on many factors. These pie charts can help us see if our horses are distributing their time in a species-appropriate way and determine if we need to make any adjustments to their lifestyle.

Equine Social Life

While horses spend comparatively little time actually socializing, their social units are among the most important aspects for their emotional well-being. Horses typically live in bands; small family units with a male, a few females, the foals, and yearlings of the past few years. Females form tight bonds with other females and try to stick together. They tend to determine who has priority access to which resources (dominance) amongst each other and they stick with this set up - so there is rarely much fighting among females, unless something has changed within the herd. The fillies tend to stay with their mothers a bit longer than colts, staying for a few years - only leaving when they've joined another family with another male. Males, as they reach adolescence and then maturity, leave their mothers and join bachelor herds. They work together to keep safe while they search for their own females - but this band changes frequently and squabbles amongst each other are pretty regular. These bands must stick together for safety in the large, open areas that are characteristic of natural horse habitat. While **dominance** determines who has priority access to which resource, need is what determines where the herd moves and when. Whoever is in need of something, goes to get it - the rest of the band follows for safety.

How does this affect the care and keeping of our horses? Understanding how a typical social unit should work can help us determine the best ways to set up our artificial 'bands'. It can help to remember that there may be more aggressive behaviors in a bachelor herd or a regularly changing group. Try to keep friends with friends and those who don't get along divided. Living in isolation is no way for any horse to live. That being said, some horses just do not get along with the others available to you at the time. Keeping them safely over a fence, but within touching/vocalizing distance of other horses is a temporary fix. When

Larkin, Punk and Marshmallow spending interspecies social time

first introducing horses together there will be a few temporary disputes over resources - once priority is determined, things tend to settle down. Providing adequate access to all resources can ease the transition and reduce fighting. Watch to ensure that acts of aggression don't continue after a horse has backed down from the aggressor. Some poorly socialized domestic horses don't know when to stop. While we most often choose our horses based on our own desires, sometimes the horses we choose don't get along with one another. Pay attention and make sure no one is outmatched or continually bullied. If your group gets along, they will be happier and more confident, as a whole. Knowing there is safety in numbers is a great comfort to them. If they don't get along, it's important to find a way for them to still be close to one another - they may not be friends, but they still seek safety in each other.

We also want to remember that we, their human companions, are a part of their social unit as well. There is no member of horse society that actively trains and modifies the behavior of another horse, so where do we fit in the social world of horses? This is not something we have an even comparison to in a natural setting, so let's think about what sort of relationship we'd like with our horse. A healthy lifestyle and a happy horse is the rock solid foundation of any good human-equine relationship. If your horse isn't happy, your relationship won't be a happy one either. Any healthy partnership is always mutual, with two companions who love and care for one another. Many human-equine relationships can be pretty one sided, where the human half makes all the demands and the horse complies to 'earn their keep'. Encouraging a more two-sided relationship requires two-way communication. This can be difficult when one member of the relationship has goals and aspirations, and things they want the other to learn and do with them. We share a special place in our horse's society, one different than any other, we are our horses' whole world. We should appreciate our place in our horses' lives, so maybe we should be asking, what type of person does my horse want me to be? What type of relationship does our horse want from us? We can work together in an active partnership for something never before achieved between two species.

How Does Your Horse Budget Their Time?

Pull out your crayons and calculators! Now that you've written your ethogram of your horses measuring how much time they spend on each behavior, we can add them up into categories and determine how our horses distribute their time. Some example categories you can use are: ingestion, elimination, rest, self-care, locomotion, comfort seeking, agonism, investigation, socializing, mating, play, appeasement, displacement, aberrant, abnormal behaviors... You can organize any way you see fit to apply to the questions at hand. We can then compare this information to other ethograms and time budgets to determine if your horse's needs are being met or if lifestyle changes are in order.

**Remember to switch the time to percentages, in this case of a 24 hour schedule
        (1 hour=4.16%)

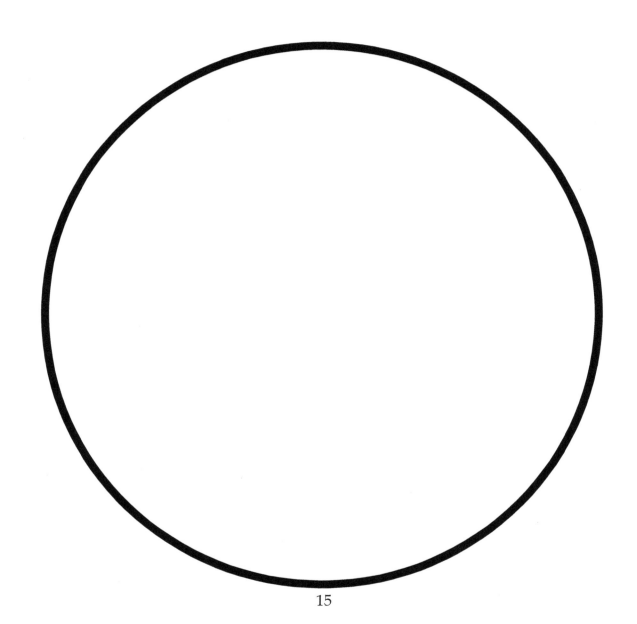

Dominance

We've all heard about dominance and leadership and how very important they are to horse training - but are they really? Old theories about dominance were developed in early observations with chickens (thus the term "pecking order"). Assumptions and theories were made about this and taken as fact. These old theories about dominance have evolved into modern (albeit misguided) training practices. These old methods often advocate the use of heavy aversives to control the animal under the idea of being a "leader" or "dominant herd member". Later these training methods softened, and through the use of threats provided the learner an opportunity to avoid the aversive, using a predictor of an aversive. They defend these practices by comparing themselves to dominant horses. Is this really as they make it sound or is this just distracting us from building our relationship on clear communication? What is dominance, really?

Dominance is related entirely to ownership, not leadership. Priority access to resources (food, water, friends, mates, territory...) comes at great cost to each individual. They must spend time, energy and risk of injury in order to earn these resources from their peers. When animals live in family units, bands, or packs, they pre-establish who earns priority access to which resources in order to reduce the cost to each individual (and thus the risk to the group as a whole). Most often, dominance is established and maintained by posturing and threatening. They do this to reduce the risk of injury in a family unit, but it may progress more aggressively if the benefits are perceived to outweigh the risk. A horse isn't born dominant or submissive, they learn to be based on the need. This happens more substantially in a domestic setting where resources are frequently limited and family units are replaced with whichever horses the human liked best.

This relationship between dominant and submissive can vary greatly. It can vary depending on the resource they fight over - my mare with sweet itch values shelter over companionship or food, so will submit to fights for food or friends but will always get priority access to the shelter. It can also vary based on mares' heat cycles; our usually submissive Clydesdale asserts herself when she is in heat and defends her 'resource' of being near our gelding. It can vary based on how the herd is composed - if two individuals want something they may fight off a usually dominant individual to get access. The dominant-submissive relationship changes regularly as well when the dominant member ages, becomes injured or sick. It can also change when the submissive one comes of age or finds themselves desperate. It all comes down to cost-benefit analysis. How badly do they want this and how limited is this resource?

"Linear Dominance"

Horse A
"Alpha"

↓

Horse B
"Beta"

↓

Horse C
"Gamma"

↓

Horse D
"Omega"

Originally it was thought all animals had what was called a "Linear Dominance" with an alpha, beta, gamma(s) and omega. It was believed that these positions were relatively fixed and determined by age, gender and breeding status. It was quickly disproven when watching animals in a natural setting. A number of other ideas and diagrams were put into place based on each research study. Now it's been determined that most species have a fairly fluid and constantly changing dominance structure.

Dominance: Power and influence over others. In our context, think of it as a temporary one-on-one relationship between two horses over who gets access over resources (food, water, friends) first. Access is usually acquired by the dominant horse though aggression.

16

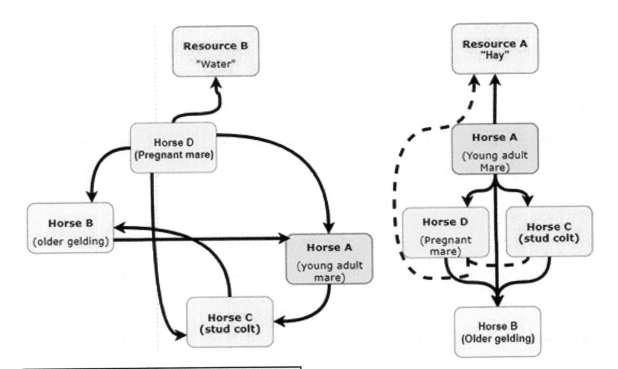

These are a few potential diagrams depicting how dominance can work with horses. Of course the possibilities are endless and relationships are ever-changing. You'll notice each situation changes based on the different resources. The resource truly effects how strongly the horse is willing to work for it. Particularly depending on how limited the resource is. The horse's wellbeing, stamina, and need for the resource can also change a preset relationship.

Resource A: is fairly linear with horse A having priority access over the others, except if horse C and horse D are together, then they have priority access to the hay, over horse A.

Resource B: Horse D has priority access to water over all the others. However while horse B has priority over horse A and horse A has priority over horse C, horse C actually has priority over horse B. This is where it can get a little chaotic.

Resource C: horse C has priority access over all the others, but horse D and horse A sometimes switch priority access, depending how they feel.

As we mentioned these are just a few of the limitless possibilities as an example of how fluid relationships are in real life.

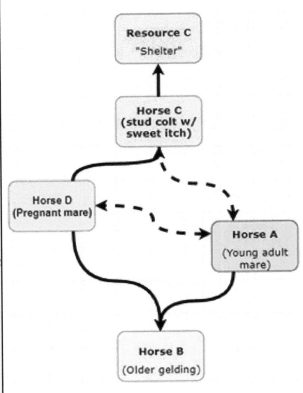

Leadership is different entirely from dominance. It was previously believed that horses had a linear leadership, meaning the most dominant horse decided when to go where and the rest followed. Modern research has shown however that horses have what we call a "passive leadership". This is where whoever has the greatest need makes the decisions, the others follow for safety. For example, a pregnant mare may need more constant access to water, so while the others don't need it, they'll follow her to the watering hole for safety in numbers. If any horse in the band spooks, the rest will surely follow, even if they don't know why they're spooking. It's safer to run than risk being wrong! So, leadership is based purely on need. They may even split up if their needs are extremely divided. Their desire to stick together is purely due to social bonds and desire for safety in numbers. The leader doesn't force the followers to follow, they follow because they must to survive. In fact, they're not really leading at all, so much as they are just satiating their needs and the others stick around because their needs match up or aren't so demanding at this time. It is ever flowing and constantly changing.

So how does this affect us, our training or handling? Inter-species dominance isn't such a thing in natural life, most individuals stick to like-species groups. While many mixed species may stick together in large herds, a dominance isn't generally determined between them. Larger species like elephants may easily intimidate wildebeests or zebra. When resources are scarce, there isn't a set dominance between the individuals. In more like-size species, access to limited resources may cause many a fight, but, because the individuals attending the dispute vary constantly, no dominance can be set. So, unless you and your horse are in a fight over the same apple, I wouldn't worry so much about which of you is dominant. In truth, we are the providers of all things to our horses. We decide when, what and how much they eat, go outside or inside, who their friends get to be and so on. **There is no need to exert dominance when we already control everything.** Knowing that we make all the decisions in our horse's lives, it's important that we take their social structure and social needs into consideration. Given substantial access to resources, a more dominant herd member can become less anxious, so they don't feel the need to hoard and defend their resources. This can make for a more peaceful herd life in general. This level of control gives us the moral obligation to meet all their needs completely and not be fighting them for the very resources we gave them! These resources are a basic right of life and not something they should need to work or perform for, these needs should always be met and never withheld for any reason (barring medical issues).

Our roles are unique and nothing as seen in nature, but it's special and beautiful when done well. What we learn from this all is that a horse-horse relationship is not comparable to a horse-human relationship. Previous training methods founded on ideas of dominance and leadership were actually a result of unintentional and often misunderstood reinforcement, punishment and conditioning. Learning about how horse social units work can be of great value in how we manage our herds. But when it comes to training and working with our horses, understanding learning theory is our greatest tool; using our brains, not brawn to influence their behavior.

Recommended Reading:
Hartmann, Elke & Christensen, Janne & McGreevy, Paul. (2017). Dominance and Leadership: Useful Concepts in Human–Horse Interactions?. Journal of Equine Veterinary Science.

P.D. McGreevy *Equine behavior—a guide for veterinarians and equine scientists* (2012). Saunders Ltd.

M.C. Van Dierendonck, H. De Vries, M.B.H. Schilder *An analysis of dominance, its behavioural parameters and possible determinants in a herd of Icelandic horses in captivity* (2017). Journal of Equine Veterinary Science.

L. Conrad, T.J. Roper *Deciding group movements: where and when to go* (2010). Behavioral Processes.

C. Sankey, M.A. Richard-Yris, H. Leroy, S. Henry, M. Hausberger *Positive interactions lead to lasting positive memories in horses, Equus caballus* (2010). Animal Behaviour.

Enrichment

There will be times we can't fulfill all of our horse's needs in a natural or obvious way. But, there are ways we can 'fake it'. We can provide enrichment in their lives to build their self-confidence, encourage play, and stir up curiosity. There are a number of ways we can enrich our horse's lives, aside from just providing food in enriching ways. We can mix up social arrangements, let them explore with all their senses around their environment, we can even give them cognitive puzzles! Please ensure your toys are safe for horses; no loops large enough to capture a hoof or anything they could potentially choke on. Pasture enrichment is great, but it's especially valuable for horses who are stalled for extended periods of time. These are not only entertaining for the horse, but it allows horses to express all their natural behaviors: pawing, rolling objects, shaking trees, and so on.

You'll notice throughout the book, we use lots of food in training and enriching our horses' lives. I've compiled a list (far from complete) of ideas for feed options to use in various situations. These are meant as additional feed to their main diet - however, there's no reason you can't use your horse's regular daily ration as part of your training or enrichment (so long as they always get all they need). Food in a bowl is boring! Make it interesting for your horse. Pay attention to which food items your horse likes best. While most horses will eat anything, there are certain feeds they'll work extra hard for. It helps to keep a chart (if you have so many horses you can't keep them all straight) of each horse's value of typical treats, low to high. There are times you'll want to use varying values, as you may need to reduce or increase the value depending on whether your horse is over-excited or disinterested. We'll get into this more later.

Enrichment Options

When picking enrichment for your horses, remember to always supervise your horse with new objects and situations. We want our enrichment to be fun and engaging for our horses - not concerning or upsetting. Be wary of any items that they could get tangled in, stuck to, hurt or choke on. The biggest key to enrichment is novelty, leaving a toy in the field for weeks isn't enriching any more. So, prepare several enrichment options and rotate them regularly.

Cognitive
Mental stimulation: puzzle feeders, positive reinforcement training sessions, stretching exercises
Novel experience: unusual food (seasonal crops), new scents, novel objects...

Social

Horses: time out with their friends, new horse friends over the fence, yard or on the trail

Other animals: meeting new animal friends, goats, sheep, chickens, ducks, donkeys...

People: their caretakers, trainers, kids, veterinarians, farriers

Activities: grooming, bathing, massage

Other: mirrors, pictures, stuffed animal toys...

Physical Habitat

Climbing: hills, rocks, ledges, dirt piles...

Substrates: dirt, sand, shavings, wood chips, gravel, straw, mud, pond, snow

Shelter: stalls, trees, lean-tos, places to get away from peers...

Sensory

Tactile: objects they can manipulate, jolly ball, door latches, leaf litter, brushes hung up for self-grooming, rubbing post, boomer balls, barrels

Olfactory: animal scents, essential oils, extracts, herbs, spices, flowers...

Auditory: music, talking, plastic bottles dispensing food, nature sounds, animal vocalizations...

Visual: novel objects, lights, sight of other animals...

Food

Types: apples, pears, bananas, watermelon, carrots, kale, romaine, endive, spinach, safe local branches...

Presentation: frozen/juice/ice cubes/electrolytes, puzzle feeder pureed fruit, shish-kabob veggies/fruits, hanging foods, hidden/buried food, floating food...

WORKSHEET

Safe Horse Treats

1. Apples
2. Apple peel (lower sugar option)
3. Alfalfa pellets
4. Bananas
5. Beet pulp
6. Cantaloupe
7. Carrots
8. Carrot top
9. Celery
10. Coconut
11. Cucumbers
12. Dandelions
13. Flax seed
14. Grapes
15. Grain
16. Hay pellets
17. Kale
18. Lettuce
19. Oats
20. Pear
21. Papaya
22. Pumpkin
23. Pumpkin seeds
24. Squash
25. Watermelon

Food Value Chart

Get to know your horse's choices and preferences with food. Practice putting different feeds out to see which they prefer. Mixing up which treats they get, in what enrichment fashion, can keep things interesting. Knowing their preferences can be a big help later in training. Try to fill in the chart below with the number of the treat you think your horse would like in which order. Then do some preference tests to see what your horse actually thinks!

This list is not complete - add any special treats your horse enjoys. This list was designed for healthy horses, if you horse has any health concerns eliminate any risky treats from the list. Make sure any changes to your horse's diet have been discussed with your vet or nutritionist, sugary, sweet treats should only make up a small portion of their daily ration.

After several trials take some notes on which treats your horse likes most and least on the chart below

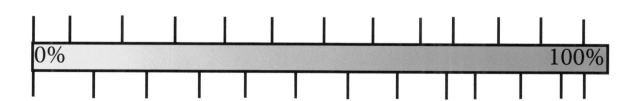

How to Build Enrichment Objects:

Box:

1. Remove all stickers, tape or staples from a cardboard box and fold the bottom shut (choose a fairly small box, not large enough for any part of the horse to get stuck on)

2. Fill it with hay and any variety of treats safe for your horse

3. Fold the top shut and let your horse explore!

Bottles:

1. Empty and clean plastic bottles (only use ones that held foods safe for horses - never any that held chemicals or poisonous foods for horses). Most work well with just the cap removed, but if this is too slow you can cut holes in the bottle.

2. Hang from fences or stall walls and fill with safe horse goodies

3. Let your horse enjoy!

How to Build Enrichment Objects:

Fruit Kabob:

1. Clean all fruits and vegetables safe and yummy for your horse

2. With a clean drill bit, spike or knife, poke a hole through the fruit/vegetables

3. String the food on a hay rope, using knots to separate or make it more difficult.

4. Hang somewhere for your horse to enjoy!

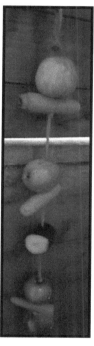

Novel Objects:

1. Put out safe, novel objects for your horses to explore and forage food out of. Dollar and craft stores are great sources for fun and cheap toys!

2. You can also practice with novel smells, food stuffs, and objects to rub on.

Domestication

Living in domestication comes with its pros and cons for horses and humans alike. We frequently question the ethics and morality of domestication. Is this really beneficial to the horse, or do we use it just for our own selfish benefits? There is a lot in the deal for us. From early civilization we've had domestic animals to serve our needs, mostly food and labor. Horses were primarily labor animals, used to transport humans and plow crops. In times of war, horses became more valuable riding and pack animals. They provided us the speed, size, and dexterity needed in war that cattle just didn't offer. Soon they became common transportation animals outside of war as well, shrinking the size of our world, by making travel easier. As uses for horses in war and transportation faded with the coming inventions of motorized vehicles and tools, horses became competition and leisure animals. We mimic history in our modern sports. Dressage utilizes the strongest and most athletic horses, as well as best controlled by the rider, just like what would be needed in combat. Jumping and racing tests the horse's agility and speed. Weight pulling competitions mimic drafts in farm work, testing their brute strength. Many modern Western disciplines mimic Old West breaking and livestock handling. The list goes on. But still we ask, what's in it for the horse to live in our domestication?

We provide horses with adequate care and protection from elements that living in nature can't always provide. As we're finding though, many of our adaptations in domestication often create more problems than benefits. Beautiful, lush and weed-free pastures can result in too much sugar, not enough movement and major health risks. As we try to give them the best we often end up inadvertently compromising their well-being. Luckily with this generation we have taken notice of these correlations and are beginning to do something about it. Setting up more appropriate domestic environments with track systems, better balanced diets, and socially appropriate herd management are just a few of the modifications we have made in an effort to improve equine husbandry. We are rapidly spreading awareness about proper care in domestication and life is getting a bit better for horses. There are many more strides our modern culture needs to make to help our beloved horses.

Domestication provides safety from predators, starvation, and weather - but it comes with other dangers; humans. Often our selfish desires result in a mindset of disposable equines. It's vital that we in the horse industry move towards thinking of horses as life time companions. It is believed that the average horse goes through over seven homes in a lifetime, with a high percentage ending up at slaughter or in other dangerous situations. These trade-offs are not much better than nature provides. So it's important we compare whether life with us is actually beneficial for the horse and make the necessary changes to ensure that it is.

The biggest benefit for us both, truly is our partnership. Horses and humans can be an amazing team. Through positive relationships we can help heal traumatic histories and empower each other to reach new levels of joy. It's important to balance our desires with our horse's needs, but together it can be a truly magical thing.

PART 2:
EDUCATING EQUINES
Why Train At All?

As we build a healthy and more natural lifestyle for our horses we may begin to question why or if it's necessary to train our horses at all. The truth is, every interaction we have with our horses is training. Learning and conditioning happens all the time, whether we are there or not, of if we intended to or not. Every waking moment of a being's life is a conditioning, learning moment (more on page: 33).

So if all interactions are training, how do we keep it kind, safe, and productive? Using positive reinforcement to train is an important first step, we'll get into detail about what that really means later. This helps keep training fun for the horse, making training an enriching and enjoyable part of their life - as well as building a strong relationship built on kindness. The next step is to look at which behaviors we're teaching and why we're teaching them. How does this behavior prepare our horses for their future? How does this behavior benefit our horses? Is this behavior just for us? If it is just for us, is it safe and fun for the horse?

There are many basic behaviors we need to build as a strong foundation with our horses, just to ensure our safety and ability to work together in the future. From here we want to work on necessary medical preparations, getting our horses ready and comfortable with their potential medical needs in the future. We want to help our horses learn about and become comfortable with daily handling, touch, farrier work, needles, syringes, and working around humans. These skills are vital for our horse's wellbeing while living in domestication. We can also teach some things that are fun and enjoyable for both of us. Building your horse's confidence in us and their world through desensitization and counter conditioning. Fun games like agility and eventually, fun cognitive training exercises can help keep our horses engaged, physically, emotionally and mentally fit.

Then we come to the behaviors that are just for us - riding, driving, cosmetic, or competitive goals. There is nothing wrong with these, we can achieve all these goals with positive reinforcement and a great relationship with our horse. This being said it's important we recognize these things are great fun for us, but may not be so much for our horses. We need to honestly look at what we're working on with our horses and whether they're really enjoying it. Think about how we can help our horses enjoy these situations more - or if maybe we need to look at something else that can be more fun for both of us. This is situational and something we need to look at independently and honestly ourselves.

As we begin influencing our horse's behavior we want to think about how we are communicating with them. How are we able to let our horse's know when they've done well, which behaviors we'd like to see more or less of. To learn this we need to understand how horses learn. Which is actually the same as how all animals learn! We learn based on consequences. We do the things that result in good consequences and avoid the things that result in unwanted consequences. Studying the science of how horses learn and adapt to their environment can enable us to train our horses with our brains, not brawn. We will focus on using positive reinforcement, which reinforces desired behaviors with something the horse loves. This style of training is focused on giving our horses a larger voice in our relationship. It's designed to influence their behavior in an enjoyable way for everyone, rather than as a form of control. Our focus is to learn ethical ways to encourage the behaviors we like more, while dissuading the behaviors we dislike. This new language will open so many doors in your training and completely change the way you and your horse view your relationship.

Overview of Using Positive Reinforcement

I have found positive reinforcement techniques to be the most empowering way to teach and guide our horses. It allows them the freedoms they need but still affords us the opportunity to achieve the goals to which we aspire. This type of training is not a method, it wasn't invented, designed, or owned by anyone. This is a way of learning. Luckily marine mammal and exotic animal keepers have done a substantial amount of research and experimenting into the most effective and practical ways of utilizing this type of learning with animals of all types. In this section, I've gathered tools, techniques, and information from a number of professional animal keepers and from years of practice with my rescue horses (and a number of other species as well!), but mostly from scientific research. We have a number of names for the type of training we use, some call it *Positive Reinforcement, Clicker Training, Reward based training, Bridge-Reward Training* and so on, we'll probably use most of these different titles throughout the section.

Clicker Training is essentially reward based training. We mark and reward the behaviors we like to encourage them to happen more. We mark the behavior with a distinct sound (or **bridge signal**) often with a clicker. The unique sound is **classically conditioned** (page: 33) to tell the horse that a reward is soon to come. Using this bridge signal we can encourage far more precise behaviors and by marking at the right time we can shape behaviors to be bigger or better in whatever way we like. We can also capture behaviors that happen naturally or encourage behaviors to happen by using a target or a food lure (page: 44).

Once the behavior has been reinforced, is happening consistently and correctly, you can add distance and duration on the behavior. This includes having the horse maintain the behavior for a specific amount of time or distance. We want the behaviors to be dependable and last as long as we need without constant reinforcement. With strong distance and duration we can reduce the frequency of our reinforcement, to a more comfortable schedule fitting our lifestyles (page: 80).

When the horse offers you their behavior completely and correctly, you can then put it on cue (a signal the horse connects with the specific behavior). You can use any cue you like, verbal, visual, tactile, or situational (page: 54). Begin by adding the cue while the behavior is being offered, until it feels like they've made the connection. Then alternate two different cues (touch target/back up for example) until they learn to differentiate the predictor/cue. At this point you're no longer rewarding them for offering the behavior, only reinforcing when the behavior was cued. You'll want to practice this in a number of situations, places and variations (from their back, from the ground, inside/outside, home or away).

This is all wonderful for training new behaviors, but what about getting rid of behaviors you don't want? While there are many ways to reduce behaviors, the most ethical options use prevention instead of punishment (page: 165). We'll change what's causing the behavior, prevent it from happening, train for the absence of the behavior, or teach a behavior that's incompatible. If it's a behavior that was being reinforced unintentionally, we can allow it to extinguish through a lack of reinforcement. Mixing and matching strategies (depending on the behavior) may be required for the most efficient results.

Clicker Training isn't always only about clicking and treating, or creating and eliminating behaviors, we aren't programming our horses like a computer. Rather, we are developing a wholesome way of working with our domestic animals that is safe and enjoyable for all involved. One way we can be more well rounded in keeping our horses happy and healthy is by providing proper enrichment in their lives (page: 19). A properly enriched animal will often have far fewer vices or behavioral problems. They're usually happier and more thoughtful; learning to problem solve and control their environments gives them self-confidence and pride.

Aversive Vs. Appetitive

Regularly throughout this book we refer to stimuli as "**appetitive**" or "**aversive**". These are big terms simply meaning "like" or "dislike". Appetitives are things we like, things that make us feel good to any degree, while aversives are anything we dislike, things that make us feel bad. Aversives and appetitives sound like they are dramatic feelings, but they can be anywhere between so mild they barely provoke a reaction to such an extreme they interfere with the learner's ability to learn or even function. We can use the learner's feelings about various stimuli to condition other stimuli, to inspire behavior, to reinforce, or even punish behaviors. These events also happen naturally, continually through their lives even without human interference.

If you take the time to observe your horses, whether in a herd or alone, you can watch countless displays of appetitives and aversives affecting the behavior and choices your horse makes. They will work to seek out and enjoy spending time with and for appetitive stimuli. For example, they'll walk to a nice patch of grass, spending time tearing it up and eating it. They may also search around for some interesting browse or spend some time socializing with a kind friend. They'll work to avoid aversive stimuli and reduce the amount of time spent tolerating the aversives. We see this often in the summer as horses stomp, shake, and roll to alleviate the irritation of flies. They'll seek out shade when they are hot or huddle together to escape the cold. This balance becomes a rather complex equation quite quickly. As the lure of the grass appetitive becomes more valuable over time as the horse becomes hungrier, it will eventually outweigh the desire to huddle with friends to keep warm, while the irritation of the bugs biting them adds up until they must stop eating to take time to roll in the mud to block some of the flies. This complex adding and subtracting of appetitives and aversives is a constant ebb and flow in the lives of all living creatures. Knowing how our horses feel about the various stimuli in their lives can help us in our training and handling.

While avoiding aversives and seeking out appetitives is a regular part of life, we as thinking, empathetic humans have the ability to choose which tools we use when influencing the behavior of our horses. Ethically we should choose to use the kindest and gentlest methods possible (page: 128). While we still want to get the job done we need to assess the behaviors we're training and determine how valuable the skill is for the horse to know. Is it for the horse's safety and wellbeing? How quickly must they learn it? Is this a cosmetic behavior or just for fun? Assessing the importance of the behavior we aim to teach and the timeliness of it can help us decide how to prioritize the behaviors we teach as well as which tools are ethical. For example, in our rescue setting we often have to perform aversive medical procedures before we've had time to properly prepare our horses for them. Sometimes we need to use more aversive techniques to ensure the future health and wellbeing of our horses. However if a behavior is just for fun or for our benefit, it's not an ethical choice to use the same amount of aversives. This can be a tricky balance to maintain and we need to look at our situations honestly, without letting our judgment be clouded by our own goals.

Over Threshold

APPETITIVE

AVERSIVE

Over Threshold

Aversive: any negative stimulus (a stimulus with undesirable consequences) to which an organism will learn to make a response that avoids it
Appetitive: An instinctive physical desire, especially one for food or drink. A strong wish or urge.

Do You Need to Use Food?

One aspect many people struggle with when starting positive reinforcement training is the idea of using food as a reinforcer. Humans have an interesting cognitive bias about using food to train animals (*"it's bribery", "they're just doing it for the food", "they don't respect you"*). I'd like to take the time to address some of these. Food is a valuable reinforcer, safe, strong, effective and ethical - the best kind! We shouldn't throw away such a valuable communication device out of cognitive bias.

I'll address these one at a time.

"Do I need to use food?" Well, no, but it is the fastest, easiest, cleanest reinforcer to use. There are thousands of reinforcers to use with the horse, food and scratches being the most common, but we have other situational reinforcers, such as opening the door, turning out with friends, and anything the horse wants in a given scenario. But what's the one thing our horses always want? FOOD! What's the one thing that makes us happy, feel good, that never gets old? Food! Scratches are most people's back up reinforcer, but the value of a scratch is usually much lower than food, and is also heavily variable, depending on the day, location, season, and so on. *Food is consistently desired, maintains a fairly level value to the horse, and is super quick and easy to use as a reinforcer.*

"Isn't food bribery?" We get this a lot, like we're some kind of mafia dealers paying off the cops with little bits of carrot. First of all, bribery is a human construct, and we have an ugly association with it due to corruption in politics and so on. But horses have no concept about what bribery is or isn't, only if it works. That being said, no, training with food reinforcers is **not** bribery, it's just like being paid. A bribe comes before the behavior, like a direct food lure. A common example is shaking a bucket of grain to catch a horse who doesn't want to be caught, or to lure a horse up onto a trailer. Food luring can work quite well in many situations, the major drawback to it is that the horses don't usually connect the behavior with the reinforcer, meaning you're going to need to maintain or increase the bribe in order to get the behavior again in the future. They can also be rather difficult to use when there are competing resources around, like grass or hay.

Bribes come before the behavior, while reinforcement comes after the behavior. When the horse offers the goal behavior we bridge (marking the desired behavior) then we pay them for it with something they value. Rather than bribery I think it helps to compare food reinforcers as a salary, a payment. We work our jobs knowing this will pay our bills. The bridge signal informs the horse that the behavior they're doing is that which is paying their bills - except in the horse's case we skip the conditioned reinforcer of money and go right ahead to paying with something they actually want, food!

"Won't food make my horse bite?" *The horse repeats the behavior that's reinforced.* If the horse investigates your body and receives food, the next time they will forage your body again. Each time this behavior is reinforced the stronger it gets, just like any trained behavior. If the behavior stops being reinforced with no alternative available, often the horse exaggerates this by foraging more vigorously, like pawing or biting - just like they might with a food producing toy. The horse is not being fresh intentionally, they're doing the behavior that worked. This is why we put such a heavy focus on building strong default safety behaviors like *stand facing forward* (page: 65) before we begin teaching other behaviors. It's why we use targets to train new behaviors, as it buys us distance from our body. Targets also give the horse the answer to the riddle without too much guess work and opportunities for wrong answers. Positive Reinforcement also gives us the ability to work in protected contact since we don't need to physically touch or manipulate the horse.

"Won't food take away from my relationship with my horse?" Most of us who are looking for more ethical ways of working with our horses are doing so because we love them and want a special relationship with them. Early in our training it can feel as if the horse is very focused on the food - because it's such a high value reinforcer, while our companionship is really not. Of course horses are focused on the food early on, it's the only consistently good thing in their life. But if we hope to modify the behavior of our horse, we can only do it one of two ways - having them work to avoid or work to gain.

We'll talk about **classical conditioning** soon (page: 33) it explains how when something with no meaning is paired with something that has a meaning the first stimuli gains the meaning of the stimuli was paired with. Just like after several times of the click being followed by a treat, the click takes on the meaning of the food - as well as all the emotional responses correlated with the food. While we can always sit in the field as a companion to our horses, becoming a neutral stimulus in their environment - if we hope to modify their behavior in any way it's going to require some interaction from us. In training a behavior we can add something the horse finds aversive, so we can remove it when the horse does our desired behavior. But how does that classically condition us and our presence? When they're with us we are adding and removing aversives - we become a *conditioned aversive*. While if when we're training a behavior we use shaping, targeting or capturing, and then reinforce the behavior with something the horse finds appetitive, how do we become conditioned then? If every time we are with them they are earning primary reinforcers and feeling good, we become a **conditioned appetitive** in our horse's life.

Very rapidly our relationship becomes appetitively conditioned, our own presence is treasured by our horses because we have been connected with all the good things in our horse's life. (page: 33) So while early on the food is all they're focused on, very quickly the relationship begins to be equally treasured. When I walk into my barn my horses buzz with joy, each horse wants to be the one chosen to play, they race us to the agility ring, they enjoy our company. The relationship is so purely wonderful for both partners. *For the first time in history we humans have a way to work with horses in a completely mutual way. It's incredible, we should rejoice!*

It's funny to me that some humans have a negative cognitive bias against the use of food with horses, as I have yet to go to a party that wasn't entirely focused around the food! Maybe it's my Italian upbringing but every special occasion, every family event, was built around the food. Birthdays, anniversaries, funerals, weddings, job promotions- all of these events are marked with food, and lots of it! Why? Because food is wonderful and makes us feel good. It seems as if adults learn this anti-food bias as they age; most children know well that feeding treats (and getting treats!) is the quickest way to someone's heart, human and animal alike.

Food Anxiety/Excitement

One of the major reasons people avoid using food reinforcers is because their horse actually has developed some anxiety or aggression around it. Many horses living in domestication struggle with food-related emotional issues, but these unwanted anxiety behaviors are symptoms of an issue we need to address, not avoid. Before we begin to address training we must first ensure our horse's lifestyle is ideal, particularly as it relates to food. There should be forage available to your horse all the time. Especially while training there should be other sources of food available. If you struggle with keeping your horse a healthy weight, slow feeders, and spreading out feeding locations can help alleviate these problems.

Horses are designed to consume food continually throughout the day. Their gut continues to produce digestive acid all the time - not just when there is food present like in humans. So this acid splashes around, giving them indigestion and eventually ulcers when there isn't an adequate amount of forage in their stomach to absorb the acid. This can make them feel as though they are starving even if they've just finished a huge amount of hay and grain an hour previously. It's not about quantity with horses, but rather duration. This feeling of starvation can be the root of most unwanted behaviors and emotional struggles for horses where food is concerned.

Most horses start out at least a little curious about the clicker training experience. Teaching a safe alternate behavior to mugging (foraging for food on our body) is usually enough to keep us both (horse and human) safe and comfortable during training with food. One key element in this first behavior though must be relaxation. A horse can tuck their chin or look away or stand facing forward, but be boiling over, trembling with anxiety or frustration at the same time. The whole point of using positive reinforcement training is to avoid those unpleasant emotions - not to re-create them in a new way.

Imagine your boss says, *"Once you complete this report I'm sure you'll get a raise"*, but when you do it, they say *"it'll just be a while longer, just do this next assignment, sorry it'll be a while more yet"* - imagine how frustrated you'd get! Each time you try harder, you get another empty promise. This is why it's vital that our rate of reinforcement is enough to satiate the horse, both physiologically and emotionally. All these details are what causes food related anxiety and the resulting unwanted behaviors.

With Viking's difficult start at life, he had a great deal of anxiety around food. Using a combination of these techniques helped Viking become comfortable with food reinforcers and opened a number of doors in his life.

What if we're sure our training is perfect and that our horse's lifestyle is perfect - but our horse is still over threshold whenever we start training? There are some horses who are so anxious around food that they can't even think or function while they desperately beg for the food. Often horses with anxieties this extreme have experienced a traumatic experience in early life, like starvation or having to constantly compete aggressively for resources. At our rescue we've dealt with a number of these cases - in some instances we could have avoided using food reinforcers, but the emotional problems the horses struggled with would have remained. Instead we worked to fix the problems, helping them overcome their desperation and in the end reducing the stress in other areas of their lives. They still need to be fed, so working through these issues is vital.

The first most important change is to not start a training session unless the horse is calm. Starting a session while the horse is at the door buzzing and pawing and tossing their head, would obviously only reinforce this behavior. So starting while the horse is out engaging in well adjusted horse things, such as grazing or resting, is best. It is also helpful to find times throughout the day when they are off being a normal horse; eating, drinking, napping, whatever, and tossing them a big handful in their bucket. This reinforces the behavior of "just existing" and takes the pressure off of training sessions as being their only source of enrichment and food/ treats as reinforcers.

When working in protected contact and on grass Viking was so comfortable with training and food reinforcers he was able to work hard with his physical therapy. While it was difficult for him this allowed him to stay optimistic and engaged.

Working outside on grass is also beneficial, or with hay available during the session to provide them with options. Starting a session just after a hard meal helps them focus, as they are likely not ravenous at that point. Because we never want them to feel that 'starving' feeling, especially while we're

asking them to interact with us, making sure they feel satiated and full first can be of great help. The better the alternative options, the less stress there is for them to get food from us.

This may vary by individual horse, but in most cases I've found, large handfuls of food with a high rate of reinforcement eases their worries. This satiates them quickly and we can slowly reduce our handful size throughout the session - but it helps take that 'I'm starving' edge off. Other horses may do better with smaller amounts fed at a higher frequency, so you'll have to experiment to find your horse's comfort level. Of course using low value treats helps too. Chaff, hay pellets, hay stretcher and so on are good lower value options (for most horses).

Viking also worked well in full contact with a high rate of reinforcement, big mouthfuls and low value feed (like hay pellets); all helped him stay comfortable and relaxed. We always made sure to start sessions with him when he was full and relaxed. It also helped for him to have a food toy available if there is no grass around.

The last thing that proved to be incredibly valuable was toys, particularly toys that provided food. If you've read the enrichment section of the book I'm sure you've seen the value of providing enrichment for your horses - as well as a few instructions on how to build some inexpensive puzzle feeders. You can use buckets with holes, hanging cones, hay nets, forage/treats hung up, cardboard boxes, plastic bags with holes - anything they have to shake, rattle or roll to get treats out of. These toys take the pressure off humans as being the sole providers of all things good (page: 19). Toys in the pasture are great, but they are especially valuable when the horse is stabled for any length of time. This is not only entertaining, but it allows horses to express their natural foraging behaviors, such as pawing, rolling objects, shaking trees and so on. It encourages problem solving and creativity, which is great for clicker trained horses! Most importantly it puts the horse in control of their environment and their food reinforcers. This sense of control brings comfort and confidence.

1. Horse has eaten recently before training
2. Has access to forage/grass during training
3. Food toy available during training
4. Train in Protected Contact
5. Safe default behavior has been taught
6. Increase RoR (Rate of Reinforcement)
7. Low value food reinforcer
8. Larger handfuls (to help satiate)
9. Start training when horse is calm

Using these techniques to ease your horse's stress and over-excitement around food will substantially reduce those unwanted frustration related behaviors. It also opens the door to using this super valuable communication device - the universal language of food!

Conditioning

Let's start with the basic **classical/respondent conditioning**; this was first studied in the iconic experiment by Ivan Pavlov with his salivating dogs. Pavlov simply paired the sound of a bell with the delivery of food. The dogs quickly learned to anticipate the delivery of food whenever they heard this bell, which was evidenced by their respondent (reflexive) behaviors - in this case, salivating.

Classical conditioning is taking any neutral stimulus and pairing it repeatedly with an aversive or an appetitive until the horse has learned the meaning, in other words **learning by association**. While there are some things we instinctively know how we feel about (food is awesome) there are many things we need to be exposed to in order to learn what they do and how they make us feel. It is in this way that we are able to adapt and respond appropriately to our environment. We use this technique in a number of ways with horses. In clicker training we classically condition the sound of the click. The sound of the click starts out having no meaning, but with pairing the delivery of food (something the learner instinctively enjoys) it classically conditions the click to predict food is coming. We call this a **classically conditioned appetitive**. We've also seen this in an aversive way many times as well. Ever seen a horse become more forward just by the rider carrying a whip? The whip is a connected to the pain it had previously inflicted, so we can say that it has become a **classically conditioned aversive**.

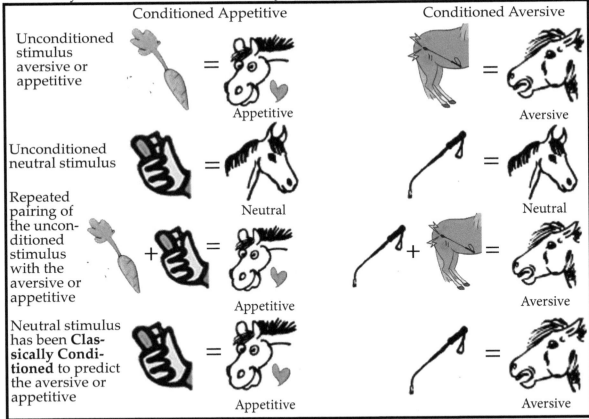

Relationships with other beings are also classically conditioned. How they feel during the time they spend with a peer will condition their relationship. This means what you pair with your presence tells your horse how to feel about having you around. If every time you're with your horse you spend time resting together, doing fun positive reinforcement games, enjoying mutual grooming - they'll connect these feelings with your presence. The more time spent together enjoying each other, the more strongly you will become conditioned as a good thing in their life. This becomes extremely important when there are times something aversive must happen, like a veterinary procedure.

The same type of conditioning happens if whenever you're around your horse you are yelling, taking them from their friends and food, or making them work. If our horse has come to consider our presence aversive it can be a serious set-back in emergency situations. Keep this in mind as you work with your horse. How are they feeling while they're with you? While we can't always make everything perfect, the more strongly we condition ourselves as an appetitive, the less damage will be done to our relationship when unfortunate things happen beyond our control. Susan G. Friedman, PhD, describes this as a **Relationship Piggy Bank**. We make regular deposits into our savings account, so in an emergency we have a solid positive history to withdraw from. Keep working on making your time with your horse as fun for both of you as you can. Luckily this type of positive reinforcement training makes this quite easy!

Classical conditioning can fade and extinguish, however, when the pairing discontinues. In the example below we have a whip conditioned to predict an aversive (pain) and a clicker conditioned to predict an appetitive (food). If these stimuli are repeatedly presented without the pairing, it will lose meaning. There is some debate over whether anything can ever become completely disconnected from the initial pairing, so long as the memory remains. This is often the cause of Post-Traumatic Stress Disorder and similar generalized anxiety disorders (when a conditioned fear response never completely divides from its correlation)(page: 33). However we can **desensitize** some things at least close to neutral (page: 136). If we click over and over without treating, the correlation fades and no longer predicts reinforcement. The same occurs when the threat of the whip is no longer backed up by an actual aversive. The correlation needs to be maintained to a degree in order for it to work as a tool in training. However, we may want to reduce the meaning of something to help them overcome fear or stress. We can take this a step further and **counter condition** the stimulus - changing the meaning from aversive to appetitive or vice versa. We will get into this further in the section on dealing with fear - though it's important to remember all stimuli can be desensitized, not just those that elicit fear.

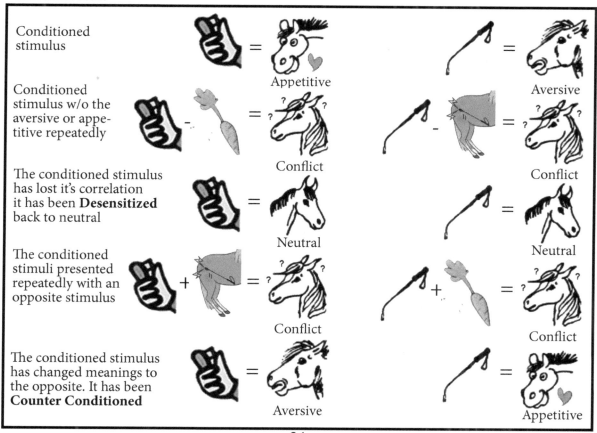

Conditioned stimulus	=	Appetitive		=	Aversive
Conditioned stimulus w/o the aversive or appetitive repeatedly	-	= Conflict		-	= Conflict
The conditioned stimulus has lost it's correlation it has been **Desensitized** back to neutral		= Neutral			= Neutral
The conditioned stimuli presented repeatedly with an opposite stimulus	+	= Conflict		+	= Conflict
The conditioned stimulus has changed meanings to the opposite. It has been **Counter Conditioned**		= Aversive			= Appetitive

34

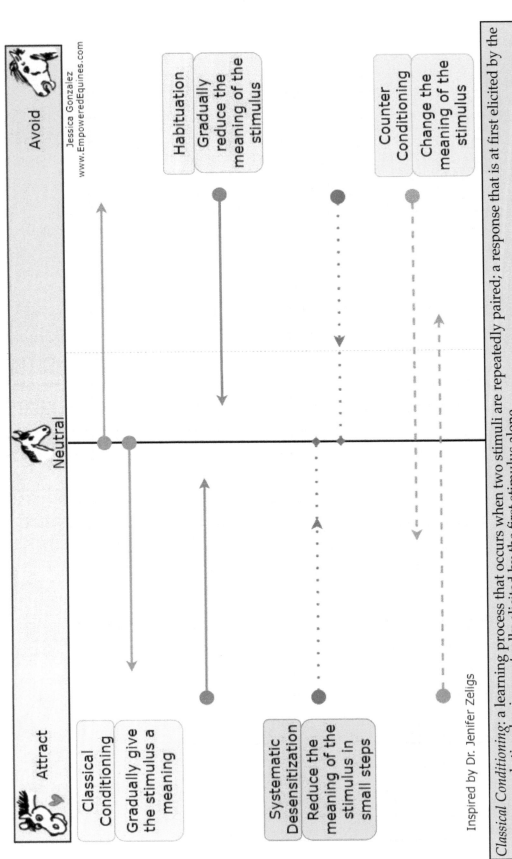

Attract   Neutral   Avoid

Jessica Gonzalez
www.EmpoweredEquines.com

Classical Conditioning
Gradually give the stimulus a meaning

Systematic Desensitization
Reduce the meaning of the stimulus in small steps

Habituation
Gradually reduce the meaning of the stimulus

Counter Conditioning
Change the meaning of the stimulus

Inspired by Dr. Jenifer Zeligs

Classical Conditioning: a learning process that occurs when two stimuli are repeatedly paired; a response that is at first elicited by the second stimulus is eventually elicited by the first stimulus alone.
Counter Conditioning: Changing the conditioning of a stimulus to it's opposite meaning through repeated pairing with an opposite stimulus
Desensitizing: systematically decreasing the conditioning of a stimulus towards neutral
Habituation: Stimulus decreases in meaning towards neutral through self-determined gradual exposure

ABCs

*While **classical conditioning** is learning by association, we also have **operant conditioning**, which is learning by consequence.* This is where the learner learns how to operate (control) their environment. This means, they learn the connections between their behaviors and the consequences. This influences their future choices and encourages or discourages certain behaviors. This form of conditioning can happen in the four learning quadrants. The learning quadrants are experienced by the learner during the 'ABC's - Antecedent, Behavior, and Consequence. These ABC's are then interpreted by the learner in one of the learning quadrants (this is happening all the time, even without thinking it through).

The ABCs happen all throughout our lives, not just when we're training. Antecedents can be anything that triggers a behavior. It can be as simple as hunger, thirst, the sight of a predator or it could be an intentionally taught trigger, like a cue. These antecedents stimulate the horse to react and they choose a behavior to respond with - eating the grass, getting a drink of water, fleeing from the predator, or responding to the cue. It's the consequence that really effects the future. Whether the consequence made the learner feel better or worse will determine whether they're likely to respond in the same way the next time. The ABCs happen regularly in nature, but can also be taken into account with our training. We cue (antecedent), the horse responds (behavior), and if it's what we want, we reinforce the behavior (consequence).

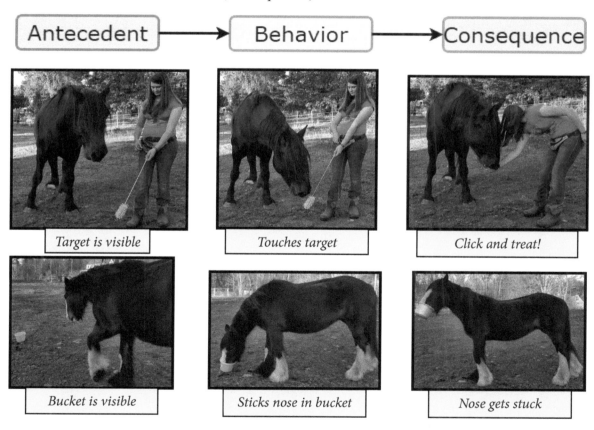

Antecedent	Behavior	Consequence
Target is visible	Touches target	Click and treat!
Bucket is visible	Sticks nose in bucket	Nose gets stuck

Operant Conditioning: A learning process in which the likelihood of a specific behavior increases or decreases in response to reinforcement or punishment that occurs when the behavior is exhibited, so that the subject comes to associate the behavior with the pleasure from the reinforcement or the displeasure from the punishment.

Quadrants

The learning quadrants are rather simple but they contain the foundation of how all living creatures learn. When a behavior happens the consequence of the behavior will either **punish** or **reinforce** that behavior. Punished behaviors will happen less frequently in that ABC scenario in the future. Reinforced behaviors will happen more frequently in that ABC scenario in the future.

A behavior can be punished in two ways, positively and negatively. This isn't "good" and "bad" punishment (there is no good punishment), but rather, in science, 'positive' simply means 'adding', while 'negative' means 'removing'. So think of 'plus' and 'minus' rather than 'good' or 'bad'. With this information we see *positive punishment means something has been added to reduce the frequency of the behavior.* In order to add something to punish a behavior, the stimulus added must be aversive to the horse, something they wish to avoid in the future. *Negative punishment is removing something to reduce the frequency of the behavior.* The stimulus removed must be appetitive to the horse for its removal to be unwanted, thus punishing.

Similarly a behavior can also be reinforced in two ways. *Positive reinforcement is when you add something to increase the frequency of the behavior* - this added stimulus must be appetitive to the horse to encourage them to want more. While *negative reinforcement is when you remove something to increase the frequency of the behavior.* The removed stimulus must have been aversive to the horse for the removal to be relieving enough to encourage the behavior to happen more.

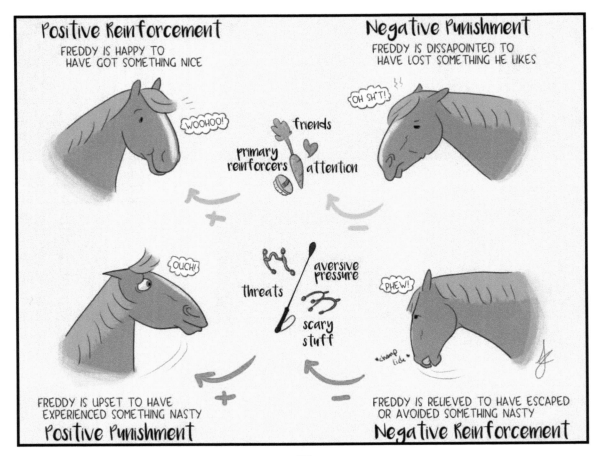

37

It's up to the learner to determine if the stimulus added/subtracted was aversive or appetitive. Only the learner can decide how to interpret the stimulus added. Some individuals will find some things reinforcing that others would find punishing, or neutral, and vice versa. So it's important to know how your horse feels about the stimulus you're using before you attempt to use it to train. If you don't know how they feel you can use the quadrants backwards to determine this. If you look at the chart below you can see the usual ABCs with the possible consequences. You can see how two of these options makes the behavior more likely to happen again in that ABC scenario, while the other makes the behavior happen less. So when you add or subtract a stimulus you can determine whether it was appetitive or aversive based on whether the behavior happens more or less in this ABC scenario in the future. Knowing how our horse feels about something can help us determine how to use it or which not to use.

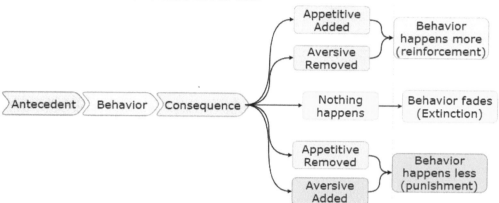

Antecedent ▷ Behavior ▷ Consequence

- Appetitive Added / Aversive Removed → Behavior happens more (reinforcement)
- Nothing happens → Behavior fades (Extinction)
- Appetitive Removed / Aversive Added → Behavior happens less (punishment)

Operant conditioning can also fade with time; if a behavior that had been reinforced is no longer being reinforced the behavior will reduce in frequency. We call this "**extinction**" as the learned response fades and eventually disappears (extinguishes). So if we look at our ABCs, this is what happens when the antecedent and behavior occur, but the consequence was not reinforcing, thus causing the A-B combination to lose value. While extinction ultimately reduces behavior to almost never happening (in that ABC set up), what often happens in the short term is what we call an "extinction burst". An **extinction burst** is when a behavior is no longer being reinforced, and the learner tries to exaggerate the behavior by increasing the intensity or adding variations to the behavior in an attempt to gain the reinforcement. Often this burst is accompanied by displaced behaviors, emotional responses, or aggressive behaviors. So long as the reinforcer remains absent the behavior will fade to almost never occurring in that ABC scenario. We will go into this further in the section on reducing unwanted behavior. However, we can use extinction and extinction bursts to help our training, when used carefully. If we are looking for an extremely specific behavior we can begin by marking anything similar, narrowing down which variation of the behavior we're reinforcing. This will extinguish the unwanted versions of the behavior and pinpoint the desired behavior. A mild beginning of an extinction burst can help achieve more enthusiasm or effort put into a behavior, if we're looking for more speed or intensity. We need to be careful when using this however, not to push too far, creating frustration or causing the learner to give up thereby extinguishing the whole behavior.

<---- Gummy Bear targeting the football

Here we used the benefit of an extinction burst to capture biting and throwing the football----->

Protected Contact

Positive reinforcement training was developed in the exotic animal/marine mammal world where the animals are generally trained in protected contact. **Protected contact** is when we do our training working from the other side of a fence, gate, stall door, or other physical barrier. Positive reinforcement is the only training method that can be used to train complex behaviors in protected contact. We don't need any physical contact with the learner to be able to communicate our intentions, which makes it such a valuable tool in the exotic animal world. This substantially reduces the risk involved with training, handling, and needing to tranquilize the animals for routine husbandry or veterinary care. They are now able to convince the animals to be an active participant in their health care and keeping, by choice. Protected contact is an equally valuable tool with horses - *even the most gentle, domestic horse can benefit from learning with a barrier.*

Protected contact is an extremely valuable tool to keep in our tool box; it's great for horses new to clicker training, new to people, new to being hand fed, new to living domestically and great for people new to using positive reinforcement techniques. It helps to keep us out of harm's way while our horses experiment, learning which behaviors will be reinforced and which won't, and while they learn to control their emotional impulses. It can also protect us while the horse learns to trust us, whether they were previously abused, mishandled, feral or wild.

It also protects the horse from us; this is especially valuable for horses who aren't comfortable with humans or who may have experienced a lot of punishment in previous interactions with humans. Horses who have been punished often will be less comfortable trying new things. Clicker training depends on the learner's desire to try to sort out what we are asking of them. This protective barrier can help horses feel more safe and comfortable offering behaviors without fear of being punished. It puts us in a position where we won't ever need to use aversives to defend ourselves should anything go wrong. Many experienced horse people are resistant to trying protected contact because they're so comfortable in full contact. It's important to remember protected contact is as much for the horse as it is for us. Often people think it's impossible to train without physical contact, but in the exotic/marine world the animals are all trained detailed behaviors like offering body parts for examination, injections, and cleaning or dental work. Horse owners can benefit from all this and more utilizing this very useful technique!

Using Protected Contact gave this rescue mule the courage and confidence to allow us to remove her embedded halter. We worked with her in protected contact whenever we introduced a new behavior. She was very afraid of humans and afraid of being punished if she did the wrong thing. This barrier gave her the confidence to try new things without anxiety.

Antecedent Arrangement

Before we begin to train a behavior we have to consider our **antecedents,** which are the events that set the stage for the behavior(s). This may sound easy, but there is much to consider. When we think about the behavior we want our horse to perform and the emotional context in which we want them to learn the behavior we can begin to make some decisions about how to prepare the environment.

- Area
- Weather
- Social
- Competing Resources
- Tools

Snow is not only fun to ride in, but also makes a safe cushion!

We want to think about the best location in which to train, whether that is in stalls, paddocks, fields, or arenas. Consider if your horse does best in an active or quiet area. Working in a big, open area can allow our horses to be more honest and have the ability to walk away if they're not engaged. On the other hand working in a smaller area can reduce the distractions and opportunities for unwanted behaviors while they figure out the new goal behavior.

Determine how much and which types of distractions are beneficial and which are detrimental for your training/developmental stage. Don't forget about weather and other external stimuli! The heat, cold, or amount of biting insects, can change how energetic horses get. If the horse is uncomfortable or frustrated by the weather or bugs it can quickly turn into a dangerous stimulus stacking situation. What about company? Think about your horse and determine if they'll be more relaxed with a friend present or if this will induce resource guarding problems. Is it best to have a friend in the same area with you, over a fence, or nowhere near?

Think about if there are any competing resources. While we would prefer if our horses didn't walk away and choose to eat grass or play with their friends over us - we also want them to be honest with us. If the training we're doing is really so boring or difficult they'd rather go eat grass, maybe we need to change our approach. It can also be comforting for an anxious horse to have some alternative resources available, which takes the pressure off of us as being the sole source of pleasure for them. In most cases I try to ensure there are at least a few food options available, or a grass or food producing toy. If the horse is anxious is around food I try to provide a higher value alternative option, so they don't feel the same anxiety of needing to earn my reinforcement, as there is another source available (page: 30). This can allow them to choose the alternate rather than get frustrated and act out.

This is a bad antecedent arrangement, these two horses don't get along so working in close proximity will be too distracting.

Now list all the tools you'll need for the exercise. How can we set up our area to make it easiest for the horse to perform the desired behavior? Sometimes using fences, ground poles, targets, walls, mats and so on we can make it obvious and easy for our horses to stumble onto the desired behavior. Ground poles are one of the best tools for shaping behaviors. You can set them up in so many ways to trigger goal behaviors, but the horse can easily step away if needed. However, when we're working on something new, we don't want so many options around that they're unclear which behavior we're working on. Until we're ready to mix them all together, then let the agility begin!

Using well known obstacles can be a great way to transfer behaviors to riding.

Create Behaviors

Now that we have our environment perfectly prepared we can begin to get our horses to do the behaviors we're looking to teach! Clicker training utilizes a number of different strategies to create the behaviors we're looking for. Each technique has particular advantages and disadvantages. Some work better for specific behaviors or for specific horses. Getting comfortable with using each of these can open a number doors in your training. With these options we can literally create any behavior our horse is

Shaping Tank to play in a pool of water

physically capable of performing and get the behaviors on cue (page: 50).

1) **Shaping:** *Clicking for approximations toward the end behavior.* This is simply asking for a bit more each time. Shaping requires an observant trainer and a clicker savvy horse. We can improve our shaping skills by having careful timing, an appropriate rate of reinforcement to keep the A-B-C chains flowing cleanly (page: 36), and clear criteria goals. It can be difficult to know when or how to stop reinforcing the less perfect attempts and start to put more emphasis on more accurate attempts at the behavior. It can take time and practice to get the hang of timing the increase of the criteria on the behavior and how to break down skills into achievable goals, but it's a great skill to master! While shaping sounds like it can be a slow process, the more comfortable we and our horses get with it the quicker and more fluid the communication can flow. With shaping we can also train any behavior that the horse is capable of - for most animal trainers it is the preferred method for extremely precise behaviors. Sometimes I'll begin a behavior with another technique - to get the behavior rolling, then move to shaping to clarify the precise goal.

2) **Capturing:** *Reinforcing a behavior that happens on its own.* This is a fast and easy way to get a big behavior on cue. If we know our horse well we should be familiar with which behaviors they do in specific situations. This way we can be prepared to reinforce them for whatever we'd like, using each click like a camera and taking pictures of the exact behavior we want to see more of. Setting up our antecedents is a really valuable tool to pay attention to when utilizing the capturing technique, it sets the stage for them to do the behaviors we wish to reinforce. For example, reinforcing when a horse happens to lie down on their own, or taking them to a nice sandy place while they're wet which can trigger them to roll, which you can then reinforce. This method is clean cut and easy to do and you can put any behavior your horse does on cue!

Capturing is the safest and gentlest way to train lying down and rolling over!

Capturing a flehmen response can put a cute smile behavior on cue!

41

3) **Luring:** *Directly following the food to the desired behavior.* Many people use this method when a horse gets loose or when trying to lure the horse onto the trailer. This method works wonderfully to get large behaviors - but takes a lot for the horse to connect the reinforcer with the behavior. While it can be difficult to remove the lure in the future or put these behaviors on cue, it can be helpful to get a big chunk of behavior that needs to be done quickly and doesn't need to be put on cue right away. Luring can also push a horse to do something they aren't quite ready for but this can also help them tolerate difficult situations, such as a veterinary procedure they weren't prepared for in advance. Be sure to pay attention to how your horse is feeling all the time to ensure they aren't being pushed beyond their comfort level.

Luring baby Nymph over a 'huge jump'

4) **Targeting:** *Following the target to induce the goal behavior.* Using a target rather than a food lure can be less distracting, as they're thinking more about their behavior. We generally start with a basic nose target which can evolve into a number of great behavior options. *We can use stationing on a target, sending to a target, and luring with a target* as ways to inspire different types of behaviors. When we **lure with a target** we can get all sorts of motion behaviors like leading, backing up, lunging, maneuvering obstacles, moving at different gaits, loading onto a trailer and so on. Standing still, **stationing at a target** can encourage standing for grooming, tacking, or veterinary procedures. Sending to targets is also extremely beneficial for movement behaviors and maneuvering obstacles, which allows them to learn how to handle each situation on their own. This also prepares them for riding or driving as they learn to move forward without the human's guidance.

We don't need to limit targeting to the horse's nose, either. We can also teach the horse to touch a **target with different body parts**, cheek, ears, neck, shoulder, knees, pasterns, hooves, sides, hind end - with this we can begin to inspire a wider variety of behaviors as well as add some precision. These can develop the horse's body awareness and clear communication between you and the horse as you work together.

Most behaviors we shape we can easily take off target and put on cue, while other behaviors we can generalize the target to other objects (like going into the swimming pool or onto the bridge). Finally for other behaviors we'll keep the target for added safety and distance.

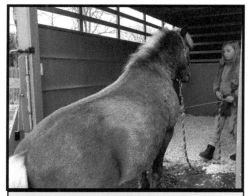
Using a target is an encouraging way to help a horse get comfortable loading onto a trailer

When you and your pony are fairy princesses you need an equally flamboyant target!

5) **Mimicry:** *We have two ways to use mimicry to train, having them mimic us or having them mimic another horse.* As such social creatures it only makes sense they're good at observing and learning from their peers. I often train one horse in front of all my others (not to make them jealous) but to help them see the goal behavior before I work on it with them. There have been times I've walked into the first training session and my horse is offering me the finished behavior the other horse was working on! Mimicking other horses is quite easy for horses to pick up on, but mimicking us (with our oddly shaped bodies) can be a little more difficult, but it's do-able. This works best with horses who are accustomed to clicker training, engaged, and comfortable offering behaviors.

Punk is comfortable with trailering, so following her good friend on board was a big help for Marshmallow

6) **Molding:** *Physically manipulating the horse's body to create the behavior you'd like.* This is a delicate technique, as it can easily become negative reinforcement with a treat on top. If the horse finds any aspect of this situation aversive, you run the risk of poisoning the behavior as a whole. Make sure your horse is entirely comfortable with you touching and manipulating this part of their body. Unlike negative reinforcement, if there is any resistance from the horse you should stop immediately (page: 44). In negative reinforcement if you let go while the horse isn't doing the right behavior, you will accidentally reinforce the wrong thing. With positive reinforcement the horse should have the freedom to move away and not partake in molding if they're uncomfortable. The reinforcer is added with the click and treat, so letting go won't accidentally reinforce an unwanted behavior as it might with negative reinforcement. Molding is useful for delicate skills like hoof handling or veterinary procedures, particularly because of how quickly this can work with a horse who is comfortable with you. While it can work quickly it can also backfire just as quickly. If your molding becomes restrictive or aversive to the horse, it may reduce their desire to comply in the future, even if it was an accident. However, due to its delicate nature it shouldn't be our go-to technique for most new skills.

We opted to use gentle molding to teach Fable to put her hoof on an object for farrier work, rather than having her target with her hoof as Fable is new to clicker training. She didn't yet understand stimulus control and we wouldn't want to accidentally teach a striking behavior. She needed her feet done so this was the quickest and safest option in this situation.

Negative Reinforcement

This book is focused on using positive reinforcement training, but for education's sake I'll also discuss the basics of how negative reinforcement is used correctly in traditional training and Natural Horsemanship. It's important we understand the difference between when negative reinforcement is being done correctly and when it's not. Often the lack of understanding of how reinforcement works, caused by pseudo-science and dominance based ideas, (page: 16) results in dangerous or inappropriate attempts at training. It is beneficial to know how negative reinforcement works, as most horses have been trained using aversive techniques understand how it's supposed to work, often our horses come with a history of previous aversive training.

In traditional training, a trainer will apply an aversive stimulus in order to trigger a reaction from the horse. When the horse moves correctly the aversive stimulus is removed, reinforcing that behavior. For example, the traditional trainer will pull on a rein connected to a bit until the horse turns their head in the correct direction and then they release the contact on the rein. Next time this aversive is applied the horse will be quicker to go to that behavior to achieve relief. This is continued until the horse learns how to consistently avoid the aversive. If the behavior fades as the horse gets accustomed to the aversive tools, the aversive will be increased. They may also increase the aversiveness of the tools to get quicker or more dramatic responses to the cue, or so the rider can use less obvious cues.

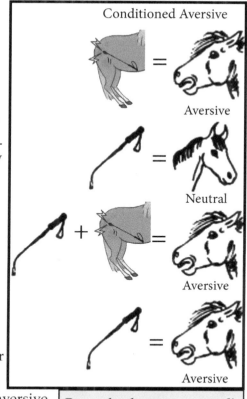

Conditioned Aversive

Aversive

Neutral

Aversive

Aversive

Remember how we can condition appetitives and aversives?

In an effort to employ kinder, less overtly aggressive tools and cues, some horse trainers have modified the types and severity of aversives; utilizing less striking and kicking, instead using forced work, repeated tapping on the horse and rope twirling/swinging to achieve their training goals. Some natural horsemanship trainers have taken to using conditioned aversives. A conditioned aversive is any neutral stimulus that the animal has learned will predict an aversive - a threat (page: 33). They do this by using the neutral/predictor signal before applying to actual aversive. We've seen this same type of training used in lab experiments where a light signals an aversive shock and the animals learn to move to avoid the shock at the presentation of the light. The light alone (previously an nonthreatening, neutral stimulus) becomes a strong enough predictor of pain. The trainer presents the threat just before the actual aversive, then they gradually increase the aversive until the horse works in the correct way to earn relief. Over time the horse learns to perform the correct behavior at the first sign of the threat. A common situation I've seen is when a trainer wags their finger at their horse to get the horse to back up, the trainer starts shaking the lead rope attached to the horse's halter, gradually increasing intensity until the horse steps backward- only at this point is the aversive stimulus removed. The horse learns that backing up relieves the rope halter pressure and that backing up at the sight of the wagging finger will prevent the application of the aversive stimulus altogether.

All this conditioning requires maintenance, so the threat will need to be backed up by the actual aversive often enough to maintain its power to alter the horse's behavior. So sadly, this technique doesn't alleviate the aversives as much as they had hoped. Luckily science has continued to progress and we have more humane training options available to us now, allowing us to leave the use of aversives behind.

Positive Reinforcers

Once we have the horse doing the behavior we want we need to find a way to get them to keep doing it. The only way to do that is to reinforce it! Reinforcement can happen naturally, when the behavior provides the horse with relief or a reward. But we can control this natural learning tool, and reinforce it ourselves. Rather than using negative reinforcement (as it requires first adding an unpleasant stimulus so we can then remove it), instead we'll just add something they like to reinforce it!

There are different types of reinforcers we can add when using positive reinforcement. *The strongest of these are* **primary reinforcers**, *which are things the learner naturally or instinctively wants and/or needs, including food, water, and reproduction.* The easiest and safest of these to control is food. Food is something we can buy in bulk and we can vary it heavily based on our horse's needs. We can monitor and control the value of the food reinforcer we're using as well. A small amount of a high value treat (sweet pellets, molasses cookies, sugar cubes, etc...) may be great for difficult behaviors, inspiring a horse to try a little more or put in a little more enthusiasm. This is a good way to inspire a higher speed or a bigger effort on a behavior. We may also opt to use a

Primary reinforcers like food maintain a relatively consistent, appetitive value. Even when a horse is full, more food is generally appreciated. Luckily for us horses are designed to be eating continually, spending much of their day foraging and grazing, which makes food an even more ideal reinforcer! Even something as simple as grass or hay pellets can be effective.

lower value food when we're shaping or working with a very high rate of reinforcement. Lower value food reinforcers fed in higher amounts can help satiate a more anxious horse, making them feel full and satisfied without adding the excitement of a high value reward. We should experiment with our horses to find how they value each of the common food reinforcers we use. Sometimes we can be surprised; my horses like sweet things in small amounts but salty things in large amounts. Practicing simple behaviors with different quantities and types of reinforcers can help us get a feel for how our reinforcement choices influence our horse's responses.

We could also use **conditioned reinforcers**, *these are things the animal has come to learn are wonderful, sometimes called a conditioned appetitive.* These include scratches, praise, and even behaviors that have a long reinforcement history (we'll get into this later when we discuss behavior chaining, page: 79). The difficulty with conditioned reinforcers is that they may change in value to the horse based on many factors. A good scratching spot may change daily or seasonally, while praise and behaviors need to be well conditioned with a primary reinforcer before they become reinforcing themselves.

Viking always loved a good scratch which it made an ideal secondary reinforcer. However, when we stopped scratching it felt very much like negative punishment to him (removing the appetitive). He would become frustrated and act out, so we only used scratching as a way to build duration between primary reinforcers in his training.

While behaviors that become conditioned reinforcers can then be used in behavior-chains they still need to be periodically conditioned with a primary appetitive.

In order to be effective reinforcers must be presented in a timely manner. Since we can't always deliver the reward while the behavior is in action, how do we connect the exact micro moment of the behavior we like with the reinforcer?

While "Jumping" might sound like one behavior, the timing of the click can greatly influence it. But each click is like a photo; when we click we are marking that specific behavior. Looking at this photo progression which of these behaviors would you like to reinforce? Think about how each could effect the future expression of this jumping behavior. Which photo would you like to see again next time?

The answer is a **bridge signal.** *This is a clear, unique signal that indicates to the learner that reinforcement is coming.* Sound is the easiest signal to use with horses, but if you're working with a deaf horse, visual markers can also be used (like a thumbs up). You can use a box clicker, a verbal bridge, or anything you'd like, so long as it won't be mistaken and will be easily heard. Many people try to use a word (but it doesn't always acquire the strength another sound does because horses have of the learned to tune out our jabbering). Using a quick, unique sound like a smooch, cluck or click is more attention catching. To start you need to "charge" your bridge signal (conditioning the sound), which is simply bridging and reinforcing again and again until the connection is made. This is OK to do with horses, but most horses are so engaged and smart that sometimes they'll start connecting behaviors right away. So to avoid any unintentionally trained behaviors, it helps to start with a simple goal behavior with a high rate of reinforcement. The marker bridges the exact moment of the behavior to the reinforcer that's soon to come. This buys us time to get out our food and deliver the treat, which enables us to get our timing down to the precise second, like a camera taking a photo.

We can use the timing of our bridge signal to increase or decrease the size, quality, distance and duration of the behavior as well. When the horse begins experimenting they slowly reach in different directions, experimenting a little, looking for a sign they're moving in the right direction. As the horse fishes around we can mark and reward as they get closer to the correct behavior. One of the biggest benefits of positive reinforcement is that the horse will increase their own criteria. We don't have to hit harder or kick more to get more out of our horses, they'll escalate the behavior themselves looking for the better answers. If you've marked a few times a behavior in one direction, that's the way they'll go and they'll escalate it until they find the consistent sweet spot. We are also able to use this to make behaviors bigger and better, by withholding the click (creating the start of an extinction burst), then catch the bursting behavior (page: 37). You want to carefully balance this and not push to the point of frustration. You can also use your timing to reduce a behavior by clicking earlier in the behavior interrupting it before it gets too big, satiating the horse to reduce their effort.

One aspect to keep in mind when using food reinforcers with horses is the importance of proper delivery. We want the horses to receive the food without grabbing for it. To help them be successful with this we want to keep our treat delivery consistent. Always feed where the *horse should be*; if they've moved since the click, keep your hand closed and extend it to where the horse was at the click and open it there. You can feed for position or encourage a bit more with your feeding.

If we've asked for a stand, feed where the horse should be. If we've asked for a back up, it helps to feed a bit behind the horse's chin, shifting their weight slightly back to further instill the idea of space. We want the horse to feel confident their reinforcement will come to them, instead of them needing to go to their reinforcer.

Other Signals

Along with the bridge signal we conditioned (that marks the exact moment the horse does the desired behavior and is going to be reinforced) we also have a number of other signals that become conditioned in our horse's life. Does your horse recognize the sound of the feed bin being opened? Or recognize that you appearing at the gate means it's time to come in? Horses learn correlations quickly because it's vital in nature to learn indicators of things they want to avoid or seek out.

There are many indicator signals we can teach intentionally that can be helpful in our training. Along with a bridge signal, we have a terminal bridge signal, a keep going signal, an intermediate bridge signal, a no reward marker, and an end of session signal. We don't need to use (in fact some I wouldn't recommend) all of these signals, but it's important to know they exist and that they may be taught unintentionally. Also think of all the other potential signals you may be teaching/using in your daily life and how they may affect your future training.

Terminal Bridge Signal: This is typically how we use our clicker (or any other conditioned stimulus we use as a click). It not only marks the exact moment the learner does the desired behavior, it bridges the gap between the behavior and the reinforcement. The learner will notice this signal and stop what they're doing to get their reinforcer. This is an extremely beneficial tool in your training and a valuable communication device to build precision and clarity in our training.

Keep Going Signal: A stimulus that is given during the behavior to inform the learner they're doing the desired behavior, but to continue this, not to stop for reinforcement. This is unnecessary but can sound awfully tempting to most horse people who hope to ride and potentially compete. Often it ends up adding complexity and confusion to training, even frustration as the learner determines what this really means. However I do find some quiet and appropriately timed "cheer-leading" can help build up a behavior effectively. While this option can sound like it might be helpful, it can be more effective and efficient to just focus on building strong distance and duration on our behaviors.

Intermediate Bridge Signal/Tertiary Reinforcer: A signal that marks and continues while the learner is on the right track, maintaining until the learner loses track of the goal behavior or completes the desired task. This is often referred to as 'Blazing Clickers', a term coined by Steve Martin and Susan Friedman in an excellent paper by the same title. This signal maintains or repeats until the behavior is ended with a terminal bridge. This allows the trainer to provide immediate feedback to the learner, and can help build duration. These can be a bit confusing, overwhelming, and unnecessary when working with horses. It can be more effective to build duration between reinforcers by chaining behaviors or chaining the same behavior to itself repeatedly.

No Reward Marker: This is a stimulus that marks when the learner is doing something unwanted, going in the wrong direction, or about to make a poor choice. This lets the learner know 'this path will not lead to reinforcement'. While there are some benefits to this, as it can reduce the amount of time spent in error, and reduce the time spent practicing unwanted behaviors, in reality the absence of a click should be doing the same job. A savvy clicker trainer and clicker horse should know that if they're not earning a click, they're not going down the right path. This is another unnecessarily complex tool that can lead to frustration or confusion.

> *Bridge Signal*: A unique signal that marks a specific moment during a behavior when the horse meets the criteria, telling the horse that reinforcement is coming

End of Session: This is the second most important signal that I find extremely important when working with horses. *This can be any stimulus that marks the time when a training session is over and the opportunity to earn reinforcement is gone.* Teaching this can help relieve anxiety, frustration and excessive offering of unwanted behaviors. It's important to not just mark the end of our sessions but to also provide a bit of food, a few handfuls on the ground or in the bucket, or a food toy to play with. This can help reduce the punishing feeling that comes with ending the session. It's very important to end the session on a good note with the horse and human going their separate ways without feeling left behind.

Duration

One of the best way to expand upon our known behaviors and make them more practical for use is to build duration, which is the length of time the behaviors are performed. Stationary behaviors can be performed for long periods of time, while behaviors that involve the horse or human moving we will build both distance and duration. In the beginning when we teach a behavior the horse will fidget and try to find the right answer until they hear the bridge. The more that bridge lands on the same behavior the more they will perform that behavior. Once the desired behavior is understood, you can begin to add the distance or duration by:

- Gradually increasing the time between reinforcing
- Fluctuating the time between reinforcing
- Reinforcing the behavior several times while it's happening, before ending it with a terminal bridge signal and reinforcement
- Chaining the behavior to itself, by cuing it again before they've stopped

To build duration on a behavior we can slowly prolong the amount of time before the bridge after the behavior begins. However this method is precarious. If we wait too long the horse may become confused or frustrated and change the behavior in an unwanted direction. As we ask for more time between clicks it can help to count, out loud if possible. We want to ensure the horse is able to maintain the behavior correctly as long as we're asking or as we slow our progress.

Another option is to reinforce the behavior continuously. Reinforcing it multiple times without ending the behavior can prolong it without the horse feeling the need to change it. This is easier for stationary behaviors that aren't interrupted by feeding. For example, when a horse first learns about farrier work it can help to feed multiple times while the horse has their foot up (you may need a second person for this). We often use this method with new rescues when we haven't had time to build long enough duration on hoof work before the need for a real farrier. We feed continuously while the horse is doing the right thing, slowly spacing out the reward until we find a comfortable rate. It's important that after this we continue to work on building duration on the behavior, so we don't need to feed continuously every time a real life situation presents itself.

When we first got Fable she could only be trimmed if she was sedated and tied in stocks. Instead we opted to feed her continuously throughout her first trim and she was perfect! This bought us time to train her properly.

We don't want to just increase the time between clicks, as this can be demotivating for the learner - if it consistently gets harder to earn reinforcement, then why try? *With each attempt go up and down in difficulty level.* If they can comfortably hold the behavior for 10 seconds, sometimes click at 5, sometimes push to 12 until 12 becomes comfortable, and so on. Keep bouncing up and down around the comfortable zone, to keep the horse encouraged and motivated. This is also where conditioned reinforcers can be beneficial. When the horse is performing the desired behavior we can use scratching and verbal praise to keep the behavior going and the horse feeling relaxed with the duration before ending with a click/reinforcement.

For behaviors in motion we can chain the same behavior to itself once or twice before rewarding. Ask for the behavior, as they reach the end, ask for it again, then reward. For example, if your horse usually backs up two steps, before they finish the second step, cue the behavior again. This chains the two "back up" behaviors together (page: 79). When chaining the same behavior together, we also want to remember to fluctuate - if the horse can comfortably perform the same behavior three times without frustration or confusion, then remember to bounce, sometimes reinforcing at one offer, sometimes pushing to four. For example, when sending to targets, at first going to each target earns them a reinforcer. Soon you can add more targets between reinforcers, they can go from one target to the next and the next.

Practicing sending Wisp to the purple frisbee, her stationary target. This built her confidence moving away from me (and the treats) during training.

With this distance and duration built up it made it easy to initiate forward motion under-saddle. Wispy knew and felt comfortable moving towards the target, even with me "behind" her.

Distance

Once a behavior is taught and understood we can begin using them in everyday situations, however some behaviors need a bit of distance in order to be practical in the real world. Sometimes we need the horse to be able to do something without us standing right next to them, this is **distance from us**. This can include doing a behavior while we move away from them, like standing stationed, or performing a behavior that moves them away from us, like going to a target. Both are valuable skills for the horse to learn. This will be important when we begin teaching mounted behaviors, as the horse needs to be comfortable performing the behavior moving away from us (even if we're 'following' on their back). It's important the horse be confident in themselves and the behavior; having some extra distance on the behavior can help them become more confident in their choices. We want them comfortable moving around and away from us/the food without worrying. We can also add **physical distance** on most motion behaviors. We start one step at a time, but we can build distance up to many steps the same ways we increase duration. For behaviors like Spanish walk, piaffe, and different types of movement, we can add duration and physical distance together. Remember to fluctuate the distance/steps as well as the duration!

Put on Cue

What is a cue, really? The cue is the communication that tells the horse which behavior we will be reinforcing right now. There is no aversive consequence for not performing the behavior. We can do this with an audible/verbal, visual, tactile, situational, or even a scent indicator. Verbal/audible cues are quite common, they can be words or sounds, like a cluck for speed. Scent based cues aren't as common in the horse world as they are in dogs, but they can be a great tool for blind horses. Visual cues can be as simple as the presentation of a target, body language, or even a more specific sign language. As horses are such visual communicators they often depend more on visual cues then any other types. If we feel our horse isn't listening to our presented cue, we should look at how we're asking physically as we may have changed something visual that they had thought was the cue. A classic example of a horse who responded to an unexpected cue is Clever Hans, a wonderfully brilliant horse who was thought to have been able to

Our sweet blind Butterfly follows the sound of jingling bell targets

perform simple math equations! As it turned out, however, he could only 'do the math' so long as someone he could see knew the correct answer. Why? Because when someone in the room recognized the right answer there was a very subtle raise of their head, as they anticipated Hans' answer. So it turns out while Hans wasn't able to do math, more impressively, he was acutely aware of the subtlest signs of human body language.

Tactile cues can look like and mimic traditional negative reinforcement commands. The difference with these and negative reinforcement is that the contact is not aversive to the horse, not even a conditioned aversive. Remember a conditioned aversive is a neutral stimulus the horse has learned will predict an aversive (page: 33). There will be absolutely no escalation of the tactile stimulus, it will not repeat, get stronger or even remain constant until the behavior is performed. Even just maintaining the physical contact can become aversive due to muscle fatigue. Just like when we use a verbal cue, we ask for the behavior once and then wait. We say "back up" - we don't prolong our word until the horse complies, "baaaaccckkkkkkk uuuppppppp", so neither would we prolong our tactile cue. We would apply it and then stop. The tactile stimulus isn't used to teach or create the behavior, only to cue it.

So why or when would we use them? I use these especially for horses who may end up with someone who doesn't use clicker training. By teaching the horse these types of cues then he/she will know how to respond to traditional 'looking' cues, but I still maintain my practice of using the least aversive tools possible, to prevent the risk of the training slipping into being unintentionally aversive.

Shaping "back up" with a target

Fading the target using hand motion to trigger the "back up"

"Back up" on it's final visual and verbal cue.

I like to teach these cues especially for halter/leading, moving over and basic handling - for times I have a pony sitter or friend handling the horses. These can also be valuable in real life situation, for example, teaching a horse to back up to tactile stimulus on the chest can teach them to back away from a stall guard, rather than run through it.

Now that we know what we can use as a cue, how do we assign it to the proper behavior? The best time to add a cue is once the behavior is being offered somewhat consistently. This means the horse has learned the behavior (with shaping, luring, capturing, targeting or mimicry) to its complete, most ideal way and offering it whenever they think it will be reinforced. For example, targeting - they have learned to touch their nose to the target, they do it just right (not biting, bashing, coming close, but not touching), and they do it whenever the target is presented. At this point we should add a cue. The addition of the cue becomes what finishes the behavior. We don't want to add a cue to early - if the behavior is still not right. If the behavior isn't completely understood you run the risk of overwhelming them with too much information to process at once or finishing a behavior while there are still unwanted elements. We add the cue simply by predicting when they'll offer the behavior and providing the cue first. For example, we can fade the target to a finger point, and then add the verbal cue and fade out our visual pointing. While you can't really be too late to add a cue, the longer you wait the harder it will be to really make the connection - or something inadvertent may have become the cue (like your body position or subtle gestures).

Because of everything stated above, I like to teach a behavior from beginning to end. I don't like to work on multiple behaviors at once, unless the situations are entirely different (inside/outside or an object brings out the behavior). Once the cue is added, you can begin to stop reinforcing the behavior if you haven't cued it. You want to try to cue it often enough to keep the horse from becoming frustrated, but you can begin adding some aspects of stimulus control very early (we'll go over this in the next section. If they remain focused on the one task, learn it completely, then you can put it on cue and add it into your regular training to utilize in behavior chains or integrate it into daily use.

Stimulus Control

Stimulus Control is the learner's understanding of the contingencies around the antecedents, behavior, and consequence (page: 36). The goal of stimulus control is to create dependability and safety with the behaviors we ask for. The behavior is said to be under stimulus control when it fulfills these four requirements:

1. When we cue a behavior the horse will always promptly perform the correct behavior
2. The horse doesn't accidentally perform the wrong behavior with the cue
3. The behavior does not happen when we haven't cued it (during an active training session)
4. The horse understands what our intended cue is and doesn't perform the behavior with the wrong cue or something else we've unintentionally added as a cue.

These criteria are important when working on most behaviors - any behaviors can potentially be unsafe with an animal as large as a horse. So it's important we know what our horse is going to do in response to our cue and our horse knows what to do to get their reinforcer!

You can determine what degree of stimulus control you want on each behavior. If you want to provide your horse more freedom of expression, more self-control in their life, strict stimulus control may not be for you. That's just fine! But make sure if you've made this decision you have your safety measures in place so you don't need to resort to aversives outside of true emergencies. This may mean you spend more time in protected contact (page: 39) or only work within fenced areas - though that may be as huge as your land allows! It's our duty as caretakers to keep our animals safe and healthy, we'll do this either with by building stimulus control into our training or using safety measures, or best yet a combination of both to meet all our individual needs.

OK, so if we decide we want a reasonably safe level of stimulus control to be able to go out on adventures, how do we achieve this? Keep in mind, stimulus control is only on behaviors within an active training session - not when the horse is on their own time.

Generally when we've taught horses a couple behaviors we'll immediately begin building stimulus control into those behaviors. We'll do this by teaching discrimination, the horse learns which cue belongs to which behavior and no other. We are simply 'proofing' the behaviors by alternating two learned behaviors until they learn which cue opens which door to reinforcement. Gradually we'll add more behaviors into this repertoire, being able to cycle through the skills we ask for with the correct behavior each time.

That being said, we don't want our horses throwing behaviors at us when we haven't cued yet, so how do we get them to just relax and wait for the cue? By asking for just that. This is why it's so important to build our foundation with a calm, safe behavior like "stand facing forward" (SFF). This is usually the first behavior I teach and return to it regularly (page: 65). Every behavior I add to the list I proof against this foundation behavior, by alternating which behavior I cue. At first we'll alternate evenly, for example: "stand", "back up", "stand" and so on. Then when they get the hang of this we'll begin alternating more randomly to ensure they haven't just learned the chain but are paying attention to the cue.

Even as we graduate to advanced behaviors, returning to SFF within a session will help maintain the patience and calmness while they wait for the next cues to be given. One big aspect about this SFF behavior is that it be a comforting for the horses. We don't want our horses to feel as though they need to 'perform' whenever we're near, offering every behavior they know. It can be stressful to feel as though they're on the spot all the time, so standing comfortably, waiting for a cue should be their default, go-to behavior when they haven't been cued.

The more skills we rotate into our training sessions the more complete our stimulus control will be. Rolling through our list of behaviors within a few minute session can be a great way to test if our horses truly know what's being asked of them or where any confusion is, we can then iron this out. This is my favorite 'rainy day' project. The more we practice stimulus control with simple, safe behaviors the easier it will be for the horse to understand the concept and practice their impulse control with bigger, faster, more intense behaviors. Some horses are naturally better at this than others and some do better with stimulus control on specific behaviors. More forward horses might need more practice controlling their desire to rush ahead - while quieter horses may need less stimulus control and more reinforcement on being creative and engaged. It takes knowing and understanding what our horses need.

Stimulus Control isn't physical, forceful control. Without Stimulus Control we have no recourse if our cues fail, so having safety measures in place is always important. We may want to work with a fence, so the horse can't get anywhere dangerous. We may use protected contact (page: 39) to keep us safe from any accidents by the horse, or the horse safe from any unnecessary punishment (it would stink to lose relationship points on punishment just because we weren't in protected contact). When we don't have safety measures like these we may want a lead rope on a flat halter as an emergency (albeit aversive) plan to fall back on until our stimulus control is dependable. When we go off property on trails, while our horses are ready and our stimulus control is predictable, anything can happen!

Our horses wear break-away flat halters and a lead rope just in case. To reiterate, this should be your fall-back plan and should be saved for true emergency situations. *It's important as well to remember to go right back after the emergency and do what you need to prevent that problem from ever happening again!*

Many Motivators

Motivation comes in many forms, from many places. We can lump these motivators into two categories, things we want to avoid and things we seek out. If we think of everything in our environment having an appetitive or an aversive value (page: 28), we can see how our memories and previous learning have conditioned us to care more about some things than others. It works much the same for horses. They go through life choosing the most salient option at any given time.

The most salient option is the one that will keep them safe and fulfill their needs. Like a math equation or a scale, if the perceived risks outweigh the benefits, they'll avoid the situation; if the benefits outweigh the risks, they'll seek it out. This changes constantly. This assessment is not just based on the environment but also the horse's internal needs and wants. A hungry horse will take greater risks to get food. A thirsty horse may avoid salty foods or seek out water in unusual places, maybe even drink something distasteful. So while we can learn what our horses enjoy and what causes concern for our horses, these can be continuously changing in value. All the stimuli in the environment are continually fluctuating in value, as needs are increased or satiated. While we like to think that we are always the most interesting and desirable resource in their environment, the truth is, sometimes we aren't. Keep this in mind as you approach your training and decide on which reinforcers to use. While the horse may learn a behavior with a very low value reinforcer in a calm environment, things may fall apart in a busier environment. When there are competing stimuli the value of doing that behavior may not be strong enough to be dependable.

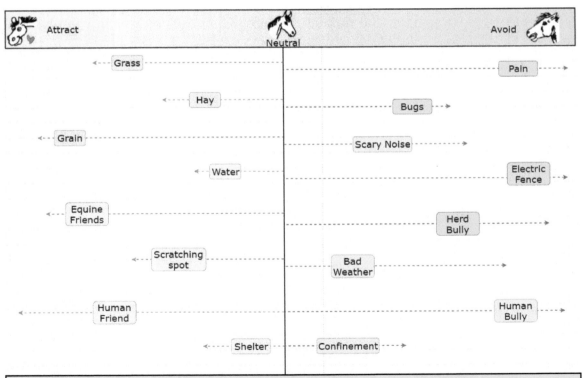

This chart shows a simple visual example of how everything in the learner's environment will be weighed into the horse's decision making process. This is just a visual representation with no actual values or scenarios attached. We can use it to help us understand how and why horses make the decisions they do. Each stimuli in this chart has a different potential value range, this can change per individual and minute to minute based on the current needs and feelings of the horse.

Generalizing Cues

Alternating behaviors can be a great practice for helping horses understand which cue belongs to which behavior and that the behavior won't be rewarded without the cue or with the wrong cue. We also want to build strong reliability on our cues. We want to make sure when we cue the behavior, in any situation the horse will do the behavior. First that comes down to us - when we look at the situation, if we had to bet $100 would you be confident your horse would perform the correct behavior? If you think not, don't risk it, rearrange the antecedents or return to some of your shaping method (maybe pull your target back out) to get the desired result.

We want strong, reliable behaviors especially if we ever hope to ride or go on adventures with our horses. So, how do we build them to be that reliable? The key is generalization, think about variations, distance, and distraction. We want to ensure the horse will perform the correct behavior when the cue is given in any way the cue might be given. It helps to have multiple people practice the same cue with the horse, so that unintended language we add don't get tied into the cue. Practice the cue in any position, location, or distance from the horse you may ever need to use it. If you plan on using the cue during riding, practice the cue from positions where the horse can't see you. If your cue is a visual, vary up where you stand, proofing where the cue works and where it doesn't.

- Distance
- Distraction
- Variations
- Locations

We also want to generalize the cues with as many distractions as possible, to help ensure they'll be reliable in real life situations. Practice when there are loud noises, visual distractions, distance from friends, whenever the horse isn't ready to focus. But remember to start with mild distractions so the horse can be successful. Be sure you'd be willing to bet all your money that your horse will be able to provide you the right answer before you cue. If not, reduce the distraction to a level where they will be successful and increase more slowly.

"I'm not telling you it's going to be easy... I'm telling you it's going to be worth it."

Definitions:
Antecedent: a preceding circumstance, event, object, style, phenomenon, etc.
Primary Reinforcer: anything that provides reinforcement without the need for learning, the reinforcer is naturally reinforcing to the organism.
Conditioned Reinforcer: are reinforcing only after the organism has been conditioned to find it reinforcing.
Bridge Signal: A stimulus that marks the desired behavior, it "bridges" the gap of time that occurs between the behavior and its reinforcement.
Cue: A discriminative stimulus - a stimulus that provides information about what to do to earn reinforcement
Command: A discriminative stimulus - a stimulus that provides information about which behavior will relieve an aversive
Stimulus Control: The behavior occurs immediately when the cue is given. The behavior never occurs in the absence of the cue. The behavior never occurs in response to some other cue. No other behavior occurs in response to this cue

WORKSHEET

To help us bring some of these complex terms and concepts to real life practice, we'll practice by thinking about some common scenarios. After reading a short description of a real scenario you'll first identify the antecedents, the behavior the horse responds with, and the consequence of their chosen behavior. With this information you can infer which operant conditioning quadrant actually took place. Then you'll compare this with whether this seemed to be the intended goal. You'll also want to think about whether this scenario was more aversive, neutral, or appetitively conditioned.

Scenario 1:

The handler wants to teach the horse to move their shoulder away from them on cue. The handler gently presses their hand on the horse's shoulder, the horse first leans into the handler's hand. The handler gradually increases the pressure until the horse moves away, at which point the handler removes their hand. They repeat this process until the horse moves away from light pressure.

List the antecedents:_____

_____

Horse's behavioral response:_____

Quadrant: _____

Conditioning: Appetitive   Neutral   Aversive

Scenario 2:

The handler wants to teach the horse to move their shoulder away from them on cue. The handler holds out a target so the horse has to take a step over to reach the target. They repeat this motion several times until the horse is offering the movement. At this point the handler fades the target and transitions to a visual cue.

List the antecedents:_____

_____

Horse's behavioral response:_____

Quadrant: _____

Conditioning: Appetitive   Neutral   Aversive

Scenario 3:

This is the horse and handler's first attempt at this behavior. The handler puts a lead rope on the horse and gently pulls downwards on the lead. The horse resists the pull a bit, turns his head, shakes it, then eventually lowers a little. The handler releases the pressure on the lead and clicks at the same time, then delivers a treat. They repeat this several times. Each time the horse resists a little before lowering their head. Sometimes the horse offers putting their head down before the halter cue, but the handler does not mark and reinforce these offers. The handler always uses the same, gentle, but firm amount of pressure on the lead as the cue.

List the antecedents:_____

_____

Horse's behavioral response:_____

Quadrant: _____

Conditioning: Appetitive   Neutral   Aversive

Scenario 4:

The handler is trying to lead the horse onto a trailer. As they approach it the horse turns and runs to the grass. The handler yells and pulls on the horse's lead but the horse gets to the grass despite this. When the handler finally gets the horse's head up by pulling, they circle back to the trailer, but the horse immediately dives back for the grass, again succeeding in getting the grass despite the flailing human behind him.

List the antecedents:_____

_____

Horse's behavioral response:_____

Quadrant: _____

Conditioning: Appetitive   Neutral   Aversive

Scenario 5:

A horse is out in the field grazing with friends. The human walks in and all the horses begin swiftly moving away. The human calls their horse and that horse recognizes their name being called, so they trot up to the human and receive a treat. The handler holds up the horse's halter, the horse knows this situation and slides his head right into the halter. The human buckles it up and feeds another treat. The two happily head off together.

List the antecedents:_____

_____

Horse's behavioral response:_____

Quadrant: _____

Conditioning: Appetitive   Neutral   Aversive

Scenario 6:

Horse is happily grazing. Bugs begin to pester the horse. As the sun rises the bugs get worse. The horse swishes and stomps the flies until finally he has had enough and he runs into his shed for relief. After a while of relief he ventures out again, but soon the annoyance of the bugs gets to be too much and he returns to his shed. This repeats.

List the antecedents:_____

_____

Horse's behavioral response:_____

Quadrant: _____

Conditioning: Appetitive   Neutral   Aversive

Scenario 7:

A horse reaches under a fence and grabs some grass. After several minutes the horse accidentally touches the fence and gets an electric zap. The horse jumps away and doesn't try to reach under the fence again.

List the antecedents:_____

_____

Horse's behavioral response:_____

Quadrant: _____

Conditioning: Appetitive   Neutral   Aversive

Scenario 8:

Horse is in a stall that opens into a field with friends. The horse stands, kicking the stall door. The human walks by the first time and shouts, "NO!". The horse stops for a moment then returns to kicking until the human comes back and yells, "NO! Stop it!" The horse stops while the human is right there, but as soon as the human moves away, the horse continues kicking. This repeats a few times. Now the human comes by with grain, the horse is still kicking and the human yells, "NO!" the horse rushes to their feed bucket and gets his grain.

List the antecedents:_____

_____

Horse's behavioral response:_____

Quadrant: _____

Conditioning: Appetitive   Neutral   Aversive

Scenario 9:

Horse stands on cross-ties, the handler cues the horse to pick up the left front foot. The horse does so, the handler catches and holds the foot for a few moments, then sets it down and feeds the horse. They repeat this for each foot. After several repetitions the horse begins picking up their foot and putting it down as soon as the human catches it, then looks to the human for food. They lose duration with each repetition, the horse becoming frustrated is now just pawing.

List the antecedents:_____

_____

Horse's behavioral response:_____

Quadrant: _____

Conditioning: Appetitive   Neutral   Aversive

Scenario 10:

A human is out filling water buckets, the horse comes over and stands beside the human. The human begins spraying the horse with the hose, the horse makes a grooming face and seems to enjoy this. The human sprays the horse for several minutes then returns to filling the bucket. The horse approaches the human again and lines up next to them, the human sprays the horse some more. They repeat this process until finally the water bucket is full.

List the antecedents:_____

_____

Horse's behavioral response:_____

Quadrant: _____

Conditioning: Appetitive   Neutral   Aversive

WORKSHEET

Answers:

Scenario 1:
This is a classic example of how to teach a behavior with negative reinforcement.
List the antecedents: Handler, a seemingly familiar environment
Horse's behavioral response: Moves shoulder away from pressure
Quadrant: Negative Reinforcement
Conditioning: Appetitive   Neutral   **Aversive**

Scenario 2:
This is a classic example of how to teach a behavior with positive reinforcement
List the antecedents: Human, a seemingly familiar environment, known targeting behavior
Horse's behavioral response: Moves shoulder away
Quadrant: Positive reinforcement
Conditioning: **Appetitive**   Neutral   Aversive

Scenario 3:
While this can look like positive reinforcement, because treats are being given, it's clear that the pressure is aversive to the horse and they are working for escape. The treat may help reduce the impact of the aversive, but may also create conflict and frustration with the behavior.
List the antecedents: Human, lead, a seemingly familiar environment, pressure, treats
Horse's behavioral response: lowers head   (seemingly reluctant)
Quadrant: Negative reinforcement
Conditioning: Appetitive   Neutral   **Aversive**

Scenario 4:
The handler is trying to use positive punishment to stop the horse from eating the grass and negative reinforcement to pull the horse onto the trailer. However, what actually happened was that the horse pulled and earned grass, which positively reinforced the behavior of dragging the human to grass. So while the human remained an annoyance, the grass was the most salient option in this scenario.
List the antecedents: Human, lead, trailer, grassy environment
Horse's behavioral response: Pulling for grass
Quadrant: Positive reinforcement (ineffective attempts at positive punishment)
Conditioning: **Appetitive**   Neutral   **Aversive**

Scenario 5:
This pair obviously have a wonderful history together! The horse knows that coming to his handler and putting his head in the halter will be positively reinforced and he was right!
List the antecedents: A herd of horses, an open field, a well known handler, a solid positive reinforcement history with some basic behaviors, a halter and lead.
Horse's behavioral response: Approaches the known human, puts head in halter, leads
Quadrant: Positive reinforcement
Conditioning: **Appetitive**   Neutral   Aversive

Scenario 6:

These annoying bugs have perfected their punishment techniques. They make it so punishing to be outside, that the horse seeks escape in a nearby shelter. Like most forms of punishment this is only has temporary results and the horse tries to go graze again. We could also refer to this as Negative Reinforcement, because the behavior of remaining in the shelter was reinforced by the removal of the irritant.

List the antecedents: A grassy field with bugs and a shelter without bugs.
Horse's behavioral response: Going to shelter
Quadrant: Positive punishment and negative reinforcement
Conditioning: Appetitive   Neutral   **Aversive**

Scenario 7:

Reaching under the electric fence was positively punished because the shock was added and decreased the frequency of the behavior. This was not negatively reinforced, like in the last scenario, because no specific behavior was required to earn relief from the shock.

List the antecedents: A field with an electric fence, grass outside the fence.
Horse's behavioral response: Avoid the fence
Quadrant: Positive punishment
Conditioning: Appetitive   Neutral   **Aversive**

Scenario 8:

The human seems to think they are punishing this behavior when they scold the horse, and the human's behavior of yelling at the horse is reinforced by the horse temporarily stopping. However the horse's behavior continues and does not stop, so it wasn't punished as the human intended. Soon we see why, because the human actually feeds this behavior. The intermittent schedule of positive reinforcement has made this behavior quite difficult to extinguish!

List the antecedents: Open stall, human, food
Horse's behavioral response: Continued kicking
Quadrant: Positive reinforcement
Conditioning: **Appetitive**   Neutral   **Aversive**

Scenario 9:

The horse's behavior was positively reinforced, unfortunately, the behavior that was correlated with the reinforcer was putting his hoof down, not keeping it up. Which was not what the trainer was intending, by using a bridge signal the trainer could clear up this miscommunication.

List the antecedents: Cross-ties, food reinforcers, hoof pick
Horse's behavioral response: Pick foot up and put it down quickly
Quadrant: Positive reinforcement
Conditioning: **Appetitive**   Neutral   Aversive

Scenario 10:

This is an adorable scenario of positive reinforcement with an unusual reinforcer.
List the antecedents: Human, hose with running water, water bucket
Horse's behavioral response: Manding - lining up with human
Quadrant: Positive reinforcement
Conditioning: **Appetitive**   Neutral   Aversive

Session Setup

Now that you're ready to start training, what should your training sessions look like?

We start by organizing our training environment. Think of all the tools you need and the optimal set up of your training area. Go through the antecedents list and make sure you've set your horse up to be successful (page: 39).

Inspire the behaviors you like with targeting, shaping, luring, capturing, molding or mimicry (page: 41). Choose an appropriate reinforcer for the moment. In a general training session food works best as it is consistent and easy to use. But we can adapt our reinforcers based on what the learner most wants in that situation (page: 45).

When the behavior is happening consistently you add distance and duration, (page: 48) and then finish the behavior by putting it on cue. Once it's on a cue you can put that cue on stimulus control (page: 51).

It's likely however you won't get an entire behavior inspired, volunteered, put on cue, and then on stimulus control all in one session. Our sessions should be short, frequent, and fun! Each session should be around 1-5 minutes, depending on the complexity of the skill and comfort level of the learner. It helps to put a limited amount of reinforcers in your bag to serve as a timer to ensure you don't overdo it. There have been times where I walk into my training session with a step in mind and I get my desired goal in 10 seconds - awesome! Reinforce it and call it good. If you keep asking for more the horse may get confused or change the behavior. We jokingly call this "greedy trainer syndrome"; when you think "that's so good, just one more time" or "you're so close just a little more" - that tends to be right when the behavior falls apart. Allow the horse time to think and process what they learned. There may also be sessions where you're just not getting what you want. These are also sessions to just walk away from. If you keep pushing you and your horse are both likely to get frustrated. Take a step back, reassess your setup and see how you can be more successful next time.

Don't forget a clear end of session signal! This is a key element that is often overlooked. When you end your session you want to make it clear to the horse that you're done training. I do this by leaving a few handfuls of food while I leave the area. Even if I plan on coming right back to do another session or clean up the area I still leave to clarify with the horse that I'm done. It's really important to leave some food as we leave as well. Remember in the learning quadrants how **negative punishment** is the removal of something the learner enjoys? (page: 37) Well what could be worse than you leaving with all the opportunities to earn reinforcers? We don't want to punish the last behavior they did - so we leave a few handfuls of food we leave to help counteract this affect. This also helps ease their anxiety or frustration during our training. If we might leave at any time (taking all the goodies with us) they'll be stressed throughout the session worried they may do something to cause us to leave. Leaving food as you go also helps ease this concern.

Try to work on one behavior at a time until it's ready to be put on stimulus control. At that point you can mix it into your repertoire of known behaviors. If you need to work on more than one behavior in a time sensitive situation, try to make the antecedents very different so the horse doesn't get confused and offer the wrong behavior at the wrong time. Finishing each behavior before moving to the next helps keep confusion, and thus frustration, out of the equation.

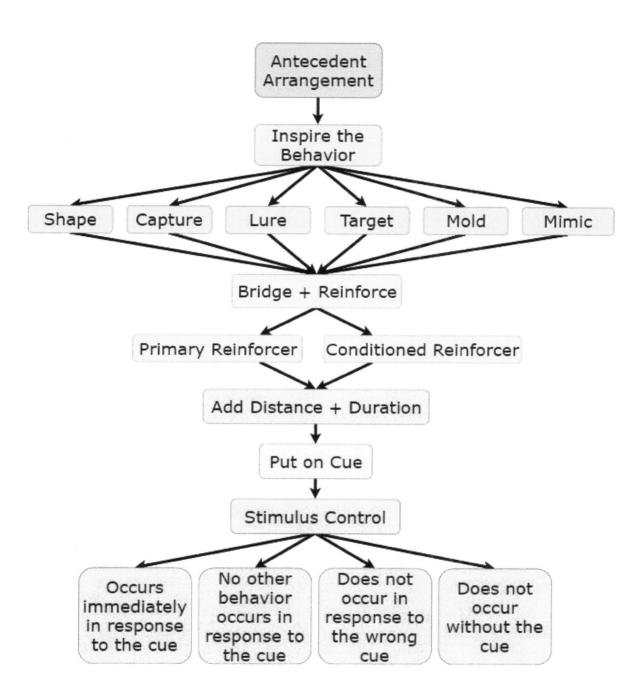

Training Plans

Organizing and planning our training plans can keep us focused on our goals and allow us to track our progress. Organizing our approach using flowcharts or checklists, which can help us decide on the exact criteria we're looking for, the best antecedent arrangement, the shaping method we plan to use, the ideal reinforcer, and the ideal cue. Being proactive by trying to identify potential problems before they occur can help us better identify solutions when things *do* go wrong.

Criteria:
> Describe the goal behavior and the steps you'll be taking today.

Antecedents:
> Write a list of ideal antecedent set up for this behavior.

Inspire:
> Determine which shaping method you think would be the most appropriate for this behavior. Try dividing it up into steps of how you'll inspire the behavior and how you'll wean off the shaping tools.

Stimulus Control:
> Think also about how strictly you want stimulus control on this behavior. Should this be done strictly if the behavior is risky if presented without a cue? More loose, something allowing more self-expression from the horse, where it's OK if it happens without the cue or doesn't always happen when you cue? There are times appropriate for both, so deciding ahead of time can help us put the appropriate amount of stimulus control on it. You'll also want to think about which behavior(s) are best to proof this cue against. If teaching back up, it can help to proof it against standing or walking forward.

> ## Example:
> **Criteria:**
> > Head low (nose close to ground)
>
> **Antecedents:**
> * Work in stall/small paddock
> * Friend in neighboring paddock
> * Have a hand-held target
>
> **Inspire:**
> > Use the hand held target to show the horse where I want them to bring their nose (close to the ground) repeatedly, until they get the hang of the behavior. When they begin offering it, fade the target and add the final cue.
>
> **Stimulus Control:**
> > Alternate with back up and SFF.

Now that we have a great training plan for each individual behavior, it can help to organize which behaviors we want to teach and in what priority order. We can organize these behaviors into checklists or flow charts. I prefer flow charts because they provide me the flexibility I like. Simply list all the behaviors you want to teach - you could go all the way to your end goal (like riding or agility) or stick with a specific situation (like a hoof care plan). If you're anything like me, you may even have smaller flow charts within a large flowchart! Organize the priority order of the behaviors, which need to be taught first in order to teach the next. Also consider your antecedents for each behavior on your list. You may want to mark which behaviors you want to teach in protected or full contact. You can color code the difficulty level of the behavior. You can even put side notes about shaping methods or special arrangements you may want (like marking down if you want to use free shaping for a specific behavior). This can keep us motivated, on task, and able to see a clear picture of where we're going and how far we've come!

In this example flow chart, I color coordinated which behaviors I think will be more diffi-cult to train, blue being the easiest down the rainbow to red being the most difficult. In the flowchart you can easily see how some behaviors build on each other. I also marked with a red background the behaviors I believe will be better taught in full of protected contact.
Along with a list of antecedents I think will help with these behaviors.

Antecedents:

- Start after a meal or time with a food toy
- Work in stall or small paddock
- Friends nearby, but divided by fence
- Alternate food available while training (or food toy)

Standing Facing Forward

Start these behaviors in Protected Contact

Station on Target → Touch Acceptance → Hoof picking → Multiple People → Pretend Vets

Follow Target → Head Down → Back Up → Leading walk → Leading turning → Shoulder Away → Hips Away

Send to Target → Send to new people → Self Halter

Wait until ready for Full Contact

Recommended Reading:

Ph. D. Jenifer a. Zeligs *Animal Training 101: The Complete and Practical Guide to the Art and Science of Behavior Modification* (2014). Mill City Press, Inc.

Karen Pryor *Don't Shoot the Dog!: The New Art of Teaching and Training* (2006). Ringpress Books.

Karen Pyror *Reaching the Animal Mind* (2010). Scribner.

Ken Ramirez *Animal Training: Successful Animal Management Through Positive Reinforcement* (1999). Shedd Aquarium Society.

Susan M. Schneider *The Science of Consequences* (2012). Prometheus Books.

Stand Facing Forward:

Standing still and calmly facing forward is a great foundation behavior that will set the horse up the horse up for success around food. It's the first behavior I teach when we are ready to go into full contact, I may teach a number of behaviors in protected contact first, but I always start here in full contact. It becomes a safe default behavior for them to go to when they aren't sure what to do or whenever you need to return to calm. It's a great skill to use to alternate with new behaviors to help put those behaviors on stimulus control. This teaches them how to relax and be patient while around food.

Antecedents:
- Work in full contact in a calm, quiet area
- A comfortable distance from friends
- Food available (hay net or food dispensing toy)

Set the antecedents to encourage the horse to be calm and relaxed. Capturing calm respondent behaviors early on with this operant behavior will allow the horse use this behavior to return to calm in the future. So work somewhere calm, comfortable, and familiar.

WORKSHEET

SFF Cont...

Shaping Process:
- <u>Shaping</u>

1. Start by standing beside the horse's shoulder, shift with them if they move. They'll likely turn to touch you or check out the treat pouch. Mark and reward any motion they make towards standing, with their head in a forward position. Deliver the treat where you want the horse's head to be (even if they lose position after the click). It may require taking the treat in your closed hand and moving your hand past their current position to deliver the treat. It will help to have your rate of reinforcement very high early on, catching them while they're chewing, before they lose position.

Fable investigating the human and the treat pouch

Fable faces forward, click and treat!

Be careful of unintentional behavior chains. Often during this behavior the horse accidentally learns to look at or touch the human, then face forward, making a little chain. If this happens break the chain by reinforcing while they remain forward.

2. As the horse grasps the concept of facing forward to earn the reinforcement you can gradually ask for more distance and duration. To build more distance, start by taking a quick step back towards the horse's hip - click and return to feed before the horse has the chance to shift position.

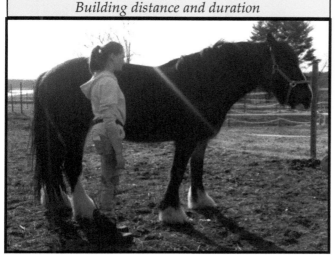

Building distance and duration

3. Build the duration and distance so you can comfortably walk around the horse's body. Practice this while you are facing them or facing towards their hip (like you would if you were going to clean a hoof). We want the horse to be comfortable with us moving around in their space, not needing to follow.

4. You can begin pairing a cue as soon as the horse begins offering the behavior correctly.

WORKSHEET

Targeting:

Touching a target with their nose can sound like a simple behavior to teach but it becomes our key to unlocking so much more. With targeting we can inspire many more behaviors from our horses or even generalize targeting to other body parts. We can use targeting to help horses become more comfortable with novel objects, stirring up their curiosity and play drive instead of anxiety. This skill is great for getting started in protected contact. This can enable you to begin shaping a number of easy and safe behaviors before going into full contact.

> *Stick like objects may be cause for concern for some horses. Starting with something new can encourage more interest.*

Antecedents:
- A quiet, comfortable area
- A comfortable distance from companions
- Protected contact
- New, novel object to target

Shaping Process:
- Capture/Target

1. Stand in front of the horse or over a barrier/partition and hold out the novel object between you and the horse. Mark and reinforce when the horse shows interest or gets close to the object.

2. Capture the moment when the horse's nose touches the target. While you're feeding remove the target so you can present the target for the next repetition.

For our blind friends we tie little bells to the target and even use some targets scented with Essential Oils

3. As the horse understands the goal, begin presenting the target in new and different places, higher, lower, left and right.

4. As the horse becomes 1consistent and accurate about touching the target you can begin to add a cue.

5. Repeat this with a few different objects to generalize the idea of targeting, it gets easier with each new object.

Head Down:

Head down is another safe, easy foundation behavior that can help a horse relax and focus while learning about positive reinforcement. This is another easy skill to teach in protected contact with either free shaping or a hand-held target.

> This is another behavior that can quickly become an unintentional behavior chain, of bobbing their head down then back up. Be sure to develop some duration on this behavior, at least a few solid seconds to reduce this.

Antecedents:
- Quiet, familiar area, comfortable distance from friends
- Hand-held target

Shaping Process:
- Targeting

1. Once the horse is comfortable touching targets in various locations you can repeatedly put the target low to the ground. Each time the horse touches it, bridge, reinforce and remove the target. Present the target low again.

2. Soon the horse will begin to predict the head down, looking low for the target. With the target behind your back or dropped away from you, make the same hand motion as you did with the target (like you're holding an invisible target). If the horse doesn't immediately get the right behavior, use the target a few more times.

3. As the horse gets the hang of lowering their head with the hand motion or begins offering the behavior you can begin to add your desired cue. Cue just before you use your target/hand motion to trigger the behavior, gradually add time between cue and trigger, allowing the horse to offer the behavior with the cue before you initiate it.

Punk touches his well known blue target

He recognizes this familiar hand motion

He knows to lower his head to earn his reinforcement

Stimulus Control:
- Once head down is consistent and on cue, stop reinforcing offers without the cue
- Alternate head down with stand facing forward and targeting, to help the horse understand the cue is the contingency for the reinforcement.

Back Up:

Backing up is an extremely important skill. Very often we need our horses to move backwards to move away from a door or gate, or to make room so we can get by. It also helps reinforce space and remind the horse its OK to move away from us (the reinforcer will still come!) This is a great skill to work on while in protected contact and can help develop safety for future full contact.

Antecedents:
- Quiet, familiar area, comfortable distance from friends
- Hand-held target

Marshmallow sees the target   *She backs up to reach it*

Shaping Process:
- <u>Targeting</u>

1. Once the horse is comfortable touching and following a target I'll use it to teach back up by bringing the target from their nose, down toward their knees. Be sure they can see and are on the target before bringing it to their knees, you don't want them to feel like your target is going to be used aversively against their legs/chest. As the target will be behind their line of vision it helps to start with it well in front of their nose, bringing it down and inward in one smooth motion.

Marshmallow recognizes the hand gesture   *She backs up for her click*

2. As the horse gets the hang of stepping backwards to follow the target you can begin fading out the target by dropping it to your side or holding it behind your back while you make the same motion with your hand as you did when you were holding the target (like using an invisible target). Mark and reinforce if the horse repeats the same backward steps. If they get confused return to using the target a few more times.

3. Once your horse is consistently backing up without the target you can begin to add a cue and continue to fade the hand gesture. Use your intended cue, then use your target/hand motion, mark, and reinforce. Soon the horse should begin offering the behavior with the correct cue.

Stimulus Control:
- Once back up is consistent and on cue, stop reinforcing offers without the cue
- Alternate backing up with stand facing forward and targeting, to help the horse understand the cue is the contingency for the reinforcement.

WORKSHEET

Leading (straight - walk/stop):

Teaching a horse to walk with us is a fundamental core behavior that is vital to living with humans. We need to be able to encourage our horse to go where we want, and when we want it for all basic husbandry and care. We'll start with just walking on straight lines and stopping on cue. These go hand in hand so we'll work on them together.

Antecedents:
* Quiet, familiar area, comfortable distance from friends
* Hand-held target
* A few simple, familiar obstacles, cones, barrels, ground poles as visual markers

You can teach this in full or protected contact. If you start in protected contact it may help to return to using the target when you go into full contact.

Shaping Process:
* Targeting

1. Start by standing beside your horse, facing the same direction, like you would when leading traditionally. Hold the target beside you, where you want the horse's nose to be when walking beside you. Take a single step and mark while the horse is walking to the target, stop to reinforce.

2. Gradually add a few steps but keep the distance short until you know how the horse feels with this exercise. Some horses are frustrated by following the target; keeping your rate of reinforcement high and the distance low will help ease their concern. Using simple obstacles like going from one cone to the next or going over ground poles can help provide horses with visual goals of where they're going and when reinforcement is coming.

3. As you add more steps you'll begin to add stopping as well. After a step or two stop with the target beside you, marking and reinforcing as the horse comes to a stop. Try to balance the amount of times you reinforce for walking and stopping.

4. As the horse gets the hang of moving forward and stopping by your side with you, you can begin to fade the target and add your cues. Add your cues just before you take the steps to walk on and to stop.

Stimulus Control:
* These two behaviors, walking and stopping, contradict and put each other on stimulus control. For more eager, forward horses, put stronger reinforcement on stopping and on walking for slower, calmer horses.
* Alternating in some stand facing forward can help relax more anxious horses as well.

Leading (turning/weaving):

Moving following a target can teach a horse to lead, weave, maneuver obstacles, even approach new situations like trailers, or anything you might encounter in the world. You'll need to work on turning at about the same time as walking and stopping (you need to turn at some point)!

Antecedents:
- Quiet, familiar area, comfortable distance from friends
- Hand-held target
- A few simple, familiar obstacles - cones, barrels, ground poles as visual markers
- Horse is confident walking/stopping with target

Shaping Process:
- Targeting

1. To encourage the horse to turn around you, hold the target out wide, luring the horse around your body.

2. To encourage your horse to make a tight pivot away from you, hold the target in and back a little while you make the wider circle and your horse pivots in the smaller circle.

3. Using simple obstacles like weaving around cones, or making figure eights around barrels can help provide horses with visual goals of where they're going and when reinforcement is coming.

4. You can begin to add any cue you want, it's rather easy to fade the target to visual hand motion/ body language cues. It's important to be aware of what you've chosen as your cues for these behaviors to ensure you remain consistent. Keep the target with you while you fade it away until the horse becomes confident in their space and timing.

Stimulus Control:
- Alternating in some stand facing forward can help relax more anxious horses

Stationing at a Target:

Standing stationed at a nose target can be an extremely useful skill to prepare for or replace the need for standing tied for vet, farrier, grooming and so on.

Antecedents:
- A quiet, familiar area
- A comfortable distance from friends
- A familiar target easily hung or attached to a wall/fence

Shaping Process:
- <u>Targeting</u>

1. Hold the target up or point to it and cue the horse to touch it. Mark and reinforce each touch, gradually ask for more duration.

2. Remember to alternate longer and shorter durations, not consistently asking for longer intervals or the horse will be discouraged. Feeding in position will help build the desired duration.

3. As you gain duration you can also begin to add distance from the horse by gradually moving away and around them while they remain stationed with the target.

Stimulus Control:
- Alternate in other behaviors while in the vicinity of the stationary target to help the horse understand they don't need to always be stationed.

Stationing on a Mat:

Standing stationed on a mat is another beneficial behavior to replace or prepare for standing tied for vet, farrier, grooming, and so on.

Antecedents:
*   A quiet, comfortable area
*   A comfortable distance from friends
*   A mat, block of wood, or anything easy and comfortable to stand on

Shaping Process:
*   <u>Targeting</u>

1. Use a hand-held target to lead the horse onto the mat. If the horse isn't comfortable stepping onto the mat, sprinkle treats all over the mat so they can explore the texture and strength of the mat without having to stand on it.

2. With the horse standing on the mat practice you're calm stand facing forward behavior. Practice this for a few repetitions then use the target to lead the horse off. Lead the horse back on and repeat.

3. Gradually build up distance and duration on this while the horse stands calmly on the mat.

4. You can begin putting this on cue as soon as you're certain the horse will remain quietly stationary on the mat.

Stimulus Control:
*   Leading the horse away and practicing other behaviors between stationing on the mat will help the horse understand the mat is the contingency for this stationing behavior.

Sending to a Target/Mat:

Sending your horse to a target or mat can produce movement in varying directions and speeds. It provides the horse with visual goals and helps the horse become comfortable moving away from you or without you (which will be beneficial when we're on their back). This can be used to teach horses to move around an area, navigating agility obstacles, getting exercise, or mimicking traditional lunging.

Antecedents:
- A quiet, familiar area
- A comfortable distance from friends
- A familiar stationary target/mat in an area with room to move around
- A hand-held target

Shaping Process:
- <u>Targeting</u>

1. Lead the horse to the stationary target and cue touching the target or stationing on the mat; mark and reinforce stationing on the target a few times.

2. Lead the horse away from the stationary target again, using a hand-held target to clarify that they don't need to stay stationed. Circle around, leading them right back to the stationary target. As you approach it cue the horse to station on the target/mat. Mark and reinforce a few times and then repeat the circle.

3. With each repetition begin to linger behind the horse, allowing the horse to go ahead of you to the stationary target. After several circles the horse should get the hang of circling around, going to the target and should gradually become more comfortable going ahead without you. Mark the moment the horse touches the target and quickly meet the horse at the target to deliver the reinforcer.

4. When the horse is comfortably moving to the target from varying distances you can begin to add a cue.

5. At this point you can begin adding more targets, sending the horse from one to the next. You can even add simple obstacles between the targets for added complexity.

Pass the Pony:

Practice sending your horse from one person to another; this can be a fun exercise to get the horse comfortable moving away from you/the food. It can also be a great tool to get them exercising, doing obstacles, and getting comfortable with new people.

Antecedents:
- A quiet, open area
- A comfortable distance from friends
- A few people with targets

Shaping Process:
- <u>Targeting</u>

1. Start by having two people holding targets next to each other. Have the horse do some targeting with one person, then have that person points to the other person and hides their own target. It can help if the person who was doing the targeting turns and faces away to avoid confusion.

2. The other person immediately holds up their target and cues the horse to touch it. After one or two targets, repeat the process backwards.

3. As the horse gets the hang of switching humans, gradually add distance between the people. If the horse gets confused meet them part way.

4. As the horse starts having fun with this you can mix it up by adding people and obstacles to the game.

Hips Away:

Moving the horse's hips away is another basic skill for being able to safely work around and handle our horses.

Antecedents:
- A quiet, familiar area
- A comfortable distance from friends
- A hand-held target

Shaping Process:
- Targeting

1. While the horse is standing facing forward, move to the horse's hip with a long hand-held target. Hold the target out to the side; as the horse turns to approach the target they'll need to first swing their hips away from you. Mark and reinforce this hip swinging away motion.

2. Repeat this until the horse gets the hang of the hip away motion, mark and meet your horse to reinforce them before they bring their front end towards you. Repeat this until you have a smooth motion without much forehand movement.

3. As the behavior becomes fluid you can begin fading the target and adding your cue. Drop or hide your target, and then stand in position and raise your hand as you did with the target. Remember if you choose to use a tactile cue (hand pressing on the hip) to make sure the horse is comfortable with you touching them there first and never escalate (prolong, repeat or increase the intensity) the tactile cue if the horse doesn't comply.

Stimulus Control:
- Once you've added the cue and faded the target you'll want to begin alternating this behavior with standing facing forward, to ensure you can still walk around the horse. It can be helpful to move your hands around their hip to help the horse clarify the exact cue for the behavior and reduce confusion and guessing.

- Remember to practice this behavior on both sides- teach each side completely before teaching the other side to reduce confusion.

Shoulders Away:

Moving the horse's shoulders away is another basic skill for being able to safely work around and handle our horses.

Antecedents:
- A quiet, familiar area
- A comfortable distance from friends
- A hand-held target

Shaping Process:
- <u>Targeting</u>

1. While the horse is standing facing forward, stand beside the horse's shoulder with a long hand-held target. Hold the target across the horse's body, under their neck, and out the other side. The horse will have to step over, but not forward, to reach the target, crossing their front legs. Mark and reinforce as the horse steps their forehand away.

2. Repeat this until the horse understands the pivoting motion. As the behavior becomes fluid you can begin fading the target and adding your cue. Drop or hide your target, stand in position and raise your hand as you did with the target. If they get confused return to using the target for a few repetitions.

3. At this point the behavior should be happening predictably and can be put on cue. Remember if you choose to use a tactile cue (hand pressing on the shoulder), make sure the horse is comfortable with you touching them there first and never escalate the tactile cue if the horse doesn't comply.

Stimulus Control:
- Once you've added the cue and faded the target you'll want to begin alternating this behavior with standing facing forward, to ensure you can still walk around the horse, moving your hands around them. This will help the horse clarify the exact cue for the behavior and reduce confusion and guessing.

Behavior Chains

Remember when we talked about **conditioned appetitives**? (page: 33) These are things horses have learned are enjoyable (verbal praise or good scratches, they've learned these things are great). Another conditioned appetitive is actually our cues themselves! After a long history of cuing the behavior and reinforcing it eventually the *behavior* becomes something the horse enjoys as well. The horse's personality and history can affect which behaviors they find more or less appetitive. More forward horses may find playful behaviors more attractive naturally, while more quiet horses may find stationary behaviors more enjoyable. With this pre-conditioning we can actually use our cues as reinforcers for other behaviors!

We can build a chain of behaviors by using each behavior to reinforce the last. Targeting or stationing on a mat are the most typical of these reinforcing behaviors for most horses, as they're usually taught early in their training and thus they have a long, strong reinforcement history. When we ask a horse to do a newer or more difficult behavior, we can reinforce it by cuing a simple, well known behavior. For example, when riding you don't want to stop and reinforce every behavior the horse does or you will never get anywhere. You can ask for *"walk on"*, *"turn left"*, *"whoa"* then click and reinforce. If each behavior has been taught individually, thoroughly and is enjoyed by the horse, each cue for the next behavior will reinforce the previous behavior. You could do any combination or number of behaviors then click and reinforce. Depending on your horse, the reinforcement history of the behavior and your goal - you can adjust these to make any chain you'd like. These become indispensable when doing agility or riding, so we don't need to stop to reinforce constantly - just enough to maintain each behavior. Remember to mix up which behaviors you use a primary reinforcer with, not always ending with the same one.

Some chains we want to be automatic and predictable. In other words we don't want to have to cue each individual step, we want it to be one fluid behavior. The best way to do this is what's called **"back chaining"**. This is a training technique in which you teach the last behavior on the list first. Usually the first behavior we teach is the one that will be repeated the most and be the most heavily reinforced. So if you teach each step backwards, each new behavior is reinforced by an easier better known behavior that's already conditioned. This minimizes anxiety and helps them feel successful as each new behavior is reinforced with the well known, more enjoyable behavior. Back chaining creates a strong link between the most work with the biggest reinforcer. If we have three steps in our behavior chain, we teach step three first, resulting in reinforcement. Once the last step is mastered you can add step two and three before reinforcement, and so on. For example, when teaching a play kick-ball, we may first teach the horse to hoof-target the ball. Once they do this well we can move the ball, the horse has to follow then kick the ball for reinforcement.

We also want to be aware that horses are highly intelligent and sometimes they create behavior chains where we didn't intend! Very often in the beginning when we're trying to teach the horse to stand still, calmly facing forward, horses may unintentionally learn to look at/touch the person, then put their head back forward. This happens when the person waits too long between clicks and the horse, being unsure what to do, turns to check on the person or try easier behaviors before they jump back to the behavior they know will be reinforced. So we've accidentally taught them that the behavior is 'touch me then look away'. We need to be mindful of our training and make sure we're not creating chains we don't mean to. If we see an unintended chain developing we can break it up by catching the behavior *before* the chain begins. If the horse turns his head to you after fifteen seconds, click him keeping his head forward at five seconds. Break the chain by reducing the distance or duration, reinforcing before the behavior before the chain begins.

> *Behavior Chain*: Using a well trained behavior to reinforce the previous behavior, linking a few together, reinforcing at the end.
> *Back Chaining*: Training a desired behavior chain in reverse order of steps, in order to make each step of the chain easier as they go.

Reinforcement Schedules

Behavior chains aren't the only way to reduce how often we need to stop to reinforce the horse. Once a behavior is taught it can be reinforced on intermittent schedules. There are pros and cons to each form of schedule. You can either choose a schedule for the ratio (how many repetitions of the behavior before you reinforce) or the interval (the duration between reinforcers). There are three common types of schedules that can be either on the ratio or the interval. There are continuous, fixed, and variable schedules.

- *Continuous Ratio*: reinforcing every time the learner performs the correct behavior.
- *Continuous Interval*: reinforcing continuously throughout the duration of the behavior.
- *Fixed Ratio*: every set number of times the learner performs the behavior they are reinforced, (continuous ratio is a fixed ratio of 1).
- *Fixed Interval*: the learner is reinforced at a set duration of time while doing the behavior.
- *Variable Ratio*: reinforcing each behavior randomly.
- *Variable Interval*: reinforcing during the duration of the behavior as random segments of time pass.

Continuous schedules are consistent, predictable, and easy for the horse to understand. It's vital when we begin to teach a behavior that we stick with a continuous ratio, and until we add duration we should always start with a continuous interval. This is especially important for horses who are anxious or easily excitable during training. The continuous schedule helps keep the learner calm and focused throughout the session. Continuous interval is a fabulous way to help a horse get through a tough situation, something for which they might not have been fully prepared. We often use a continuous schedule of rewarding when our new rescues need to stand calmly while being seen or treated by the vet. However, we can't always remain on a continuous schedule for everything - not only for health reasons (very fat horses!) but also for practicality of use. For some animals a continuous schedule can lose its value the longer it continues, it gets boring and loses its allure. I haven't found this to be the case with most horses (they always seem pretty happy about getting treats to me!).

Fixed schedules are always an option but I have learned they are rarely very useful. Horses are smart and they catch onto patterns quickly (this is a survival mechanism). If you only reward the behavior in certain situations, specific times, places, or amounts of time, the quality of the behavior will deteriorate during the predictable non-reinforced times. For example if I reinforce every 30 seconds, after a reinforcer the horse may not do the behavior right away, might not do it as well, until close to the 30 second mark. If I only reinforce when they perform the behavior in a clicker session, but not in regular life, the behavior may be flawless while training but deteriorate when you really need it.

Variable schedules can be extremely valuable if done with some intuition and common sense. While variable means random, we don't have to be so literal. I like to be variable, but pick and choose the best offers of the behaviors, the most like what I want to reinforce. This sort of variable schedule can help maintain and improve the behavior as opposed to just choosing randomly when to reward (which may lead to some messy timing). The unpredictability of these schedules can be stressful early on for horses. Try to reduce your variability very slowly, start by just not accepting poor attempts at well known behaviors. A horse who is insecure or has food anxiety may need some of the food anxiety methods working in place before beginning a variable schedule.

Personally, I find when I've finished training behaviors I keep them on close to a continuous ratio. If I've cued the behavior, I generally reinforce it. Sometimes I'll use a secondary reinforcer instead of a primary though. I find when I finish a behavior I keep it on a fairly variable interval, reinforcing at different durations, unless the behavior predetermines the duration (like jumping).

Body Awareness

When we talk about equine body awareness we are discussing not just their proprioception, but their balance, coordination, sense of touch, and their gross and fine motor skills. We want to empower the horse not just to be aware of themselves but to be in control of their entire body.

In training we can teach the horse behaviors we understand to be biomechanically correct, but these are just solitary, stand-alone behaviors. Rather than just showing the horse how they should be posed and how they should move, we need to teach our horses the concepts as a whole. To better understand their bodies, how they function, how they feel, and how they can use this knowledge to keep themselves healthy, safe and sound.

What is proprioception anyway? Try closing your eyes and touching your nose with your finger. Did you find it? This is proprioception in action. A healthy horse should naturally have a good sense of proprioception. Some things can affect this to varying degrees, such as neurological conditions and even medication. We can see this natural proprioception in examples like the horse being able to carefully find and scratch their ear with their hind hoof. Some horses are more aware of themselves than others. Some also have difficulty knowing where they are in relation to objects around them. This can obviously become dangerous should they crash into, trip over, or side-swipe an object at high speeds or with great force. We can help build our horse's self-awareness with exercises like body targeting. This can not only help them become aware of their body, but how to maneuver it within their environment. You'll notice some body targets are very precise - these can really help develop the horse's fine motor skills and coordination.

We can also help develop a solid sense of balance and coordination with positive reinforcement exercises using a variety of obstacles. This can help build awareness and control of where they're placing their feet, bending their body, and shifting their weight. These obstacles aren't designed to teach any specific behavior, but rather teach them about themselves and how to handle like situations. We can also teach them some fun games to play - pick up, toss, and kick their toys, play fetch, basketball, and even dance! We can also use games to help keep our horses engaged, having fun, and experimenting with what their body is capable of. All this practice prepares a horse for endless life situations, whether it be dealing with rough terrain on the trails, feeling balanced and comfortable with a rider, or being an active participant in their health care.

Body targeting can also build a horse's confidence with being touched. The following worksheets provide some guidance on how to teach body targets, but please be aware these are not written for horses who aren't ready to be touched yet. If you're working with a horse who's not comfortable with touch, take these exercises much slower, with a much higher rate of reinforcement. Working in protected contact also allows the horse a higher level of consent and ability to move away if they find this difficult (page: 39). You may want to play with which order you teach the body targets, with which the horse is comfortable with at the time. While these can help a horse learn about touch, you want to ensure this is taken at the horse's speed with their comfort in mind.

Proprioception: A sense or perception, usually at a subconscious level, of the movements and position of the body and especially its limbs, independent of vision
Gross Motor Skills: control over the large muscles of the body
Fine Motor Skills: the use of precise coordinated movements
Biomechanics: the study of the mechanical laws relating to the movement or structure of an animal

Cheek Target:

Body targeting can be a valuable tool when dealing with health, husbandry care, self-confidence, and body awareness. Cheek targets can help a horse become comfortable with touch and can be your first step in teaching your horse to station against your hand for things like eye and ear exams.

Antecedents:
- A quiet, familiar area
- A comfortable distance from friends
- A hand-held target

> *Body targets are great for teaching in Protected Contact.*

Shaping Process:
- <u>Targeting</u>

1. While the horse is standing facing forward, stand beside the horse's face with a hand-held target. You can try using your hand as a target, instead of a physical target, but I find our hands mean too many things to our horses. The physical target is easier for them to understand; you can later transition to the hand target. Hold the target up by the horse's cheek. When the horse wiggles about mark and reinforce anytime they get close to or touch the target with their cheek. It can help to feed the reinforcer further away, so when they return to a neutral head position they may bump their cheek into the target.

2. Repeat this until the horse grasps the concept and begins intentionally bringing their cheek to the target. Make sure your target/hand is soft so they don't unintentionally hit themselves when they target it. Mark and reinforce each touch.

3. As they get the hang of the behavior and are actively touching their cheek to the target you can gradually switch the target to your hand by holding gradually closer to the top of the target.

4. As they predictably bring their cheek to your target/hand you can begin adding your cue. Teach this behavior completely on each side before teaching it again on the other side. While they may pick up on the second side more quickly, most horses don't easily generalize to both sides.

Stimulus Control:
- It helps to alternate this with nose and other body targets to help differentiate your cue.

Ear Target:

Body targeting can become a valuable tool when dealing with health, husbandry care, self-confidence, and body awareness. Ears are an especially sore subject for some horses. If this is an issue for your horse, start with other body parts first to build familiarity with the concept of body targeting.

Antecedents:
- A quiet, calm area
- A comfortable distance from friends
- A hand-held target

> *A soft feather duster or a glove stuffed and put on a stick is a great option for body targeting.*

Shaping Process:
- <u>Targeting</u>

1. While the horse is standing facing forward, stand beside the horse's face with a hand-held target. Hold the target up by the horse's ear. When the horse wiggles about mark and reinforce anytime they get close to or touch the target with their ear. It can help to feed the reinforcer further away, so when they return to a neutral head position they may bump their ear into the target.

2. Repeat this until the horse grasps the concept and begins intentionally bringing their ear to the target. Mark and reinforce each touch.

3. As they get the hang of the behavior and are actively touching their ear to the target you can begin adding a desired cue. You can also gradually switch the target to your hand by holding gradually closer to the top of the target.

4. Teach this behavior completely on each side before teaching it again on the other side. While they may pick up on the second side more quickly, most horses don't easily generalize to both sides.

Stimulus Control:
- It helps to alternate this with nose and other body targets to help differentiate your cue.

Chin Target:

Body targeting can be a valuable tool when dealing with health and husbandry care, as well as self-confidence and body awareness. Using a chin target sounds a little silly but it can be a valuable skill to teach a chin rest behavior for vet exams, as well as the ability to maneuver their head.

Antecedents:
- A quiet, comfortable area
- A comfortable distance from friends
- A hand-held target

Shaping Process:
- <u>Targeting</u>

1. While the horse is standing facing forward, stand beside the horse's face with a hand-held target. Hold the target up behind their chin when the horse wiggles about mark and reinforce anytime they get close or touch the target with their chin (even if it's just some whiskers touching). It can help to feed the reinforcer up high, so when they lower their head they may bump their chin into the target.

2. Repeat this until the horse grasps the concept and begins intentionally bringing their chin to the target. Mark and reinforce each touch.

3. As they get the hang of the behavior and are actively touching their chin to the target you can gradually switch the target to your hand by holding gradually closer to the top of the target. You can begin to add some duration and slight movement as they learn to rest their chin on your hand.

4. When the horse is reliably offering the chin target you can begin to add your desired cue. You'll want to really generalize this cue, cuing from both sides and in different locations, so nothing unintentionally becomes built into the cue.

Stimulus Control:
- It helps to alternate this with nose and other body targets to help differentiate your cue.

Hip Target:

Body targeting can be a valuable tool when dealing with health, husbandry care, self-confidence, and body awareness. Hips are a big body part and it can be quite intimidating when they start swinging their big bums towards us. Make sure you're ready to finish this behavior when you start to teach it, don't stop half way leaving a big hip swing on no stimulus control.

Antecedents:
- A quiet, open area
- A comfortable distance from friends
- A hand-held target

Shaping Process:
- <u>Targeting</u>

1. While the horse is standing, calmly facing forward, walk beside their shoulder and face towards their hip, as if you were going to pick up a front foot. Make sure the horse is comfortable with the target moving around their body and hips, and that they have no aversive correlation with this. If the horse reacts in any way to the target moving around try using a different target or counter conditioning the target first. Hold the target out and touch it to their hip, mark and reinforce several times.

2. When the horse gets used to the cycle of the target touch resulting in reinforcement, begin to hold the target out an inch or so away from their hip. They may shift, lean or step towards it. They may try a number of other behaviors, stepping forward, backing up, moving their hips away. Just try to stick with them or patiently step away while they try to sort it out. If the horse can't find the right motion in a try or two go back to just touch, click and treat.

3. Repeat this until the horse begins more confidently moving their hips to bump the target. Gradually begin moving the target further away. I find it important to only ever ask for one step, and try to catch this behavior at exactly one step each time. If the behavior gets too large it could become a hip-check and accidentally knock into you. So keeping it small, one step per cue, will keep everyone safe.

4. As they grasp the concept of this behavior you can begin to put it on your desired cue.

Stimulus Control:
- This is one behavior that easily happens too much and can be dangerous if done out of context, so be sure to immediately put it on stimulus control as the horse learns the behavior.
- Alternate this behavior with stand facing forward while you walk around them and touch their hip.
- Alternating this behavior with hip away will be difficult - it can be confusing for horses to coordinate this, so wait until hips target is completely finished and on cue before trying to alternate with hip away. Keep practicing and stay patient as they learn to discriminate the cues.

WORKSHEET

Shoulder Target:

Body targeting can be a valuable tool when dealing with health, husbandry care, self-confidence, and body awareness. Shoulders are a big body part and help control the front end of the horse. They don't generally throw their forehand around quite as wildly as their hind end, but we still want to ensure we finish this behavior promptly.

Antecedents:
- A quiet, comfortable area
- A comfortable distance from friends
- A hand-held target

Shaping Process:
- <u>Targeting</u>

1. While the horse is standing, calmly facing forward, stand directly in front of them and hold the target out beside their shoulder. If the horse isn't comfortable with the target moving around like this spend time counter conditioning it or use a different target. Touch the target to the horse's shoulder, mark and reinforce, repeat this a few times.

2. When the horse gets used to the cycle of the target touch resulting in reinforcement, begin to hold the target out an inch or so away from their shoulder. They may shift, lean or step towards it. They may try a number of other behaviors, such as stepping forward or backing up. Just try to move with them or patiently step away while they try to sort it out. If the horse can't find the right motion in a try or two go back to just touch, click and treat.

3. Repeat this until the horse begins more confidently moving their shoulder to bump the target. Gradually begin moving the target further away. A solid step is plenty here.

4. As they grasp the concept of this behavior you can put it on your desired cue. If you want your cue to include your body in a different position (or generalized to many positions), after repeating the behavior a few times, gradually begin moving your body position to your desired goal.

Stimulus Control:
- This behavior isn't as much of a safety concern as hips toward, but it will still help to alternate with standing facing forward and shoulders away.

Knee Target:

Body targeting can be a valuable tool when dealing with health, husbandry care, self-confidence, and body awareness. Knee targeting can become a nice exercise for precision work - or a fun 'Spanish walk' behavior.

Antecedents:
- A quiet, comfortable area
- A comfortable distance from friends
- A hand-held target

Shaping Process:
- Targeting

1. While the horse is standing calmly facing forward, stand beside their shoulder (well out of the strike zone). Touch the target to the horse's knee, mark and reinforce each touch a few times.

2. As they begin to make the connection you can gradually hold the target further out. If the horse is struggling to get the idea, try leaning or stepping forward to encourage them to take a step. When their knee bumps the target, mark and reinforce.

3. As the horse begins picking up their knee to hit the target you can shape the behavior larger or smaller how you like.

4. Once the behavior is working as you intend you can add your desired cue. Teach this equally on both sides.

Stimulus Control:
- This behavior can get very out of hand and be quite dangerous when it happens unintentionally so you want to implement stimulus control right away.
- Never reinforce the behavior without it being intentionally asked for, from the very beginning.
- Alternate this heavily with standing facing forward, nose target, and other behaviors.

Spin:

Doing a twirling spin around is good dexterity practice and a simple fun behavior to work on in a small area.

Antecedents:
- A comfortable area to work
- A hand held or stationary target.

Shaping Process:
- Targeting

1. If the horse is small enough you can bring the target over their back. When they turn to reach it bring it back towards their hip. At first you'll want to mark and reinforce the first steps turning away from you, but you can rapidly extend this up to a full spin with the target.

2. If the horse is too large to do this, or having trouble getting the hang of it, you can put a stationary target behind them, sending them to the target and then calling them back to you on the other side. At first you may need to meet them part way to deliver the treat, but gradually you can lure out the rest of the spin.

3. As the horse gets the hang of spinning around you can fade the targets and transition to your final cue.

Yes/No:

Teaching your horse to nod their head "yes or no" can be a fun trick at demonstrations and shows, allowing the audience to ask questions or participate too! It's also a good stretch.

Antecedents:
- A comfortable area to work
- A hand held target

Shaping Process:
- Targeting

1. Make sure to teach one completely before teaching the other, so the horse can clearly differentiate the cues. Using the target bring the horse's head up and down or side to side, mark and reinforce after each repetition.

2. Practice this until the horse starts to catch on and these behaviors become smooth and well understood. Reduce your target influence by switching to a hand gesture similar to your targeting gesture.

3. Once they begin offering it freely you can add a final cue. Think carefully about what you want your cue to be, so you can use these in a fun, but practical sense.

Bow:

A bow is a great deep stretch of the forehand and adorable way to end any series of tricks. Your horse deserves the praise and admiration after a sweet bow to the audience!

Antecedents:
- A comfortable area to work
- A hand-held target

Shaping Process:
- Targeting

1. Practice cuing your horse to pick up a front hoof repeatedly until the horse begins smoothly lifting the leg with a simple gesture or point. Then practice cuing the horse to lower their head using the target or use the cue, if you have this on cue.

2. You can gradually begin asking for these two behaviors together, using the target to help them put it all together.

3. Once they get the hang of these two behaviors working together and stretching a bit more, you can begin to add your final cue.

Spanish Walk:

This front leg stretch is great for forehand awareness.

Antecedents:
- A comfortable area to work
- A hoof/knee target

Shaping Process:
- Targeting

1. Practice cuing the front leg targeting both legs while you stand on one side. Alternate which leg a bit at a time.

2. As the horse gets the feel for this, you can begin adding some forward motion as you do hoof/knee targets up front.

3. This can take coordination and balance so be patient as your horse gets the hang of this. If they need to take a few regular steps between leg targeting.

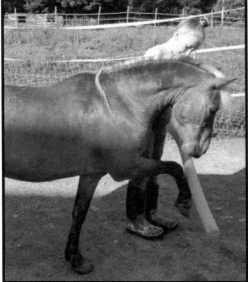

WORKSHEET

Different Terrain:

Getting your horse used to moving on different types of terrain and substrates can be extremely valuable tactile experiences for horses, preparing them for possible situations.

Options:

• Yoga mat	Box/Kid's pool filled with:
• Box mattress	• Sand
• Memory foam mattress	• Mulch
• Plywood	• Plastic bottles
• Wood platform	• Foam cubes
• Tarp	• Water
• Snow	• Gravel

Shaping Process:

1. Using your target lead the horse up to the new footing/substrate and allow them to investigate. If safe to do so, scatter some treats on the ground to encourage them to investigate the footing.

2. Using free shaping or your target encourage your horse to step up onto the new footing and experience how it feels underfoot.

3. As they get comfortable, let them dig, play, and investigate the substrate and then practice walking them over it, circling on it, and backing up on it.

Blind Butterfly exploring the stress relief mat with her whiskers

Platforms:

Platforms are a great way to help your horse learn depth perception and how to negotiate stepping up and down from different heights (like getting in and out of a trailer). It also helps them learn where their feet are in relation to the objects around them.

Options:

- Bridge
- Reinforced pallet
- Stairs (layered reinforced pallets)
- Soil/sand filled tire
- Large rocks
- Tree stumps

Shaping Process:

1. Using your target lead the horse up to the platform and allow them to investigate. If safe to do so, scatter some treats on the platform to encourage them to find the height and density of the platform.

2. Using free shaping or your target encourage your horse to step up onto the platform and negotiate how to step on and off an obstacle of this height.

3. As they get comfortable practice walking or trotting across it, backing up, even turning around on the obstacle, learning to find the edges, and keeping their feet where they belong.

Ground Poles:

Going over ground poles can help a horse practice their depth perception and stepping over various heights and even sometimes landing on new terrain. This can help them practice their balance and spatial awareness of all their legs as well.

Options:

- Ground pole
- Raised ground pole
- Uneven, half raised ground pole
- Wide ground pole (triangle or two together)

Shaping Process:

1. Using your target lead the horse up to the ground pole and allow them to investigate, especially if it's decorated.

2. Using free shaping or your target encourage your horse to step over the pole.

3. As they get comfortable alternate the ground poles, with some that don't roll, some that are wide, or a few in a row, some raised and some uneven. You can also practice them at varying gaits.

Pathways:

Practicing behaviors with barriers like ground pole pathways can provide a new level of precision to your training. If you're having difficulty getting your back up straight, or getting your turning smooth, or developing a nice bend around turns using ground poles to guide your path can really help you prepare for a variety of situations.

Options:

- Path
- L-shape
- Circle
- Maze

Shaping Process:

1. Leading your horse through an L-shaped pathway, while you remain outside the ground poles can be a good exercise for developing a healthy spatial distance and coordination around turns.

2. Using a straight path of two ground poles you can use as a guide to develop straightness and spatial awareness, forwards or backwards.

3. Zig-zag mazes can take this up a notch. They can provide a challenging path to help guide your turns, turning tightly towards and away from you. To make it more difficult try to stay inside the maze poles with your horse.

4. The circle paths can also be a valuable tool to help develop a smooth bend around gradual turns.

WORKSHEET

Ground Pole Patterns:

Making patterns with the ground poles can allow you to get creative with your training process and help the horse coordinate and balance around bends and tight turns.

Options:

- Spiral
- Triangle
- Square
- Letter X

Shaping Process:

1. Using your target or your leading cues, lead the horse over and around the ground pole obstacles.

2. Practice different gaits and patterns to help with balance, coordination and spacial awareness.

WORKSHEET

Jumping:

Once a horse is comfortable playing with ground poles and various low obstacles you can try raising the bar! Teaching horses to jump over small jumps, no higher than the height of their front knees, can keep a horse limber and agile. It can be a great asset to further develop their depth and height perception and adjusting their pacing.

Options:

- Cross Rail
- Log
- Raised ground pole

Shaping Process:

1. Using your target, practice trotting up to and over small obstacles to encourage a jump. When using this technique it helps to bridge/click while the horse is going over the jump, then when they land, and then come to a halt to feed. This is where the bridge signal really becomes important, marking what we want even if there is a long gap before feeding.

2. You can also practice sending them to a target on the other side of the jump, allowing them to pick their own speed and find their own pacing. Again in this situation mark when the horse goes over the jump and then feed as they reach the target - otherwise you may inadvertently teach going around the jump.

3. These jumps can also be put in patterns and combinations to further test coordination, balance and proprioception.

Teeter Totter:

Teeter totters can be exceptional tools for helping horses balance and get comfortable with terrain moving under their feet.

Options:

- Teeter totter
- Round table
- Moving platform

Shaping Process:

1. Once the horse is comfortable walking onto a variety of platforms and terrains, you can lead your horse onto the teeter totter. Allow them to walk on and off several times, step off the sides if needed, and don't worry if they rush off the first few times they feel the movement.

2. As they get comfortable practice leading them over at walk and trot and even backing up over it.

3. When they're really good you can shape them to lean their weight back and forth on the teeter totter, controlling the direction it goes. This is a great core building and balance awareness exercise!

Wacky Noodles:

Pool noodles make amazing tools in the agility ring! They are a wonderful way to get the horse used to tactile stimulation all over their body. They help the horse learn the idea of something that looks solid being squishy and flexible.

Options:

- From side to side (car wash)
- Hanging down (door frame)
- Sticking up from a jump

Shaping Process:

1. Start with the obstacle set as easy as possible, fewer pool noodles, or set far apart. Lead the horse up and allow them to investigate the object. Cue them to touch the noodles to help encourage them to feel it.

2. As the horse becomes comfortable, practice leading them around the obstacle and through the obstacle. If it's too difficult reduce the number of noodles and increase the distance between them.

3. As the horse becomes comfortable moving through and around the obstacles, increase the difficulty of the obstacle by adding noodles or placing them closer.

4. You can also practice sending the horse through the obstacle to a target or person on the other side.

5. Get creative and have fun!!

WORKSHEET

Play Ball:

Engaging with toys and objects in new and creative ways can teach your horse spatial awareness, dexterity, and coordination with objects in their environment. Playing with a ball offers a number of opportunities for manipulating objects with their mouth and hooves.

Options:

- Kick the ball
- Pick up the ball
- Nose the ball
- Drop the ball

Shaping Process:

1. Start with basic nose targeting with the ball object, allowing the horse to see how the ball moves and feels with their nose and whiskers.

2. With shaping you can fine tune this to pushing the ball around with their nose.

3. Exaggerate this to pushing the ball into a net or basket.

Play Ball:

Engaging with toys and objects in new and creative ways can teach your horse spatial awareness, dexterity, and coordination with objects in their environment. Playing with a ball offers a number of opportunities for manipulating objects with their mouth and hooves.

Options:

- Kick the ball
- Pick up the ball
- Nose the ball
- Drop the ball

Shaping Process:

1. From here you can shape the horse to practice kicking the ball; some horses will naturally offer pawing the object when the click is withheld for just touching. If your horse doesn't do this you can place the ball at the horse's feet, encourage them to step forward, and mark and reinforce when they bump the ball.

2. From here you can shape marking when the kick the ball forward, rather than backward

3. You can teach them to kick the ball back and forth with you or kick it into a net!

Play Ball:

Engaging with toys and objects in new and creative ways can teach your horse spatial awareness, dexterity, and coordination with objects in their environment. Playing with a ball offers a number of opportunities for manipulating objects with their mouth and hooves.

Options:

- Kick the ball
- Pick up the ball
- Nose the ball
- Drop the ball

Shaping Process:

1. To teach them to bite/hold the ball with their mouth, make sure the ball is deflated enough for them to bite, or has a handle to hold onto with their mouth. Hold the ball up and cue nose targeting. Gradually shape towards nosing, and then biting the ball. Some horses are more naturally inclined to biting objects - if your horse isn't you can try putting molasses or apple sauce on the part you want them to bite. Mark and reinforce as they bite onto the ball.

2. You can shape this to carrying or throwing the ball, placing it in specific containers or tossing it into a net.

3. Get creative and have fun!!

Painting:

Painting is a creative way to develop your horse's coordination and spatial awareness. It's also really fun!

Supplies:

- Canvas
- Non-toxic, washable kids paint
- Thick wood paint brushes

Shaping Process:

1. After learning the basic picking up and holding an object you can generalize this to a paint brush or anything you can think of!

2. As they're holding the paint brush build the duration and add in some movement.

3. From here encourage them to target the canvas; having a person holding the canvas can help early in the process.

4. Mark and reinforce each time the paint brush hits the canvas. Build up on the motion and duration of this fun skill.

5. Get creative and have fun!!

Color Discrimination:

Don't forget to exercise your horse's mind as well as their body. Discrimination exercises are a great 'rainy day' project. Teaching our horses names of colors can be a great way to get your horse paying attention to cues, learning vocabulary, and cognitive thinking. Horse's vision picks up blues and yellows most clearly, but they are also able to discriminate reds.

Antecedents:
- A comfortable area to work
- Blue, Yellow, and Red cones/balls/cards

Shaping Process:
- Targeting

1. Hold up the blue target and have the horse target it repeatedly. As they begin offering the target, name the target "blue".

2. Repeat this with the yellow target.

3. At this point hold up the two targets with the blue one held closer to the horse. Cue the horse to touch the blue target several times. As they consistently target the blue one, slowly bring the two targets closer together.

4. Switch which hand your targets are in, holding the blue closer to the horse again, work on blue again as you gradually bring the two targets closer together.

5. Repeat this process with the yellow target. Practice with the yellow target held on both sides.

6. As they get the hang of yellow, begin alternating your cues evenly. As they get this correct start mixing up your cues unpredictably.

7. At this point you can introduce "red" the same way you got started.

Object Names:

Teaching our horses names of objects in their world can be a great way to get your horse paying attention to cues, learning vocabulary, and cognitive thinking.

Antecedents:
- A comfortable area to work
- A curry comb, a hard brush and any other object you'd like to name.

Shaping Process:
- Targeting

1. Hold up the curry comb and have the horse target it repeatedly. As they begin offering the target name the target "Curry".

2. Repeat this with the hard brush target.

3. At this point hold up the two targets with the curry comb held closer to the horse. Cue the horse to touch the curry comb several times. As they consistently target the curry, slowly bring the two targets closer together.

4. Switch which hand your targets are in, holding the curry closer to the horse again, work on curry again as you gradually bring the two targets closer together.

5. Repeat this process with the hard brush. Practice with the hard brush held on both sides.

6. As they get the hang of the hard brush, begin alternating your cues evenly. As they get this correct start mixing up your cues unpredictably.

7. At this point you can introduce any other object you like the same way you got started.

8. You can even begin to give these objects meaning. After they target a specific brush you can brush them with it a bit, allowing the horse to not only learn the word but the purpose of the objects.

PART 3:
EMOTIONAL EMPOWERMENT

Emotions

Any of us who have enjoyed time with horses know how intelligent and emotional they are. Luckily the scientific community is catching up. Science is focused heavily on what can be observed, measured, and documented. Unfortunately, that's extremely hard (or impossible) to do with emotions! With humans we can ask each other how we feel, but we have no way of knowing if 'sadness' or 'happiness' feels the same in each of us. With horses it can be even harder; they can't communicate how they feel in words. All they can truly show us is if they find something attractive or worth avoiding. For generations we were seriously limited in our ability to study animal emotions. *Thankfully, with ethologists, biologists, behaviorists, neuroscientists, and many others coming forward with more and more information on animals as a group (and equines more specifically) people have truly begun to open up to the idea of animals being thinking, feeling, sentient beings.* We are now able to understand animal intelligence and emotions in a deeper and more accurate way than ever before.

Emotions can be inferred through physical expression, language, and behavior – many scientists have been driven to categorize these and find the physical source of these emotions. Darwin was among the first to attempt this categorization, and he did so by using observable expressions. He organized all emotions within these observable categories: Joy, Sadness, Pride, Shame, Fear, Anger, Disgust, and Contempt. This early research opened the door for further study and understanding into emotions of humans and more generally in the animal kingdom as a whole. I'm going to focus a bit more specifically on the modern neuroscientist, Jaak Panksepp's model of emotion as this is the most useful when discussing horses. It's also well categorized and easy to understand. The rest of this section directly references research written about in his books listed at the end of this section.

Panksepp's research has shown that the primitive sub-cortical regions of the brain are the same among all animals studied. What this demonstrates is that all the species studied have the same physical source of their emotions. These emotions are not only apparent in these regions but are able to be triggered when the appropriate region of the brain is stimulated. More animals are being included in these groups as studies progress; as research expands, ideally empathy and understanding will follow. Knowing how our animals' feelings mirror our own can help us empathize with them and support them throughout their lives, when being handled, and in our training.

Emotions run deep, coded into our genes, providing a basic set of instinctive behavioral action patterns and a set of unconditioned triggers. **Instinctive behavioral action patterns** *are behaviors that animals are born understanding and knowing how to do. These are behaviors like finding a teat, suckling, standing, running, mating rituals, yawning, and so on.* There are also **unconditioned triggers**, *animals are born knowing how they feel about these stimuli.* From birth they understand their love for their mother, their satiation from food, their fear of predators, and caution around the unknown. This means horses are born with the ability to understand their environment from an emotional point of view, knowing what they enjoy, what they fear, and so on. Later in maturation with higher brain activity the behaviors and emotional arousal can become understood, learned, and regulated. Species all mature at different rates - horses are born not only physically mature, but mentally as well (compared to humans). These strong instincts can help them independently meet their own needs and keep themselves safe before life experiences have taught them all they need. The animal becomes a learner, not just instinctively reacting to their environment. They grow, adapt, and change to their world. Their instincts aren't lost or overruled, rather they work hand in hand with the learned triggers and behaviors.

Emotional responses to certain environments and stimuli can change and adapt through classical conditioning just as we've described in the previous section on learning (page: 33). It's important to recognize that emotion and behavior are both triggered by the environment but occur independently from each other. While often certain emotions correlate with certain behaviors, (like fear is typically accompanied by freeze, fight, or flight) the behaviors happen as a result of the environment and are driven by their consequences. Each individual's learning history can alter their behavior in various situations. So while it's typical for a prey species like a horse to freeze and then flee from a predator, if flight doesn't provide escape from the threat, they will fight to defend themselves. If this

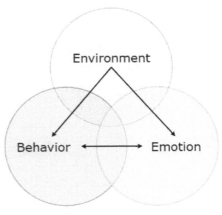

happens enough the horse will more quickly resort to fighting for safety. The emotion of fear, is also triggered by the environment (the predator) - but does not influence the behavioral response. The emotion does not equate to or cause the behavior, because the behavior can change through learning - but the two are often paired together (thus fear does not always equal run). We can't weigh or observe the emotion without invasive hormone measuring and brain scanning tools, but we can make educated guesses based on common emotion/behavior correlations that are formed through learning. With training we can also change behavioral/emotional correlations, teaching a horse to stand still or lower their head when afraid. This may not outweigh the respondent reflex of startling - but can help when the situation turns more operant (page: 114). It's important to remember that this conditioning and learning happens both artificially, as in something that is intentionally planned by humans, and in nature without intention or design.

So if emotions can't easily be quantified, and behavior can be trained independent of emotion, why should we care about them? Empathy and compassion alone should make us want to care about their emotions. That being said, there are some practical reasons. Some emotional/behavioral correlations are deeply ingrained in a species and require careful understanding. We also know certain emotions are naturally aversive or appetitive, which also affects our learning (page: 110). The emotions the learner feels as a result of the environment can inform the learner whether they want to change or maintain the environment through their behavior. Then the consequence will also be interpreted by their emotion, determining if the consequence is aversive or appetitive. I'm not going to go too deep into the neuroscience, but I'd like to discuss the way these emotions are categorized and how they affect us, our horses and our interspecies relationship.

The purpose of these emotions is to tell the animal from the inside out how well they are doing in their mission to survive and reproduce.

Emotional Systems

Panksepp's emotional systems are RAGE, FEAR, PANIC, SEEKING, PLAY, CARE, and LUST. We capitalize the emotional categories to differentiate the terms from common language. So, when we write FEAR, we know we're referring to the entire emotional system, not just the general feeling. Panksepp organized emotions into these seven systems by referring specifically to the neurocircuitry based on the location in the brain and the function it evokes. We can stimulate these emotional tendencies by triggering a specific neuroanatomical location (place in the brain) with electrical or chemical impulses.

Emotions are not all or nothing, they ebb and flow, and they can build or can dampen each other. There are levels to all emotions. When all emotions are functioning at low levels the animal is content and calm. When one or several begin to increase in intensity those emotions are felt more strongly. If you look at the image, you'll see a visual example of how emotions could flow. This is a graphic based on no real data, it is just to help us visualize the concept. The center white spot is complete calm, which might only be able to be achieved through meditation or quiet rest, while the most intense color at the edge of the wheel represent the most dramatic, extreme level at which we can feel the emotion. It's rare, if ever, that we just feel one emotion, pure and in the absence of any other emotion. Imagine an extremely emotional situation you've experienced recently. Try to think back to how you felt - it's usually a combination of several feelings. Each system has an important job to do in our mission to survive and pass along our genes. Some emotions we actively work to avoid feeling, others we seek out and enjoy. Lab testing with a variety of species has shown that it's fairly universal how these emotions are interpreted (as aversive or appetitive). Aversive emotions (FEAR, RAGE, and PANIC) are designed to warn us and protect us from potential risks (physical or social). These systems protect us, and while we dislike how they feel, they play a vital role in our lives. If possible, most living creatures would choose to feel only the attractive emotions. CARE, PLAY, and LUST let us know we're doing well in our mission to survive, our needs are being met, and we can enjoy life's pleasures (like reproduction). These emotions all interact with one another, and some work together to make a stronger reaction. For example, when the FEAR system is engaged, and the animal is not finding safety, RAGE will step in to provide the extra help needed. These emotions can also work to reduce one another. If the learner is feeling isolated, which engages the PANIC system, comfort from friends and family can engage the CARE system which can ease the social anxiety.

The SEEKING system is unique, this system is our motivation to act and respond to our environment. While this system was originally called the "Brain Reward System", we've come to find it's also responsible for interpreting consequences for behaviors that seek relief. This system is responsible for how we categorize the stimuli in our environment. It ties in with all other emotional systems, seeking out the good feeling emotions and avoiding the aversive emotions. SEEKING is vital for our ability to function and survive, but situations like chronic illness, stress, or learned helplessness can diminish this system, resulting in depression of varying degrees. This system also requires regular satiation, or it will begin to trigger the RAGE system. When we have a need we just can't meet, when we think we earned something we're just not getting, when restrained or unable to find relief, we become frustrated and angry in a last-ditch effort to meet our need.

In the chart on the next page we organize and explain the emotional systems. Each emotional system has a job, a function it performs to help a living organism survive, thrive, and reproduce. There are specific triggers for each emotional system, some instinctive and some conditioned from their life experiences (all different for each species and individual). We've also listed common equine behavioral correlations to the emotional system as well as extreme responses. We separated these behaviors because as they reach an extreme the behavior becomes harder to influence through learning. We might call many of these reactions "over threshold".

Recommended Reading:

Jaak Panksepp *Affective Neuroscience: The Foundations of the Human and Animal Emotions* (2004). Oxford University Press.

Jaak Panksepp, Lucy Biven *The Archaeology of Mind: Neuroevolutionary Origins of Human Emotions* (2012). W. W. Norton & Company.

Kenneth Davis, Jaak Panksepp *The Emotional Foundations of Personality: A Neurobiological and Evolutionary Approach* (2018). W. W. Norton & Company.

Kiley-Worthington, Marthe. *The Mental Homologies of Mammals. Towards an Understanding of Another Mammals World View.* (2017). Animals.

Affective System	Function	Causation	Equine Expression	Extreme Equine Expression	Aversive or Attractive
RAGE	- Protection - Predatory	- Desperation - Physical irritant - Restraint	Pinned ears, bite threat, striking, rear, chase, kick threat, pacing	Bite, kick, fight	Aversive
FEAR	- Defense - Safety	- Pain - Threat	Avoidance, freeze, alert, huddle, flinch, appeasement, jaw snapping, self soothing, defensive posturing	Bolt, fight, startle, eliminate waste	Aversive
PANIC	- Social bonds - Grief	- Separation - Social loss - Death - Loneliness	Calling, head tossing, spinning, loss of appetite	Weaving, pacing, pawing, withdrawing (internalize)	Aversive
SEEKING	- Produce action - Motivate	- Desire - Want/Need	Approach, avoid, tactile investigation, visual searching, flehmen response, smelling	Digging, foraging, browsing, problem solving	Attract/ Aversive
PLAY	- Learning - Fun - Social bonding	- Social cues - Joy - Satiation of other emotional needs	Circle, frolic, jump, leap, prance, stamp, bounce, toss/shake, carry object	Nip, fight threat, pull/tug, neck wrestle, chew object	Attract
CARE	- Social bonds - Maternal nurturing	- Maternity - Positive relationship	Nose touch, huddle, nuzzle, nudge, sharing resources,	Mutual groom, nicker, nurse, lick	Attract
LUST	- Reproduction	- Heat cycles - Arousal	Masturbation, erection, calling, herding, scenting feces, mount attempt	Presenting heat, mating	Attract

The Emotional Side of the Learning Quadrants

So now that we understand how the emotional systems work and are expressed in horses, how does this influence our training? With their research neuroscientists were able to determine whether organisms found a system aversive or appetitive/attractive. With this information about the emotional systems we can determine how they function in traditional learning quadrants.

In the quadrants chart I included which of Panksepp's emotional systems are involved in which learning process. You'll notice SEEKING is in both positive and negative reinforcement, both require the horse to behave in order to earn what they like or find relief from something they don't. They must seek out the answer to the problem at hand. How do they make the aversive stop? How do they earn the appetitive? On the other hand, the goal of punishment is to stop/reduce a behavior which effectively puts a temporary stop to the SEEKING system.

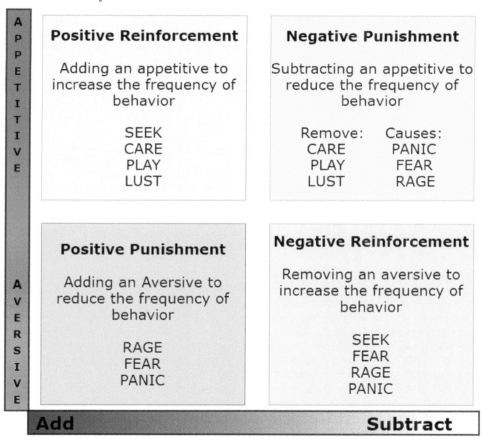

With positive reinforcement we know we need to add an appetitive to increase a behavior, typically we use food or scratches. These things make the horses feel good as they trigger the CARE or PLAY system. Regular hand feeding seems to be received by the horse much like nursing, and in fact many horses will return to old behaviors they learned to get their mothers to let them nurse when we first start clicker training. Scratching mimics mutual grooming, a great display of CARE between equine friends. We also involve the PLAY system quite heavily in positive reinforcement, mostly with the behaviors we ask for. Movements like running, jumping, and exploring new things engages PLAY, when taught thoughtfully.

While positive and negative reinforcement share the SEEKING system, the similarities end there. Negative reinforcement requires the horse to feel FEAR, RAGE, or PANIC to some degree in order for the removal of these emotional triggers to be relieving. If a horse is being chased by a predator, their FEAR system will become active at the same time the horse will chose a behavior to relieve the threat (freeze, fight, flight...). If the behavior results in a relief of threat, and thus the FEAR, the behavior will be negatively reinforced. They'll also remember the antecedents around this scary situation and be more alert when these warning signs are present.

In training, however, we must first coerce the horse to feel the stimulus is aversive enough that they seek escape. The relief from this aversive feeling must be valuable enough that it increases the behavior's frequency. For example, we may add the conditioned aversive of a whip tapping their skin, which triggers the FEAR or even RAGE system. When the horse does the right behavior, we relieve (remove) this emotional stimulus. We typically use the FEAR system during training with negative reinforcement, often utilizing their flight response to get results through the expression of avoidance behaviors. Typically we use things that resemble **unconditioned triggers**, *which are things horses instinctively know to avoid, like swinging rope motions or crouching/predatory postures*. We may also use a mild pain aversive like physical pressing, tapping, pinching, or pressure points. Usually a horse's first response to pressing is to lean into it to remain balanced, but when the pressure becomes strong enough to be so aversive they must react, then they move. When they move the way the trainer desires the aversive is removed and they learn how to avoid the pressing. Despite it being physically mild, *the emotional impact remains the same*. The level of FEAR elicited by the trainer's command must be aversive enough that the learner seeks relief. So, we must maintain the conditioning of the aversive tool we may be using for it to continue to elicit these strong emotions.

Typically, we want to avoid triggering the RAGE system in horses during training (though relief from RAGE can be a common negative reinforcer in a more natural setting), however, there are times trainers will use RAGE to trigger behaviors they want. Most often trainers use this in the form of irritation or annoyance (repeated tapping or pressing) to trigger the behaviors they want and inspire enough aversion for the relief to be valuable. We can also use RAGE to trigger more advanced skills like rearing, bucking, or chasing a human at liberty.

That being said, more often RAGE tends to be an outcome of negative reinforcement, usually in the form of frustration or self-defense. When a horse feels FEAR, they respond with previously correlated behaviors such as, freezing, fleeing, or fighting - whichever they believe will keep them safest. Most horses have learned that freezing or fleeing works in correlation with the FEAR system, but some may be more naturally inspired to fight (like stallions) or may have learned fighting is more effective in their early life. We see this often with horses who have learned to bite or kick, because more timid handlers have left them alone out of fear (or because they were injured). While trainers typically try to provoke the flight response to inspire the behaviors they want, if the horse doesn't find the relief they are looking for (due to poor timing or insufficient release of pressure), RAGE will be triggered, which is typically correlated with agnostic behaviors. We see this occasionally with lesson horses. The unskilled riders kick the horse to go, but simultaneously pull on the reins (because they are balancing with their hands). The horse doesn't know how to earn relief from the conflicting aversive aids, so instead they buck, rear, or just stop. When negative reinforcement is done well, the trainer should keep the horses seeking escape (FEAR), but not yet stirred up enough to fight (FEAR/RAGE). If they do try to fight in self-defense as opposed to flight, and it works to find them the relief they're seeking, it will progressively become their go-to response. If both fight and flight responses fail the horse, learned helplessness will set in.

111

PANIC is another aversive emotion, exhibited typically in the form of separation anxiety- it is what keeps horses sticking together in a band, as this keeps them safe emotionally and physically. Being separated from their friends and family is extremely aversive. We rarely utilize PANIC in our training, but there are some old theories of isolating horses so that they become so desperate for companionship, human companionship becomes much more valuable. We also need to be aware of how strong an emotion like PANIC can be for horses and have empathy for their situation when they are separated from their domestic bands when re-homed or when we ask them to leave their social unit for things like trail rides or competitions.

Positive punishment also requires FEAR, PANIC, or RAGE (but not so they can be relieved as reinforcement); these feelings are being added to punish or stifle behavior. In most training situations we use FEAR to punish - either with an extreme threat or actual pain. They must believe the behavior will cause them to be at risk for the behavior to decrease. Some Natural Horsemanship trainers have really understood this, using phrases like "make them believe they're going to die" or "make sure they're more afraid of you than anything else". There are times PANIC also reduces behavior, for example wandering from the herd or risking being cast out of the herd is a threat to their safety and wellbeing. We all want to fit in, especially when our survival depends on it. While FEAR and PANIC are punishing to the horse, RAGE is often the outcome. When one feels isolated or at physical risk the RAGE system can easily be triggered, which is why our horses can have aggressive outbursts after experiencing punishment. This is usually met with stronger punishment until the outbursts cease, though it's safe to infer the RAGE is still there, just stifled by FEAR.

Negative punishment is a bit more complicated; some emotional responses need to be relieved, which causes other emotions to be stirred up. Negative punishment removes something the horse enjoys - this would be something that involves the horse's SEEKING, CARE or PLAY systems, things they need to thrive. The removal of these things that the horse enjoys is what feels aversive enough to punish the behavior. When these emotions are forcibly removed or replaced, this triggers RAGE or PANIC. When CARE is removed (friendship or companionship) PANIC sets in. When PLAY or something the horse needs to survive is taken away it provokes RAGE in defense. The PANIC and RAGE are aversive enough to make the horse unlikely to try that behavior again.

Remember, the learning quadrants and the emotions connected to them are for all living things capable of learning - not just horses. You may be able to relate to many of these scenarios with situations in your own life. As you can tell both punishments and negative reinforcement involve the aversive emotions, while positive reinforcement alone involves the more enjoyable emotions. While we all learn from all quadrants all throughout our lives, we need to remember there is a difference between natural learning situations and contrived. In contrived situations we have an ethical decision to make. We as trainers have the ability to choose which quadrant we'd like to use to teach. There are so many aversive things that happen in our horse's lives, (bugs, heat, social conflict) we don't need to be aversive as well. I don't want my relationship with my horse to resemble one they have with an annoying bug, overbearing heat, or a threatening bully in the herd. Rather, I'd much prefer my relationship to be one of a loving companion, engaging their CARE and PLAY systems.

Our goal should be to use the positive reinforcement quadrant as much as possible when training our horses. Not only for good behavior, but for a happy, healthy relationship and the emotional wellbeing of the horse.

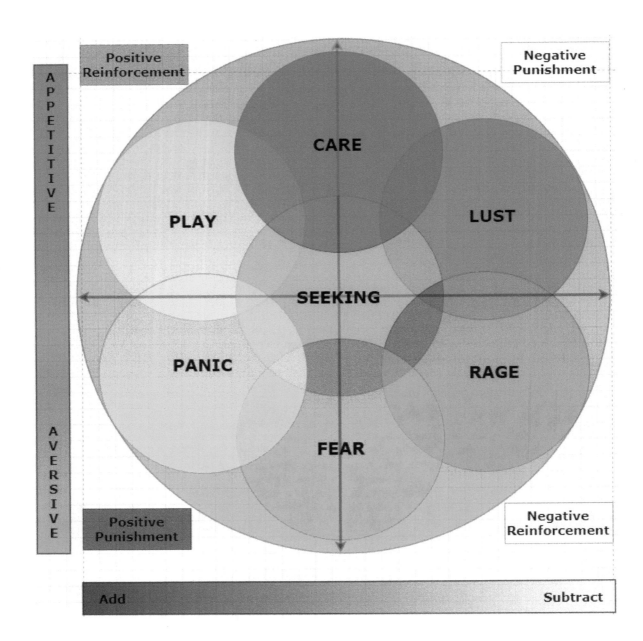

Respondent Behavior

In science it is required that we look at behavior analytically and without emotion. It's important we do this so we can see the truth through our, usually, very biased eyes. No matter how much we try, we often just see what we want. So, taking emotion and subjectivity out of the equation can help us be more honest. When we look at our animals, we frequently project and anthropomorphize (assign human attributes) to justify our ideas. How often have we heard *"My horse loves to jump"*, when really, he's just thrilled to be out of his stall? *"My horse is such a princess"*, when really, they just don't like to wear tack that doesn't fit or *"My horse loves his bit"* - when really, it just means "this is the only thing I can control him in". We frequently assign opinions to and place labels on horses - to justify our own desires/choices.

It's so important to look at behavior honestly. Understanding operant behaviors and how they work in the ABCs and learning quadrants can inform us of how a horse feels about a situation, but it can only generally tell us if the horse finds the scenario aversive or appetitive. If they work to avoid the stimuli/scenario we know the situation is aversive to the horse, while if they seek out or work to earn the stimuli/scenario we know the horse finds this situation appetitive. When we see the behavior change we can then see what is reinforcing it or punishing it. However, without assumptions or risking anthropomorphism we can't determine much more about how the horse is feeling.

It's absolutely vital that we don't forget the emotion part! Just because we don't want to make assumptions doesn't mean we should forget about how a horse feels. *Many behaviors correlate with specific emotional systems, though learning history can mis-align these. It's important we don't make assumptions on emotion based on behavior because of this, but we can use this knowledge to make educated observations.* How do we look at this honestly? How can we include the emotion without adding in our own bias and assumptions? There's no way we can look at another living being (even another human, even the human closest to you) and know that they feel each emotion the same as we do. There's no way for us to look through someone else's eyes and feel with someone else's emotions. That being said we can connect the dots to make some basic inferences.

In the last section on learning theory we discussed only operant behaviors, behaviors we can modify, but are there other types of behavior? We have artificially divided behavior into two categories, so we can better observe, study and influence them. **Operant behaviors** *are those that animals have learned to use to operate their environment.* These are the behaviors we can reinforce and put on cue through the learning quadrants and ABCs. **Respondent behaviors,** *however, are those that are reflexive and not under voluntary control (normally).* These are behaviors like salivating, increased or decreased heart rate, breathing, shivering, flinching, startling, and so on. These start out instinctive, unconditioned, just physiological responses. They can't be trained, but they can be classically conditioned, which is why "classical conditioning" is sometimes called "respondent conditioning". Remember Pavlov's dog salivating at the sound of a bell? The bell was classically conditioned to predict food - resulting in the respondent behaviors connected with the anticipation of food (salivating).

Luckily studying respondent behaviors gives us more information about how a horse feels. Based on comparing the respondent behaviors expressed by your horse with where they would occur in an unconditioned setting, we can determine more accurately how our horses are feeling.

Respondent Behavior: a reflex that occurs in response to a specific external stimulus. All organisms have an inherited response ELICITED by environmental stimuli.
Operant behavior: Occur when EMITTED behaviors are weakened or strengthened by the consequence. Shaped by the ABCs and learning quadrants.

Because respondent behaviors are less under voluntary control, and less influenced by learning history, their correlations with the emotional systems tend to be a little stronger than operant behaviors. We can use these to better infer information about the horse's emotional state. This takes studying and understanding the species and individual we're working with. This is another place ethograms can be extremely helpful. We can see the difference between a "standing calmly" behavior and a "standing alert" behavior - not from the behavior 'stand', but from all the respondent behaviors happening alongside (the facial expression, the muscle tension, the breathing rate, and so on). However, many respondent behaviors aren't always very obvious or even well understood. Without a stethoscope we may not know when a horse's heart rate has increased. Without taking blood or connecting electrodes we can't monitor their hormonal or other physiological changes. So, we'll only ever know a portion of the picture. While it's still important to refrain from making assumptions, we can begin to read emotions with a bit more accuracy.

Let's look at an example and break this down. Situation: we scratch our horse's withers and our horse stands still, relaxes their body muscles, stretches their neck a little, elongates and wiggles their top lip. Operant behavior: standing still. Respondent behaviors: relaxing body, elongating and wiggling top lip. So if we take these behaviors and compare them with our ethograms, we'll see that standing still can happen just about anywhere, but the respondent behavior of elongating and moving their top lip matches up with auto-grooming/mutual grooming. If we look at what categories the grooming behavior appears, it generally occurs in bonding/socializing situations. With this information we can infer that the CARE system is active - but remember, this is just an educated guess, without fancy tools, we can't know for sure.

"An organism's behavior may appear totally under operant control, yet there is always an underlying respondent component"

~Bob Bailey

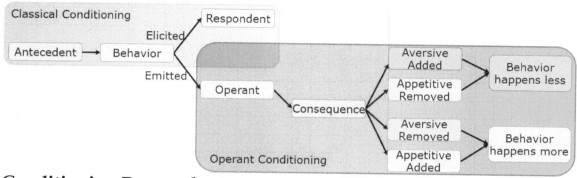

Conditioning Respondents

Aside from just being able to better measure what our horses are feeling, respondent behaviors are also important in our active training. We can't train a respondent behavior (we can't train a horse to startle, flinch, drool, tremble, or increase their heart rate, etc.), however, respondent behaviors are classically conditioned and become a part of the big picture. It's important to remember that operant and respondent/classical conditioning are never happening alone or in short bursts but are both happening all the time (not just in contrived training sessions).

When we reinforce a behavior we are not just capturing the physical, operant behavior - we are also encompassing the respondent behaviors, at least in part. When we reinforce "stand with high heart rate, tension in your jaw, rapid breathing" it is a different behavior than "stand, breathing softly, relaxed eyes". In fact, they're so different often the learner doesn't even realize it's the same operant behavior being performed. We run quite differently when we are chasing the bus we are about to miss, than when we are being chased, or when we're enjoying a run for exercise. If you picture these three behaviors, the operant "running" will be the same in each, while the respondent behaviors will be very different. The same person running in each of these scenarios will look very different. The same applies for our animal learners. "Back up happy" and "back up scared" are two completely different behaviors in the learner's mind, even though "back up" is the behavior while "happy" and "scared" are feelings.

We must first be aware of this correlation. When we are training a behavior, if the horse is upset (for any reason - even unrelated to your training) these aversive emotions are being tied into this behavior (as expressed by the respondent behaviors that may get wrapped up with it). It's vital that we remember that emotions should be among the criteria we're encompassing. We should ensure when we mark the behavior the horse is not only performing the correct behavior, but doing so in the right state of mind (as best we can determine based on the respondent behaviors).

This works in both directions - if the horse is soft, relaxed, and feeling good while we teach a behavior, this behavior will correlate, even elicit these pleasant emotions in the future. So we can take advantage of this correlation to bring comfort to an uncomfortable situation. We can train simple comfort behaviors, in a safe and secure environment, building in the relaxed, content emotions, so we can refer to this behavior to help relax the horse in high stress situations, like going to the vet's office.

When we approach altering emotions in training we want to look at our ABCs again. The operant behaviors are inspired by the Antecedent and altered by the Consequence. The respondent behaviors are only elicited by the Antecedents (page: 39). Respondent behaviors can't be reinforced to happen more or punished to happen less. *However, the reinforcer/ punisher could become antecedents in themselves, in that they elicit emotions as well.* Punishing a horse for spooking, reinforcing a horse for being happy, doesn't influence the likelihood of that emotion happening more or less, just the behavior. There is a common myth that if you comfort a frightened animal or child it will reinforce the fear, but this isn't what is happening. Your comfort helps change their feelings in the situation but does not cause the emotion to happen more. *If you feel the learner begins showing fear more after you've helped them, it may not be that they are more afraid, but they are more comfortable showing you how they feel and asking for your comfort when needed.* While reinforcing a horse for being happy won't increase the likelihood of the horse being happy in the future, it can reinforce the operant behaviors related. Just as well, punishment can't reduce the likelihood of the horse spooking in the future - it can stifle the operant behaviors related. The reflexive behavior will continue, but as they fade, like a gradient, the operant behaviors will take over and can be influenced. We see this often when a horse's flight response has been heavily punished. While they are still frightened, the bolting behavior has been stifled. You'll see horses dancing in place, eyes wide and alert, respiration and heart rate through the roof even as they comply with their rider's cues.

This all being said, we don't want to just sit and wait for the horse to be feeling the right emotions to begin our training. We can ensure we're wrapping in the ideal emotions by setting up the environment and antecedents to help encourage the learner in the right direction. If we're looking to encourage PLAY, or CARE, or SEEKING, if we want the horse to be excitable or exhibit soft, relaxed levels of these emotions - we can prepare our training scenario to match appropriately. When we write our lesson plans and antecedent arrangement we should keep in mind our emotional criteria as well. We can even use our reinforcement to set up the emotional situation we're looking for. Feeding larger quantities of lower value food can be comforting for horses. We can also use scratches and affection to soothe them as reinforcement. Even how we feed the reinforcer can change how they feel; we can use active tossing treats for excitement or calm hand feed-

ing and rubbing the withers to help relax an anxious horse. There's a lot we can do to influence how our horses feel before and during our training session. So work actively to keep them in the zone you're looking for.

We can take this a step further and condition our antecedents! Depending which direction we'd like to encourage our learner, we can take the time to prepare the learning environment in the emotional state we'd like. This may sound complicated, but it can be as simple as a "security blanket". By spending our relaxing, happy grooming time in proximity to a specific object or location, we can pre-program the object or location to be perceived as safe by the horse. Doing this can set up our learner to feel relaxed when we train new behaviors. We could also use a large open field with obstacles to encourage playful and fun behaviors! This sort of conditioning happens often unintentionally when we use targeting. Very often we see horses go to their target when they are stressed; the target has become so heavily conditioned as a good thing (appetitive) that it can help soothe them.

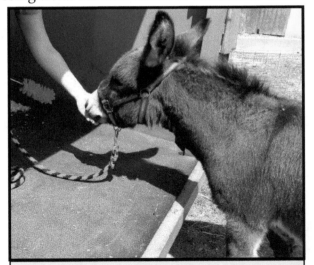

While operant conditioning can overshadow emotional behaviors, it can't influence the respondent behaviors. Sunflower desperately wants to touch her target to get her treat, but her fear of the trailer is evident in her respondent behaviors. With a higher value reward or the addition of an aversive we could overshadow how aversive the trailer is and get the operant behavior we want (getting on the trailer). But this wouldn't change her feelings about the trailer right away. This type of conflict between how they feel (respondent) and how they've been taught to behave (operant) can be extremely stressful for the learner. So we need to change the antecedents. We need to start much further from the trailer.

A horse's peers are also subject to classical conditioning. Just like anything, how they feel when they're around someone (human or animal) will encourage them to want more or less time with them, to seek out their company or flee from them. They'll come to know how someone's presence will affect them, how they feel to have them around. Their presence alone can change how a horse feels as well. We've often seen this with veterinarians and farriers - horses rapidly learn how to recognize them as often the experience can be quite aversive for most horses. But it doesn't need to be that way. *Remember this as you spend time with your horse, what emotions are you being paired with?*

When we make emotion a criteria, we can consider how we condition our tools, our environment, and most importantly ourselves. With awareness of how we affect our horses and how they're feeling when we're around we can determine how we're conditioning ourselves. Does your horse greet you with delight? If not, it might be time to start thinking about how your horse feels when you're around and what you can do to improve these experiences. Having ourselves be attractively conditioned (someone safe, comfortable, and fun to be around) we have already taken a huge step towards conditioning our antecedents to encourage positive emotions during training.

When someone
else's happiness
is your happiness

That is Love

www.EmpoweredEquines.com

118

WORKSHEET

Observational Skills Part 2

Let's practice our ability to see and list respondent behaviors objectively. We've already described and identified the operant behavior, label, function, causation, development and evolutionary history for the images below. This time we'll list the respondent behaviors seen. We'll research the respondent behaviors in ethograms and consider the information we've already learned about the behavior to determine which emotion(s) we're seeing - using Panksepp's categorizations.

Remember these are best guesses based on a single photo taken as a moment in time. I tried to choose photos that showed as much of the "complete" picture as possible - without any hidden surprises. But we should remember when looking at other photos there is often a great deal of detail left out, so while we take our best guess it's just a guess. Watching short video clips can expand our operant and respondent behavior list substantially and can add a great deal more clarity to the situation and better understanding of which emotional categories we're seeing.

Respondent behaviors: lower heart rate, slower breathing, soft facial muscles, relaxed body muscles
Emotional category: CARE (of self)
Added details or questions: Pony is resting or sleeping, emotional systems are all on low.

Respondent behaviors:_____
_____
_____
Emotional category: _____
Added details or questions:_____
_____

Respondent behaviors:_____
_____
_____
Emotional category: _____
Added details or questions:_____
_____

Respondent behaviors:_____
_____
_____
Emotional category: _____
Added details or questions:_____
_____

Respondent behaviors:_____
_____
_____
Emotional category: _____
Added details or questions:_____
_____

Respondent behaviors:_____
_____
_____
Emotional category: _____
Added details or questions:_____
_____

Practice using
your own photos

Respondent behaviors:_____
_____
_____
Emotional category: _____
Added details or questions:_____
_____

Inappropriate Behaviors

Ideally, we'd only see our horses displaying behaviors indicative of a happy and fulfilled life - but, unfortunately, we live in the real world. There are some unhappy emotional behavioral displays that are just a part of a full life for a horse. But, where is the dividing line? What behaviors, in which situations, are not acceptable? What do we do if we see them?

As social creatures, horses are bound to run into a few disputes when interacting with each other. When arguing over resources we'll see agonistic behaviors (fighting/competing). These behaviors may include acts of aggression, threats, attacks, retreat, and appeasement behaviors. Remember, dominance is only related to family units of like-species and in temporary relation to who has priority access to which resource (page: 16). So, these disputes may be settling who has current priority or rearranging a previously settled order. These are natural and, so long as both sides settle down quickly, there's little to worry about. Some horses have social troubles, due to poor upbringing, and don't understand or don't accept another horse's appeasement behaviors. They may continue to aggress well past winning and even hurt the other. It's important we don't allow these horses to injure or bully other horses. Some horses may have the opposite social difficulties, not standing up for themselves, and allowing themselves to be bullied out of access to all resources. If there is plenty of access to resources and plenty of space to avoid each other there shouldn't be disputes, otherwise you may need to consider dividing those horses. There is a line between natural possessiveness and bullying. All horses are entitled to safety and security - even from other horses, if the case may be.

We also want to watch these aggressive and appeasement behaviors during interactions with humans. Aggressiveness towards humans is almost always a sign that something has gone terribly wrong in their world. If you experience aggression of any sort immediately stop what you're doing and look for potential pain issues. If needed, call the vet for further clarification. Most acts of aggression are defensive, either of their physical self or their external resources. So, pain, fear of pain, and the resources they require to meet their needs are the first things to check when aggression presents itself. Determine if all their needs are being met and there's nothing they feel the need to defend. Most often, we can fix these problems and prevent aggression from happening again. However, if the aggressive behaviors have been unintentionally reinforced or become habit we may need to teach a safe alternative behavior the horse can do to earn reinforcement, making aggression unnecessary. We'll go into this more soon (page: 164).

Sometimes however, aggressive behaviors are actually an attempt at play, like sparring. This can be fun for your horse, but very dangerous for us small humans. It's important play behaviors have a healthy outlet - either another horse to rough house with or toys like yoga balls, barrels, trees, and food toys that allow the horse to paw, kick, and bite. We also need to teach appropriate alternative behaviors to redirect the horse to safer options for when we're working together.

We also want to be aware of our horse's appeasement behaviors - licking, empty chewing, averting gaze, turning head away, yawning, slow blink, and so on. Unfortunately, these behaviors have commonly been misinterpreted as a horse being polite or "thinking". However, horses only offer an appeasement behavior when they feel threatened by another animal, if they are stressed, or frightened. These behaviors are usually calming or self-soothing. We should be careful never to make our horses feel this way, if we can avoid it. We need to take these signals seriously and not dismiss them, so, take note when you see an appeasement behavior and reassess your training plan.

There are some even more concerning inappropriate behavioral expressions that we see often at over-crowded or poorly managed farms. If you've ever been in a barn where the horses are left a period of the day without food or are confined to stalls for long periods of time (or even a horse who has spent a long time on stall rest), you may have seen some stereotypic behaviors. **Stereotypic** behaviors *appear to have no function but can be self-stimulating or self-soothing for the horse. They're often repetitive and continuous until something interrupts the behavior.* With horses, we mostly see behaviors like cribbing, wood chewing, weaving, pacing, tongue sucking, lip flapping, or even masturbating. Most of us can relate to this. While we don't crib, we may resort to the use of drugs or other vices. There are more mild versions as well, some of us bite our nails or twirl our hair. We may not realize that these habits were formed to relieve stress or boredom, as they often stick around even after the stress has passed.

If you've been at one of these barns during feeding time, you may get to see a huge display of **superstitious** behaviors as well. *These are actions the horse has inadvertently learned when they were unintentionally rewarded.* Humans have lots of superstitions that many of us still believe! Maybe you found a particularly shiny penny and the rest of the day went really well. You may attribute your good day to finding the penny. Horses make these unintentional connections as well. We see them most often at feeding time as the whole barn erupts in a display of behaviors that they each think will get them their dinner faster. Many horses whinny, screech, paw, pace, kick walls, bite bars, or attack their neighboring horses (if they can see each other). I've even seen some horses who feel the need to urinate at feeding time! At one point in their life they must have been doing this behavior out of boredom or coincidence when they got their food. Now, it's become a superstitious habit.

We often call these stereotypic or superstitious behaviors "vices" as though the horse is being "fresh" when, in truth, they are clear signs of depression, anxiety, and a need for control in their lives. Once these behaviors are learned, they are very hard to undo. They often take a long time in a healthy lifestyle before the behaviors begin to fade (if ever). Ideally, we'll keep their needs met and these behaviors won't begin to appear. So, be aware and keep a close eye on your horse's emotional displays and what you may be unintentionally teaching them.

Agonistic: behaviors that are associated with fighting/competition: submission, aggression, threat, retreat, and attack are all agonistic behaviors.
Appeasement: Kind actions by one horse that reduces the likelihood of threatening behavior from another horse. This usually involves trying to make themselves small, share resources or mimic behaviors made by foals.
Stereotypy: a repetitive or ritualistic movement, posture, or utterance.
Superstition: A behavior that was unintentionally reinforced or punished, when there is no real correlation between behavior and consequence, accidentally causing the behavior to increase or decrease in frequency.
Displacement Behavior: occurs when an animal is torn between two conflicting drives, activities often consist of comfort movements, such as grooming, scratching, drinking, or eating.

Conflict

Another place we see inappropriate behaviors is when a horse is feeling conflicted. Conflict comes in three forms: approach-approach, approach-avoidance, and avoidance-avoidance.

- Approach-Approach - the horse has to choose between two things they want.
- Approach-Avoidance - the horse needs to decide if they want to tolerate something unpleasant to gain something desired.
- Avoidance-Avoidance - the horse must choose the lesser of two evils.

We see these quite often in our horses' lives and, as usual, some degree of this is just a part of real life. We, as caretakers, can help reduce conflict in our horses by providing clarity. Most mild forms of conflict are met with some hesitation, then a decision. However, there are times when the conflict is extreme. It is in these situations that we will see what's called "displacement behaviors". This is when they display a behavior that doesn't make sense at the moment, for example, scratching, grooming, or head shaking. When we ask a horse to do something they're not comfortable with, or leave something they enjoy, they may hesitate and then display a displacement behavior before making up their mind. This may not seem like a big deal, and while these behaviors were identified and understood for a long while, it wasn't until recently people found a use for them in research. We can use and measure displacement behaviors to determine how much anxiety, stress or conflict our horse is feeling at the time and recognize conflict when we may not have realized before. When working with your horse, noticing a displacement behavior can make you aware when a horse is just complying to earn reinforcement, but is not truly comfortable with it.

Learned Helplessness

The right to choose can be ever empowering to our horses not just in their living situation, but also in our training. A horse who feels 'out of control' of themselves will tend to be more anxious and unpredictable during work with humans - unless the horse has sunken into a state of learned helplessness. When a horse feels they have choice, they often put in a great deal of effort and try harder, than when they feel forced or compelled. We are frequently told that we need to gain our horse's trust by exerting control and that when they allow us to control them, this is a display of their trust. When often, the opposite is true. We can't hope to control our horse when they can't control themselves. A horse can't trust your control, if they don't have trust in themselves. Rather than attempting to control our horse through escalating pressure or the use of aversives, we should empower our horse with self-control and choice, regularly throughout their life. Horses are frequently trained to a point of "learned helplessness" so we can have complete control over our horses, even in extreme situations. In this case, the horse relinquishes all control to us, giving up their right and ability to defend themselves. So, if it gives us more control, is learned helplessness in our horses such a bad thing?

Learned helplessness truly is as bad as it sounds. This is when the horse has reached a point where they truly believe that they are helpless. They feel so out of control of themselves and their world that they have given up trying to find escape or hope. This mental state is akin to extreme depression and hopelessness. This is beyond fear. From a Panksepp point of view (refer to the emotions section of the book), this is when the SEEKING system shuts down. This system drives all behavior, all desire, the ability to go on. Without an active SEEKING system, the rest falls apart, not just emotionally, but physically. Learned helplessness is typically caused by prolonged or regularly repeated feelings of complete lack of control. It can happen when the learner is exposed to many, seemingly inescapable aversives over a period of time. This phenomenon is not exclusive to horses or prey animals, but all creatures. Humans are not exempt; examples of childhood abuse, domestic violence, kidnap victims, and other such traumatic experiences often result in the same feelings of helplessness and lack of control, with the same prolonged symptoms.

There is a famous experiment carried out by Seligman and Maier (1967) that examined the phenomenon of learned helplessness in dogs. The experimenters looked at three groups of dogs (non-escape, escape, and control groups) and two phases for the dogs to go through. The first phase gave all the dogs in non-escape and escape groups electric shocks through the feet (not including the control group). The dogs in the escape group had the ability to press a panel to stop the shock. The dogs in the non-escape group did not have any way to avoid the shocks. The second phase was to put each dog from all the groups into a shuttle box, a box with two chambers they could jump between. They classically conditioned a warning the electric shock. The dogs in the escape group quickly learned to jump to escape the shock.

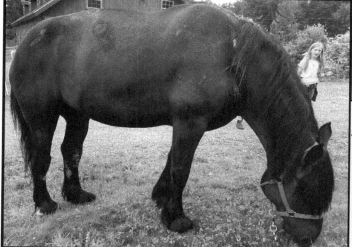

An animal living in chronic pain or submitted to extreme pain due to injury or illness can also induce Learned Helplessness. This was Gummy Bear just after he came off the slaughter truck, living in chronic pain and being worked as hard as he was put him in a state of learned helplessness.

Most of the dogs in the control group did, as well, while the dogs in the non-escape group did not seek escape or try to jump away from the shock. The first phase of inescapable aversives clearly reduced their ability to learn how to escape, even when the option was made available to them.

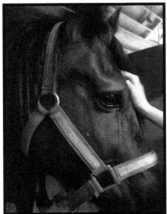

Their eyes frequently tell it all, Gummy Bear's eyes truly showed the emotional struggle he was going through.

Many trainers work to keep their horses in a state of learned helplessness so they don't fight during aversive training or try to flee when spooked. This can be done through a large, extreme trauma that shows the horse they have lost control. Some trainers have used laying a horse down forcefully until the horse stops trying to get up or tying them out to a tree or patience pole until they stop fighting. It can also be done with a subtler approach, through having control taken away in small ways on a regular basis. We see this when horses are chased around a round pen or through the use of phased escalation of aversive pressure with no relief. Over time, learned helplessness sinks in. There may be times you see horses working completely loose in a field, but obviously complying to aversive training. It may look like the horse is there willingly, when in fact they're feeling quite helpless. Is it much like abused children, hostages, or prisoners who don't attempt escape (even when given the option) because they have given in to their circumstances. If they do find their way out of this situation, there is often lasting emotional damage (to both the humans and animals). Most often we see it as a complete lack of "try", the desire to keep going. They're afraid of failing so they simply don't try. We see this quite often with our rescued horses. *Many of them struggle to offer even the simplest behaviors. Curiosity and playfulness fall to fear and hopelessness.*

We can help horses like this overcome their past or their pain by providing them a healthy lifestyle, with enrichment and play. Stir up their SEEKING system by encouraging them to try and succeed. *If your horse is having a hard time with something try not to think of it as them being disobedient or fresh, try not to take it as a personal slight or that they don't trust you. Realize that your horse is struggling to handle a situation, empower them by giving them the tools to be a better version of themselves. Build their self-confidence, encourage play, boost curiosity, and teach them to trust themselves.* Many of our rescues come to us with a degree of learned helplessness, at least around humans. Some have come to the extreme where even with food available they have no desire to try to get it, and often we have to put the treats right to their lips. Many will stand quietly, afraid to move, until we've gone learned helplessness it helps to reward any effort. We'll spend the first phase of positive reinforcement training in protected contact, rewarding any attempt, even any movement, eye contact, any form of connection. Our goal is to help them learn that it's safe to try, and worth the effort. In a situation like this it's even more vital that punishment is removed entirely from their lives.

Gummy Bear having fun learning to touch a target to get treats!

Tonic Immobility

A further, more extreme technique for controlling, in this case restraining, horses is the use of Tonic Immobility. This behavior is a bit of a phenomenon that continues to be studied. The basic defense strategies for most horses is freeze, flight, fight - I've frequently felt we ought to add an extra freeze at the end. We often see horses stop, standing alert, listening, smelling, and watching, deciding whether to run, this is the first freeze. They'll start to flee in an effort to escape, but if that fails and they're caught or cornered they may try to fight the threat at hand. If fight and flight fail and the animal believes they can't possibly escape or win the fight, they will freeze again, in a different way. They are no longer alert, in fact they're the opposite, they seem glazed over, paralyzed, they are no longer responsive to external stimuli, their heart rate and blood pressure drop. This immobility is almost a trance-like state - however the experience seems to be remembered. Science has labeled this freezing behavior "**Tonic Immobility**". You've probably seen images like this in wildlife documentaries, of prey animals caught by predators, becoming stock-still.

Though this phenomenon has been studied frequently, the reason for it is still not fully understood. Most often we see it in prey animals, when they've been caught by a predator. It may be a defense mechanism they use to reduce physical harm once caught by the predator, in case they do find means to escape. Most predators' natural reaction is to continue attacking when there is movement (think of a cat playing with a toy) but when the movement stops they may reduce their grip or not attack so violently, potentially giving the prey a chance to escape. However, another theory is that this paralysis provides an emotional escape for the prey, allowing them to 'zone out', blocking out the fear or pain of the situation they're in. There are people who think they are hypnotizing animals by laying them on their backs. Other theories relate this to mating, where a male will use these pressure points to immobilize the female to reduce risk of injury if she were to resist.

Humans are no exception to this when faced with overwhelming stress or pain - there are scenarios of child abuse, domestic violence, assault, and humans who were trapped (building collapses and such) who have also experienced Tonic Immobility. As terrible as this is, we've been able to talk with these humans and begin to get a firsthand account of how it feels and how it effects their life. They've explained how in this state they've "de-realized" or "depersonalized", where they feel cut off from reality or from themselves. Sometimes this dissociation can reduce the impact of the memory of the experience. But the experience is definitely remembered as something to be avoided. These experiences can lead to Post Traumatic Stress Disorder in humans and repeated experiences can lead to Learned Helplessness and trauma induced emotional disorders.

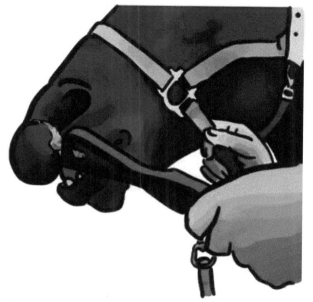

So why would we ever do this to horses? Why would we ever want them to feel so helpless? Simply put - it works. The twitch has been used for decades in war and on the farm as a successful tool for restraining large animals like horses, during surgery and medical procedures - before they had safe sedatives and pain relief. A twitch is a band, chain or rope that is twisted tight around the horse's top lip. The top lip of the horse is loaded with nerve endings for precision while picking up food (ever seen a horse find a a single piece of hay in a pile of shavings?). When squeezed tight the pain and feeling of entrapment induces a state of Tonic Immobility - keeping the horse still during any procedure. There are many common defenses of this tool, that it's *"just a distraction"* or *"is just used to release endorphins"* - but the distraction and, the cause of the release of endorphins, is the same - *Pain*. It's safe to conclude that while this tool may work and may have been the only option in the past, it is now outdated and thoroughly unethical to use, barring life-threatening situations where chemical restraints aren't possible. Humans have also used other techniques to induce Tonic Immobility in horses, in the form of laying them down and other physical restraints. In these cases it is usually in an attempt to demonstrate the human's level of control and manipulation over the horse, reducing the horse's likelihood to try, fight, or resist during future aversive training. Often people phrase this to sound like they're displaying dominance over the horse, to justify their actions. But as we've already discussed, this isn't how dominance works, what they are really doing (even if they don't know it) is utilizing learned helplessness as a training tool.

Tonic Immobility is not only emotionally shattering, with possible life-long side effects, it's also extremely risky physically. While in this state the heart rate and blood pressure drop, which can cause an animal to go into shock if prolonged or when they come out of it. If the horse feels they can escape at any point (even when we are intentionally letting them go) they may do serious damage to themselves, or the human as they attempt to shake free. They may also be in such a panic they crash into things or fall. Ultimately, while these techniques can work for restraint, they should be our final, last resort in life-saving situations, never to be used lightly or when there are any other options available to us (like sedatives). Ideally, we should always be prepared to do as necessary for our horses, with proper medications, sedatives, pain killers, and environmental adaptations to prevent us from ever needing to resort to this option.

What are Equestrian Ethics?

When we venture down this path we can feel lost. As we learn more about how to be kind and treat horses well - suddenly we are stricken by the realization that most are not treated so well. As we learn not just about more ethical training techniques but about animal emotion, cognitive abilities, and social structure we realize how often these things are ignored or overlooked for personal gain. So many chose to remain ignorant because it's easier. We simply cannot learn more about kindness without also seeing the cruelty.

It can hurt to try so hard to learn about the good, only to find out there is so much bad. It can be overwhelming, drowning us at times. It can make us want to lash out with violence to fix it all! But we know that won't work. We need to remain focused on the kindness and not let our growing awareness of the cruelty poison us. This maybe harder to do than it sounds.

It can help us to quantify and measure aspects of our horse's welfare to determine our own individual moral lines. With our growing knowledge we can make more appropriate decisions for the good of our horses, rather than for our own internal personal desires. We must all come to our own conclusions on how much, of what, is acceptable and under what circumstances, but we have some guides to help us make these decisions when we're unsure.

It can help to first recognize the species-specific challenges horses face to determine which moral issues we are likely to be faced with. We know that in domestication horses have basic welfare needs that must be met. The least we can do for horses is ensure that all their physical and emotional needs are met. It shouldn't stop there. We also need to look at our interactions with our horses and consider the impact on them of what we ask them to do for us. We need to ensure our training, interactions, and what we ask of our horses doesn't cause any suffering, pain, or emotional risk. This may be more easily said than done, but it's our responsibility to take this into consideration for the wellbeing of our horses. Even before we train a behavior, we need to determine: who is this behavior for? Who does it benefit? If there is no benefit for the horse, we need to assess if there is any risk or detriment to the horse. From here we can determine the necessity of the behavior, whether it's ethical to train it or to what degree. We can also identify some adaptations we can make to reduce the risk or aversive impacts of our actions and requests of the horse.

Love shouldn't be conditional on what I can do for you

www.EmpoweredEquines.com

True love continues long after the work is done

To address and make decisions on ethical situations with our horses we need three things - research, empathy, and action. We need to ensure we continue to educate ourselves to make the best ethical decisions for our horses at all times. There is new research on the benefits and detriments of tools, training techniques and housing methods being published constantly.

Staying aware of this can help us ensure we're making good choices. Compassion and empathy should be our drivers to do what's best for our horses, and our gauge to measure honestly if our choices are as moral as we believe they are. Finally, there's action. We not only need to utilize our education and compassion, but we need to share what we have learned with anyone open to hearing about it.

We also struggle with the reality of domestication. We can't always meet all our horses needs in the most ideal ways. Many of us board or are restricted in how we can keep our horses and need to meet the requirements of the farm at which we board. While we should always, always strive to be better people and provide a better life for our horses, we must accept our limitations and do the best with what we have. As our knowledge grows we will be able to improve our training, handling, and keeping. There are a few models to help guide us on our path to choosing the most ethical options. Each decision should be made individually by ourselves in relation to our individual horse. These guides can just help us make our own personal decisions, as it relates to training.

LIMA

"**Least Intrusive, Minimally Aversive**", is a principle that we should apply to our handling and training, it was developed by Steven Lindsay (Lindsay, Steven. *Handbook of Applied Dog Behavior and Training Vol 3*). This is designed to help us examine what we're asking of our horses and how we're asking, then choose the least invasive and least aversive options when training. In this context, the term invasive refers to anything physically interfering with the horse's body, personal space, or that takes away from their welfare requirements. We need to take this into particular consideration when choosing the tools we use with our horses and our aspirations for working with them. Keeping LIMA in mind can help us look at our options from an objective point of view and potentially find gentler, kinder, or less intrusive ways of achieving the same goal. It can also help us to assess whether this is really something we feel deserves this level of intrusion or aversiveness.

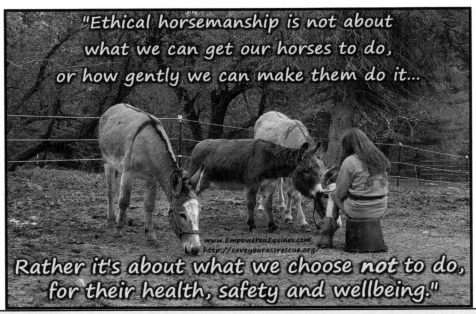

"Ethical horsemanship is not about what we can get our horses to do, or how gently we can make them do it... Rather it's about what we choose *not* to do, for their health, safety and wellbeing."

www.EmpoweredEquines.com
http://saveyourassrescue.org/

Keep in mind, with all behaviors, what your horse is physically and emotionally capable of. Just because with Clicker Training we can convince them to perform a behavior doesn't mean they're ready for it. It's our job as caring horse-parents to keep their safety and physical comfort in mind. If you find your horse becoming reluctant or stressed with a behavior stop and assess if they're really ready for this one. Think about ways to make them more physically and emotionally prepared or determine if this isn't an appropriate skill for this horse.

Humane Hierarchy

If our goal is to train all of our behaviors with positive reinforcement, what do we do if that's not working? Is it ethical to use negative reinforcement? What if we must? To this we refer to the **Humane Hierarchy**, developed by Dr. Susan G. Friedman. This is a flow chart of the most ethical approaches to altering behavior and what our back up contingencies should be. We want to try each step in the flow chart to its fullest, exhausting it completely before stepping down to the next level. We also want to determine how vital it is that this behavior is done and how quickly it must be done. Determine who this behavior is for (is it for you or your horse?) and how soon must it be done.

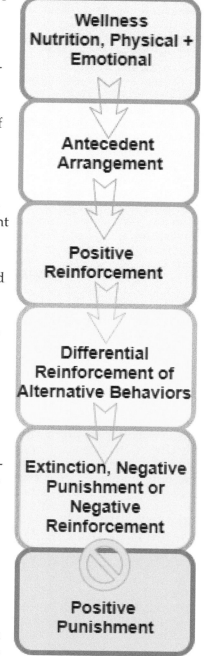

The humane hierarchy begins with considering the horse's internal antecedents - the horse's physical and emotional wellbeing. When we prepare to train a behavior, assess if the horse is physically and emotionally ready for this behavior. If there is a problem behavior we would like to reduce, ensure this problem isn't the result of an emotional, physical, or nutritional need before attempting to fix it with training. If there is a problem behavior or difficulty getting a desired behavior, look into hiring a vet, nutritionist, body-worker, or other equine professional to see if there is something externally causing your trouble.

From here we can arrange the antecedents; we talked about this in depth already (page: 39). Should you want a horse to perform a specific behavior, you can arrange the environment to encourage the correct behavior. Using fencing, ground poles, targets, stations, resource placement and so on we can make it easy for our horses to stumble into the correct behavior. If there is a behavior you are looking to reduce, see if there are any antecedent changes you can make to fulfill the need and prevent the unwanted behavior.

If we've checked to ensure all their physical, nutritional, and emotional needs are met - but the unwanted behavior is still occurring, the desired behavior isn't happening, or we want to get the desired behavior on cue for use. This is when we implement positive reinforcement training. We've already discussed in detail how to elicit, reinforce, put on cue, and put under stimulus control behaviors we want with the use of positive reinforcement. But we can also use positive reinforcement to prevent unwanted behaviors. A brief overview of options includes training an incompatible behavior or training the absence of the behavior. We'll discuss this in further detail soon (page: 165).

This is my usual stopping point - I try hard not to proceed beyond this. If you feel you must, be sure you've done the best you can, exhausted all the creative options, and tried contacting a professional for assistance. Decide how important this behavior really is - is it for you or your horse? Is it for safety or fun?

If there is a behavior we must prevent or eliminate, and we've exhausted all the other options, we can try using extinction or negative punishment. Remove anything from the environment that may be reinforcing this behavior and allow the behavior to extinguish (page: 37). Remember there may be a burst before extinction. If this isn't safe to allow we can use negative punishment, removing ourselves and anything the horse finds appetitive when the behavior is performed. We may resort to this if our horse presents a dangerous behavior during training and we've missed the opportunity to take our necessary safety precautions - we may need to remove ourselves and our reinforcers from the environment. This not only negatively punishes the behavior, it also keeps us safe from the potentially dangerous behavior. Be aware this can result in a great deal of frustration in the horse, causing more anxiety during training. It really should be a last resort. If you've exhausted all your options - but this behavior must happen, we may need to investigate the use of negative reinforcement. It's important to remember that negative reinforcement isn't wrong to use when done with care. We want to work to eliminate the need for the aversive as quickly as possible and ensure we aren't creating frustration or a lack of clarity, we don't want to make the situation any more aversive than needed. This requires careful calculations and an honest look at your horse and training goals to determine if this is really necessary or beneficial. Remember with negative reinforcement we want to apply a strong enough aversive to stimulate the desired behavior and outweigh any external influences with a prompt and complete removal of the aversive when we achieve the desired behavior.

If all of our previous efforts have failed us - if we have found ourselves in a terrible situation and for our safety or the horse's wellbeing we must get this behavior to stop, we may need to resort to positive punishment. Remember positive punishment is not 'good punishment', but rather we're adding something aversive to reduce the frequency of the behavior in the future or stop it in the moment. I will go more into the risks that come with this soon and the dangers involved (page: 167). It should be our absolute last option and it should be a lesson learned. If we find ourselves in a position where we must use this, stop and forgive yourself, emergencies and accidents happen. But we should reassess the situation and come up with a plan to prevent us from ever being in this situation again, whether it be preparing our horse to handle this particular situation better or not putting our horse or ourselves in this position again.

Which jobs are so important? This becomes an ethical decision, and science alone can't answer these questions for us. Each person will have their own ethical line as to how far they're willing to go to accomplish each behavior. Some behaviors are purely for us, our enjoyment or our ability to compete - these behaviors we should be very conservative with how far we're willing to go. If there's nothing in it for the horse to perform this behavior, we could at least add something in it for them (like positive reinforcement). However, it may not be something we're willing to resort to aversives to achieve, while if the behaviors are for our horse's own good we can take our time to prepare them and build the behaviors as best we can with positive reinforcement. Unfortunately, sometimes there is a time rush or an emergency situation where we may need to use aversives. In these health and safety concerns, with an emergency time-restraint we may need to fly down this humane hierarchy rather quickly. Remember our relationship piggy banks, where we deposit lots of good experiences and positive history of our training? (page: 33) These aversive situations would be considered an emergency 'withdrawal' from our piggy bank. Ideally, we'll have a strong enough history of deposits that we won't be 'in debt'. If we do find ourselves withdrawing more than we put in we need to ensure we spend the time making more 'deposits' of good experiences and positive training. We each need to determine our own ethical line in relation to the importance of the behaviors we're asking of our horses and how far we're willing to go to make those behaviors happen.

131

Transition Troubles

For those of us with a long history of traditional or natural horsemanship training the transition to positive reinforcement may be difficult. I struggled for years during my transition. I truly did not want to believe this option was viable or appropriate. I was riddled with guilt, thinking about how if this method works then there is no justification for the terrible things I had done before. While I've never been comfortable whipping or using harsh tools on my horses, there were times I took the plunge to get the job done, to make my horse *"respect"* me. Self-doubt tore me apart, making me think I would never be good enough or smart enough to understand all the nuances of learning. There are people in the world who thrive on making others feel inferior - at these sensitive times of change it's easy to believe the cruel words of others. I was consumed with fear, fear that I was going to ruin my horse, fear that if this doesn't work then what else is there? Maybe it was me- I'm just not good enough. I knew I needed to make the change but fear that I wouldn't be able to change completely, or quickly enough overwhelmed me - or that my horses would never forgive or trust me again. I had no way to tell my horses that *"no really, it's different this time"*, *"I won't ever punish you again"* - it takes time for this trust to come, and with all my relapses and self-doubt it took longer.

Learning anything new that goes against a strongly held belief is going to be uncomfortable, even painful at times - but it's always worth it for self-growth. The phenomenon that causes us to feel so terrible, to deny things we know are true, just because they go against something we used to believe is called **"Cognitive Dissonance"**. It's common, it's normal and it's OK to feel this way! But it's also important we accept that this is what the discomfort is and that it's worth it to move past.

Every time things didn't work out the way I planned, every time my emotions got the better of me - my feelings of inadequacy would bubble up and tear me apart. I'd want to go running back to all I ever knew before - often doing so and causing major setbacks in our training and relationship. Every small mistake felt earth shattering. In the end though, my desire to be better for my horses and with the support of caring friends who understood what I was struggling with, I pushed past this and found myself on the other side. A side full of hope, excitement, new opportunities and beautiful, dream-like relationships with my horses. It was worth the trouble, it was worth the discomfort and it was wonderful.

I wanted to share this and include this in the book because I find this is a struggle most of us go through when making this transition. Even if things go smoothly, it's never easy to change. Despite how difficult it can be, it will be and is worth it to open your mind and continue learning. Don't let yourself be discouraged by people with bad attitudes or by mistakes and your own self-criticism. Bumps happen on every new road, but they smooth out over time and it is worth it. We are here for you. *That relationship you end up with, based on communication, clarity and understanding is worth every bit of it.*

You can't fix yourself by breaking someone else Train with Kindness

Do not be dismayed by the brokenness of this world.
All things break. And all things can be mended.
Not with time, as they say, but with intention.
So go. Love intentionally, extravagantly, unconditionally.
The broken world waits in darkness for the light that is you.

~L.R. Knost

www.EmpoweredEquines.com

Handling Change

As we delve into the world of equine emotions one of the biggest aspects many of us become focused on is FEAR. FEAR in horses is a common issue during training and handling. Being flight animals, they can have a fast and sudden response to concerning stimuli - which can be dangerous when we're working in full contact or while mounted. Humans have also taken advantage of a horse's flight response in training for generations (in some cases intentionally breeding faster, more reactive horses to progress in some sports). Of course, in our modern world and positive horse training we want to avoid making our horses feel any real fear. Not only can we avoid using fear as a training tool, but we can also help our horses become open to change and new things with a more optimistic outlook. The goal is to reduce the risk to horse and human from explosive fear responses, as well as ensuring our horses get to live a happy and comfortable life. Unfortunately, FEAR isn't an emotion that's easily avoided with horses, so we need to learn how to handle it.

As prey animals, horses are extremely observant about their environment and know immediately when something has changed, any change being a potential risk. Horses who have been observant and quick to react are the ones who survive through the challenges nature presents to them. Unfortunately, this can cause trouble in domestic life. Things change, especially if we want to go anywhere new! In the past humans have tried to stifle a horse's response to FEAR. In an attempt to make horses safer when in contact with humans, we've used tools that cause pain to control the horse's movement and try to reduce spooking. Sounds a little counter-intuitive, right? If they're afraid why would we do exactly what they're afraid of, add pain? Unfortunately, pain has worked in the past to control them, the physical force and pain contains the behavior of the horse. The human becomes the worse of the two threats, so they comply. The aversive consequence of not doing what the human asks outweighs the aversive consequence of the environment. To put it simply, they chose to avoid the more concerning stimuli - the human and their tools. But do we really want our horse to be more afraid of us than everything that could possibly occur in their environment? Remember how our horse feels while they're with us is how we become conditioned in their mind.

So how do we keep ourselves safe when the horse becomes scared and their behavior becomes dangerous? We have many an option. Protected contact is an underutilized tool but can be valuable for horses and humans alike when dealing with fearful situations. Don't forget to utilize this! It can provide a level of choice and control for the horse allowing them more freedom of expression as they learn. It also keeps us safe while they learn.

Wisp meeting a new stuffed animal friend. Not sure what to make of it at first, she investigated on her own time and discovered he was kind of cute!

Our goal should not be to stifle their expression, nor to try to control them - but rather put them in better control of themselves. We want to empower them to know they are safe, have choice and the ability to control their reactions. We want to show them that new may not be scary, but fun. We can build their curiosity and develop a self-controlled, positive outlook on their environment. Learning that change, that new, can be fun, engaging, and rewarding.

Stimulus Stack

Before we get into how to train and deal with fear responses I'd like to talk a little about what fear is. FEAR is one of the primal emotions, hard wired to drive all animal's self-preservation. One of the biggest problems with fear is that it lingers in the brain and takes a long time to wear off. The hormones that trigger the FEAR system do not fade quickly even after the stimulus goes away or after it's been determined the stimulus is safe. If the horse startles at a bird flying out of the bush they know quickly the bird isn't a concern and stop being afraid - but the hormone is still lingering in their body.

What happens now is what we call "**Stimulus Stacking**". When one fear-invoking experience happens and doesn't have time to wear off before another experience occurs, the effects of the two combine. This can result in situations where *"he exploded for no reason"* or when your horse reacts to something they normally never do (maybe a funny colored bucket or a jump they're usually good with). When the flapping bird causes the horse to startle, but he contains himself right away, then a few minutes later you ask him to jump a jump he's usually fine with (but may have some lingering anxiety about) that lingering concern can be too much for them to handle at this time - while their hormones are on overdrive from the previous concern. While usually the mild anxiety about the jump isn't enough to stop them from going over it, this time it's enough because it added to the flapping bird.

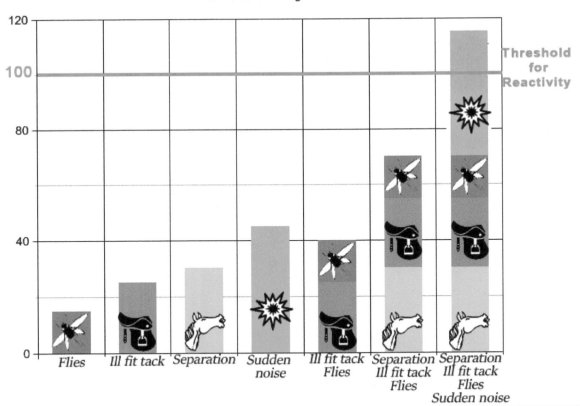

In this example of a stimulus stack you can see how the horse is only mildly concerned about each individual stimulus, but when they each accompany one another they can be too much to handle. This is a theoretical stimulus stack, based on no real data. Each individual stimulus may be so mild that the horse actually shows almost no signs of concern until they combine. If fear behaviors have ever been punished, they may have learned not to express that fear - until it becomes too much to handle, which can make it extremely difficult to see when a stimulus stack is building in order to break it down before the reaction.

We call this reaction a horse going "**over-threshold**". It is the moment where their instinctive behavioral reaction to fear becomes an uncontrollable reflex and not a thought-out behavior, and learning cannot happen while over threshold. Previous fearful stimuli have stacked up and weren't noticed or given ample time to reduce before another was added, sending the horse over threshold. This happens especially often when a horse is punished for showing fear behaviors - they learn not to show the signs of fear, until it become a reflex and they can't control it, leaving us with very little warning. We want to be constantly aware of stimulus stacking and be sure after little frights we've allowed the horse to relax before asking more of him. Luckily time isn't the only way to reduce a stimulus stack. *While adding experiences that induce FEAR can push a horse over threshold, introducing experiences that feel good can help this stack break down more quickly.*

Dealing With Fear

The FEAR system feels terrible, and we want to reduce fear in our horse's lives, but we can't just lock them in a padded room, right? They also need to learn how to live successfully in the human's world. How do we approach this in a kind and thoughtful manner?

There are four basic techniques we can utilize to help us help our horses overcome fear; **flooding, habituation, systematic desensitization,** and **counter conditioning.** Our goal is not to remove every fear producing stimulus or teach them to ignore their instinct to defend themselves (through the freeze-flight-fight responses), nor to teach them to tolerate every individual stimulus in the world, but rather to help them build a sense of self confidence and encourage curiosity.

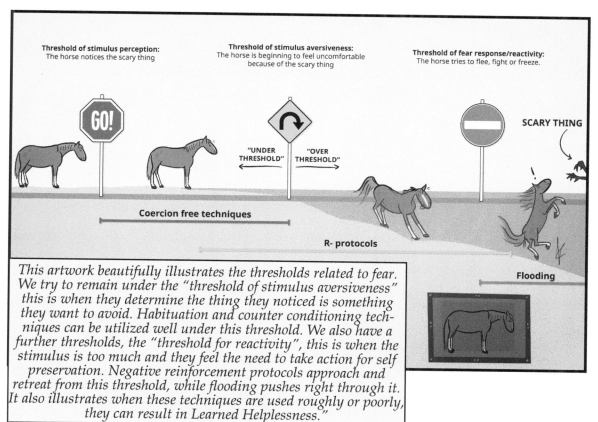

Threshold of stimulus perception:
The horse notices the scary thing

Threshold of stimulus aversiveness:
The horse is beginning to feel uncomfortable because of the scary thing

Threshold of fear response/reactivity:
The horse tries to flee, fight or freeze.

SCARY THING

"UNDER THRESHOLD" ← → "OVER THRESHOLD"

Coercion free techniques

R- protocols

Flooding

This artwork beautifully illustrates the thresholds related to fear. We try to remain under the "threshold of stimulus aversiveness" this is when they determine the thing they noticed is something they want to avoid. Habituation and counter conditioning techniques can be utilized well under this threshold. We also have a further thresholds, the "threshold for reactivity", this is when the stimulus is too much and they feel the need to take action for self preservation. Negative reinforcement protocols approach and retreat from this threshold, while flooding pushes right through it. It also illustrates when these techniques are used roughly or poorly, they can result in Learned Helplessness."

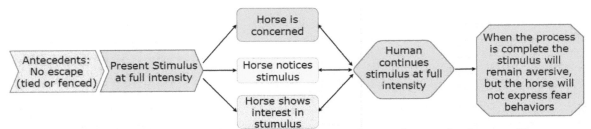

The first option I'll mention is common, but when we learn about what's actually happening, emotionally, we really ought to look elsewhere for a more ethical option. **"Flooding"** *is when the horse is exposed to the full extent of the feared stimulus in a situation where escape is limited or unavailable.* This form of fear therapy was designed for humans to overcome phobias. In therapy the human patient would practice relaxation techniques they had learned previously while being exposed to high levels of the object they fear. This was done to show the person that their fear was irrational. This, however, is dangerous and cruel when done to animals or people who can't speak for themselves to stop the experience, learn the relaxation techniques, or understand that this is a controlled, safe experience. *This technique requires consent, understanding, and the ability to control the scenario - which isn't an option with animal learners.* When this technique is used on horses many people tie the horse or put them in a small, inescapable area (like a stall or round pen). Then they expose the horse to the stimulus allowing the horse to react until the horse reaches exhaustion or the trainer punishes the horse's reaction. They do this continuously until the horse stops reacting to the stimulus. Often this happens not because the horse has seen that the stimulus is not something to be feared, but rather that they've learned that the stimulus is inescapable and that they have no control over their situation. The learner discovers nothing they do can alleviate the fearful stimulus, so they simply stop trying (a degree of Learned Helplessness).

A common example of flooding is when a trainer holds a tarp, waving it in the center of the round pen until the horse stops trying to run away. This is done repeatedly with different stimuli until this sense of helplessness lingers and generalizes into real life scenarios where the horse has more choice. Even in complete freedom they can still feel they have no choice or control. Not only is this method extremely stressful to the learner, it's also ineffective in most cases without a great deal of maintenance and generalization. In this case, the horse's fear response is simply stifled or overshadowed. However, when the fear becomes strong enough, becomes stacked, or the antecedents change, the horse can shake out of this state and become dangerously reactive.

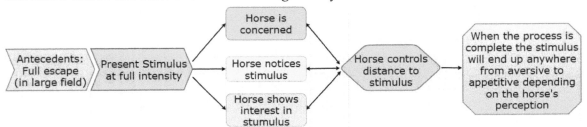

A less intense option is **"Habituation"**. *This is where the trainer also submits the horse to the full extent of the stimulus (for example, a whole tarp open and exposed) - except in this situation the horse has complete control over their exposure.* The horse should have enough room to avoid the stimulus completely, where they can be completely comfortable away from it. The horse is allowed to approach, investigate, and interact with the stimulus on their own schedule. They're able to choose how much of the stimulus to tolerate. This should be done without external influence, nothing pushing them to go closer which can create conflict and stress. With this method, the horse has complete control. It can be very slow, and the fear of the stimulus may never actually resolve. It works well for horses who are curious and self-confident, but horses who have low curiosity, horses who are more shut down may choose to just never take the risk.

While habituation is extremely useful and can be a great tool - sometimes we need to work a little faster. "**Systematic Desensitization**" allows us to help our horses approach their fears more directly. To use this method, we start with the stimulus reduced to the smallest degree we possibly can (in the example of the tarp we would fold it as small as we can). If it makes noise, turn the volume down low, if it's large, make it as small as possible and so on. The horse needs to be in a comfortable situation with the ability to express themselves fully and room to leave if we miss their signals. It requires an observant trainer to work with the horse, someone who understands the subtle signs of stress and conflict. Simply add the stimulus at this smallest amount possible, allowing the horse to become comfortable with this. As they become comfortable and show signs of relaxing, remove the stimulus to allow them some time of relief - so the repeated exposure of the stimulus doesn't stack. Repeat this process as the horse becomes more comfortable with the stimulus, and then you can gradually increase the intensity of the stimulus. It's important we keep the stimulus at such a low level that the horse is never reactive to it, if they become reactive it'll slow the process. There are some techniques which take the stimulus closer to the reactive, over threshold point, before relieving it. *This is a more dramatic negative reinforcement desensitization technique, which can get out of hand far too quickly. Each time the horse gets close to threshold the longer it will take for the horse to return to baseline.* This borders on flooding and can often slow our process or poison the experience. While this can work quickly, it's vital that this is done with a patient and observant trainer, working at the horse's speed - if pushed over threshold this can rapidly become flooding and set progress back again.

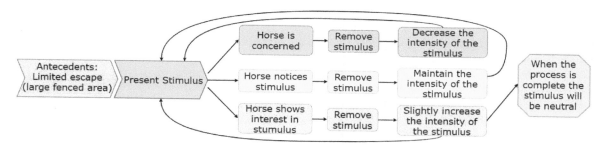

Unfortunately, all these methods can only bring a stimulus up to neutral, at best. However, we must ensure we finish introducing each stimulus, making sure the horse views the stimulus as a neutral object and not let the process linger at the halfway point, so that the horse still views the stimulus as somewhat aversive. Otherwise, we run the risk that the stimulus becomes a part of a stack. This is where "**Counter Conditioning**" comes in. *We want to not only bring the horse's perception of the stimulus to neutral but bring it all the way to the appetitive side of the scale. We can do this by pairing the stimulus repeatedly with an attractive stimulus.* It sounds straightforward to just give the horse things they love in the presence of the scary stimulus - but it's not exactly that easy in practice. Simply covering something scary in treats is likely to result in a great deal of conflict and stress while they decide how to handle this situation. Luring them into a situation they aren't comfortable with just to get something they want can run the risk of poisoning the appetitive, rather than counter conditioning the aversive. While this technique can work wonders to convince our horse to no longer fear something, but love it, it needs to be done with care.

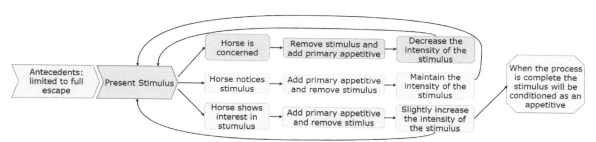

We can mix a bit of systematic desensitization in with our counter conditioning to help our horses work through their fear quickly and completely. If the stimulus is highly aversive, adding an appetitive alone will trigger conflict. So we should start by shrinking the stimulus to its smallest, least aversive version, like we did in systematic desensitization and begin counter conditioning from this level. If the stimulus can't be reduced in size or volume (like a scary bush) to be less aversive we can use distance from the stimulus to reduce its impact. This will help us tip the scale towards the appetitive side. Each time we present or approach the stimulus, we add an appetitive and remove the aversive. Work at each level until the horse is eagerly approaching and showing interest in it before moving to the stimulus' next level of intensity. With this we'll be able to ensure he horse isn't just hiding their fear, but actually has changed their opinion about the stimulus, so it can no longer become an accidental piece of a stimulus stack. It's important to remember that FEAR is an emotional system that is triggered by the environment. This is something the animal can't control, it's respondent, involuntary. We can't accidentally reinforce fear or teach a horse to pretend to be fearful. Comforting your frightened horse, bringing them good things, and helping them self-soothe will only help your horse and in no way cause them to be more fearful. If you comfort your horse and the horse begins to show more fear towards things, it's only because they are feeling more comfortable using their voice. A horse who was previously shut down, stifling their fear because they are more afraid of what the human may do, may become honest when comforted instead of punished when afraid. This is good, if our horses can be honest with us we can better help them learn to become comfortable in themselves and their environment.

Rather than trying to punish the fear, flood out the fear, or train expressions of fear away with negative reinforcement protocols, we can help teach our horses to be open and curious around novel situations and objects. With a mix of habituation, systematic desensitization, and counter conditioning we can help a horse learn how fun 'new' can be, while remaining well below the threshold for stimulus aversiveness. If new experiences are an opportunity to earn good things, then all things new become fun in themselves!

Recommended Reading:

Ralph Adolphs The Biology of Fear. (2013). Current Biology.

Franklin D. McMillan, DVM (2002) *Development of a mental wellness program for animals*. Journal of the American Animal Hospital Association.

Stankowich T, Blumstein DT. *Fear in animals: a meta-analysis and review of risk assessment.* (2005). Proceedings of the Royal Society B: Biological Sciences.

Franklin D. McMillan, DVM, DACVIM Bernard E. Rollin, PhD *The presence of mind: on reunifying the animal mind and body* (2001). Journal of the American Veterinary Medical Association.

Tarp:

A tarp is a great tool to introduce horses to early on; it's unpredictable, noisy, and blue is a vibrant color for horses. Introducing the horse to a tarp can help them learn about the desensitization process. It can prepare horses for when they experience plastic bags, construction, tarp covered hay, and blankets.

Habituation:

1. Tie the tarp to corner of paddock, somewhere the horses can easily avoid. Put a rock or something heavy on it so it doesn't move around.

2. As the horses get comfortable with the tarp, after they have investigated and felt it you can remove the weight so they can see it move.

3. When they're comfortable in the proximity of the tarp you can begin desensitizing and counter conditioning.

Desensitization/Counter Conditioning:

4. Fold the tarp up as small as you can manage, in a way it doesn't move or make noise.

5. Practice having the horse target the tarp. Mark and reinforce any approach or attempt at targeting until they're completely comfortable targeting all over the tarp. Each time you reinforce, remove the tarp (hide it behind your back) so you can re-present it with the next repetition.

6. Make crinkly sounds with the tarp while the horse targets or stands facing forward. Keep a high rate of reinforcement while the tarp makes noises.

7. Gradually unfold the tarp; slowly increase the sound and motion of the tarp. Keep your sessions short and sweet. The horse should be excited and eager when the tarp comes out. If they show signs of conflict, slow down and break this down into smaller chunks.

8. Move the tarp around their body while they stand calmly facing forward.

9. Lay the tarp out with weights holding it down and scatter treats on top for the horse to explore.

10. Gradually move the weight to the center of the tarp so the sides can flap and blow in the wind.

11. Begin introducing the tarp in a variety of circumstances, around the agility obstacles and other places in their environment.

Hula Hoop:

Hula hoops, particularly the noisy ones, can be a fun object to teach horses about. They can be a fun toy in the agility ring and prepare the horse for surprising objects in their life.

Habituation:

1. Tie a hula hoop to corner of paddock, somewhere the horses can easily avoid. Make sure the hoop is cheap and will break easily if the horse plays with it.

2. When they're comfortable in the proximity of the hoop you can begin desensitizing and counter conditioning.

Desensitization/Counter Conditioning:

3. Hold the hula hoop just below the horse's nose level and encourage some basic targeting and standing facing forward. Mark and reinforce any interaction with or any time the hula hoop makes noise.

4. Gradually start to rattle the hoop (if you have the noisy ones), reinforce each time the hoop makes noise.

5. Keep a high rate of reinforcement as the horse engages with the hoop.

6. You can shape the horse to hold, rattle, even toss the hoop themselves.

7. Make sure the horse is comfortable with the hoop moving all around their body and stepping into it like a stationing mat.

8. Begin introducing the hula hoop in a variety of situations, such as in the agility ring and games.

Ball:

If you want to do all the ball exercises and train all the fun games that involve the use of a ball, it may require some desensitization first. Balls are great objects to get a horse comfortable with, as many objects roll and bounce and behave unpredictably. They can also be great enrichment and training tools!

Habituation:

1. Attach a ball to the corner of the paddock, somewhere the horses can easily avoid. Either tether it or put something around it to prevent it from rolling.

2. As the horse gets comfortable with the ball, investigates and feels it, you can remove or loosen the tether so the horse can see it move.

3. When they're comfortable in the proximity of the ball you can begin desensitizing and counter conditioning.

Desensitization/Counter Conditioning:

4. Holding the ball still, allow the horse to touch and investigate it, eat some treats off it or target it.

5. Maintain a high rate of reinforcement as you gradually roll the ball around, left and right, then towards and away, reinforcing with any movement of the ball.

6. Practice gentle, low bouncing the ball, reinforcing each bounce. If the horse shows any signs of conflict or stress, immediately reduce the criteria.

7. Allow the horse to practice nudging and moving the ball around on their own. Mark and reinforce any interaction and engagement.

8. Practice rolling the ball around the horse's body while they stand calmly facing forward, mark and reinforce any movement from the ball, especially as you get further behind the horse or out of their vision. Allow the horse to move freely if they feel the need to turn to face the ball. Stay slow and keep a high rate of reinforcement. You want to ensure the horse is comfortable with the ball all around them, in case it should roll under their feet.

Umbrella:

Umbrellas are a real cause of concern for many horses, but if they live among humans they're bound to see some, or something similar. Umbrellas are surprising, noisy, and large sometimes.

Habituation:

1. Tie a closed umbrella just outside the fence of the paddock, where the horse can see and touch it, but not entangle themselves.

2. As the horses get comfortable with the umbrella open and hanging in the same spot, make sure it's out of reach where they could poke their eye with a tine. This is just so they can see and explore at their own time.

3. When they're comfortable in the proximity of the umbrella you can begin desensitizing and counter conditioning.

Desensitization/Counter Conditioning:

4. Close the umbrella and tie it flat so it's as small as possible. Mark and reinforce anytime the horse engages with the umbrella or targets it.

5. Practice targeting with the umbrella and moving it around their body, try using it like a regular hand-held target.

6. As they get comfortable, untie the umbrella so the fabric can swish and move, but don't fully open it yet. Encourage the horse to practice targeting with it open and noisy. Reinforce when the umbrella makes noise or flutters.

7. When they're feeling comfortable and enjoying the umbrella, slowly slide the umbrella to open it, don't allow it to pop, restrain it as it opens. Mark and reinforce any curiosity and investigation.

8. Work on this until the horse is calm and comfortably targeting while the umbrella is open. Gradually open the umbrella more quickly and allow it to make more noise. Reinforce promptly each time the umbrella pops open.

9. Always keep a careful watch that the tines of the umbrella are not going to poke the horse. Keep a high rate of reinforcement as the horse engages with it.

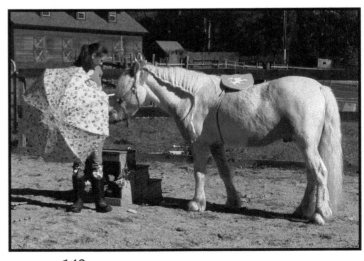

Wet Sponge:

Helping a horse get used to the feeling of being wet and being washed with a bucket of water and a sponge is a good way to slowly progress towards full hose baths. This is also beneficial preparation should you need to clean a wound.

Habituation:

1. Providing a pool with water to splash in can be a great way to let the horse explore getting wet on their own time.

Desensitization/Counter Conditioning:

2. Start with your horse standing calmly facing forward while you go over touching/brushing the horse.

3. Practice scrubbing your horse with the dry sponge all over to get them accustomed to the feeling. Mark and reinforce while the horse stands calmly as you rub them with the sponge.

4. Reinforce the horse as you splash around and make noise with the water.

5. Dip the sponge and ring it out until there's no more dripping. Mark and reinforce with a high rate of reinforcement as you begin to rub them with the damp sponge. Start somewhere your horse is very comfortable with and gradually move to more difficult areas.

6. As your horse gets comfortable with this allow the sponge to be wetter until it's dripping wet. Try not to let the water tickle your horse as it rolls down.

7. Maintain a fairly high rate of reinforcement. If the horse gets uncomfortable and needs to move away, slow down, and decrease the criteria.

WORKSHEET

Hose:

Getting a horse comfortable being hosed is not only beneficial for bathing them but also preparing them in case they should ever need to be cold hosed due to an injury.

Habituation:

1. If it's safe to do so, putting the hose on trickling into the field (somewhere that won't turn into a mud pit) can be a good way to let your horse learn about hoses.

2. As the horses get comfortable with the hose in that position prop it up so it sprays more.

3. When they're comfortable in the proximity of the spraying hose you can begin desensitizing and counter conditioning.

Desensitization/Counter Conditioning:

4. First we need to introduce the hose while it's off. Using a hose with a garden spray nozzle that allows you to mist or shower can make it more comfortable and easier for your horse to get used to.

5. Allow the horse to explore and target the head of the hose while its off.

6. As the horse stands calmly facing forward, move the hose all around them, letting them get accustomed to the squiggly rubber hose. Reinforce fairly frequently to make this a comfortable and easy game for them before we step it up a notch with the water.

7. When they're comfortable with the hose moving all around them, turn the hose on its lowest setting. Allow the horse to go back to targeting it with the hose pointing away from them.

8. Move the hose all around the horse again, without touching them with the water, while they stand facing forward. If they get concerned slow down.

WORKSHEET

Hose:

9. Keep your rate of reinforcement up as you let the water trickle onto their hooves and pasterns. Allow them to wiggle and move away if this is surprising or uncomfortable. Mark and reinforce any attempt to stand calmly again.

10. Using the mist or gentle shower head you can gradually move up and down their legs, belly and chest. If the horse is particularly itchy in any spot, try that area. It may help to have an additional person reinforcing at a high rate.

11. It can help to spread this over several sessions, especially if your horse isn't very comfortable with this right away.

12. As they get comfortable begin spraying the rest of their body. Don't spray their face, (unless they like it) wipe this sensitive area with a cloth or sponge.

Clippers:

Introducing our horses to clippers isn't purely a cosmetic desire, but may also be necessary for medical reasons, like clipping hair away from a wound.

Habituation:

1. Set the clippers somewhere just outside the paddock, turned on, so the horse can get used to hearing them from a comfortable distance.

2. If you have a horse comfortable with being clipped, allow the other horses to watch and hear, and make sure to heavily reinforce the horse being clipped, so the others see how awesome it can be.

3. When they're comfortable in the proximity of the noisy clippers you can begin desensitizing and counter conditioning.

Desensitization/Counter Conditioning:

4. With the clippers off, but plugged in, practice moving around the horse while they stand facing forward. Continue reinforcing as they get comfortable.

5. Allow the horse to target the back end of the clippers, reinforce any interest.

6. When the horse is comfortable with the clippers all around them, hold the clippers a good distance away from the horse and turn them on the quietest setting, or use your quietest set you have.

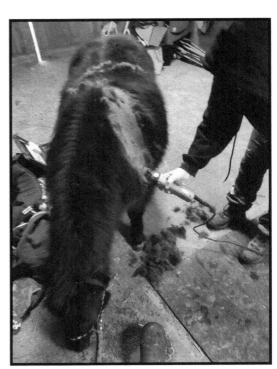

7. Practice a few times turning on the clippers, reinforcing heavily, then turning them off. Repeat this until the horse begins to predict the reinforcement with the sound of the clippers turning on.

8. As the horse gets used to the sound keep them on longer and gradually move the clippers closer to the horse. Keep a high rate of reinforcement while moving the clippers around. If the horse begins to get concerned reduce the criteria.

9. Every few reinforcements turn off the clippers and take a short break, allow the horse to relax, and practice some easier behaviors.

Clippers:

10. As the horse gets comfortable with the clippers turned on moving all around them you can take the next small step. Holding the clippers on in your hand touch the horse with the back of your hand, letting them feel the vibration. With a high rate of reinforcement and frequent breaks, practice this all over their body.

11. As they get comfortable feeling the vibration through your hand, go through the same procedure with the butt end of the clippers, keeping a high rate of reinforcement and taking frequent breaks.

12. From here they should be ready for actual clipping. It may help to have an additional person reinforcing for this. Keep your sessions short and sweet; if they get concerned, slow down and go back a step.

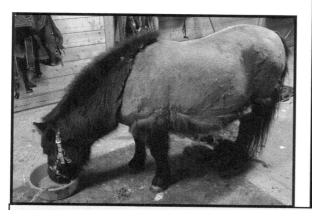

Marshmallow had mites and fungal infections when she arrived, so we clipped her to help treat her skin problems. So please excuse the terrible clipping!

Trailer:

The trailer is probably one of the biggest and most difficult tasks for us to handle, especially for seasoned horses who have learned to hate the trailer. While working at liberty is usually best for desensitizing, we don't always have the opportunity to practice trailer loading in a large, fenced area. If you need to use a lead because you're outside of a fenced area, be careful not to use it to try to pull the horse into the trailer or block the horse from getting away if they want. Using a longer lead or lunge line can help but may be hard to manage.

In this "how to" I'm going to jump right to preparing with a trailer, but if your horse has a history and isn't ready for this step or if you don't have access to a trailer, you can make an artificial trailer. If you use two jumps and hang blankets or tarps from them you can create pretend "walls" which you can move progressively closer together. You can also use a platform to practice stepping up and backing off the trailer.

Habituation:

1. If you can have a trailer in a fenced area, allowing your horse to explore it at liberty, while supervised can be fabulous. Unfortunately this isn't usually the case. The best we can usually do it allow our horses to see and examine the trailer from the other side of their fence.

2. If you have a horse who's good with the trailer, allowing the other horses watch them load while getting lots of treats can be a great way to get everyone curiously engaged.

> *A key to remember when working on any fear-related issue is to break it down as small as possible and work in many, very short sessions. Even mixing it into your regular sessions in a tiny way can help speed up progress. Don't dwell on desensitizing, doing one minute every now and then usually makes more progress than an hour of drilling!*

Desensitization/Counter Conditioning:

3. When you're ready to get started with your real or pretend trailer, lead the horse towards the trailer, marking and reinforcing as you move towards the trailer. Find the line where the horse begins to show acute awareness, tension, or hesitation (do not wait for them to get nervous). Stop there, feed a few times, then walk away. Repeat this several times, circling towards and away from the trailer. Mark and reinforce heavily the entire time you're approaching the trailer, then walk away. Each time you make these circles towards the trailer, don't try to get closer each time, sometimes do an easy circle or two. Allow them to approach, reinforce what they're comfortable with, then walk away.

4. As you practice you circles, when they get close to the trailer, mark and reinforce any signs of curiosity or engagement with the trailer. Allow them to walk around the entire outside of the trailer. If they're comfortable with it, allow them to eat treats off the outside of the trailer.

Trailer:

5. As they're standing comfortably near the trailer and not worried about it, someone else can begin opening and closing the trailer doors and latches. Allow the horse to watch, reinforce heavily with each noise or movement. Circle the horse away and back towards the trailer with the doors opened and closed and from different directions.

6. With the loading door open practice approaching the entrance of the trailer and when they're comfortable enough to stand near the open door they can eat food off the trailer floor.

7. As the horse gets comfortable eating off the floor of the trailer and walking around the outside of the trailer you can begin playing with targeting. If you've generalized your target cue you can encourage your horse to target different parts of the trailer, the latches, the door, the outer frame, the tires, anything!

8. If you haven't been using a target for leading before, using one now can really help. As the horse follows the target toward the trailer and reaches the entrance, practice having the horse target left, right and all around without having to step into the trailer. While they're doing this well circle away from the trailer.

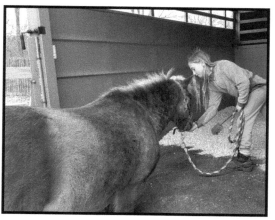

9. Open the trailer as wide as possible, re-move or open dividers, open windows and extra doors (if you have a small human door, you can open it, but block it so the horse doesn't try to exit through this door if they get scared). At this point you can begin using the target to encourage the horse to reach or step onto the ramp or up into the trailer. Mark and reinforce the moment their hoof touches the new floor. If they get even one hoof in, circle them back out. Even if you feel like the horse would happily walk all the way in, circle them back out. You don't want them to push themselves over-threshold just to get the food, only to find themselves in a panic - ruining your progress.

10. As the horse gets comfortable stepping their front feet into the trailer practice having the horse touch a target in all directions while standing with their front feet in. Build up the duration of time spent in the trailer, even with just a foot or two, don't keep pushing for more.

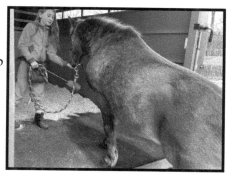

11. When the horse is comfortable standing with their front half in the trailer, then circling back out, you can begin to ask for more. Encourage a step or two more, keep an extremely high rate of reinforcement to continue to classically condition the trailer as an awesome place to be.

12. As the horse gets the hang of stepping in, circling or backing out, begin to spend more time in the trailer, targeting around, being rein forced, before backing or circling out again. Soon you can begin spending time in the trailer practicing different skills having the trailer just as a side aspect of your training.

13. Now that the horse is comfortable hanging out in the trailer you can begin to move things around, practice swinging the latches, rattling the doors, and moving the dividers. Reinforce heavily as the horse remains comfortable and bring the horse out repeatedly during this. As they get comfortable you can practice arrang-jm all the buckles they'll need and closing the doors. Keep a heavy rate of reinforcement while you prepare them for any of the added noises and barriers they'll need to get used to.

14. When they're comfortable standing in their position, with everything adjusted correctly you can prepare them a delicious mash or feed pan, set it up in front of them, and step out of the human door. Allow the horse to happily eat what they like, then help them out of the trailer before they're completely done. Practice this for various durations.

15. From here you can begin to add some movement! When they're all loaded and tucked in with their yummies, about 2-5 minutes, up and down the driveway, unloading them just where you loaded them up. They may be a bit upset after this movement, so reduce your criteria the next few times.

16. You can practice going quiet, easy, familiar places when you can, some where safe if you need to spend time reloading. After each real ride, make sure to practice multiple approaches to the trailer and pretend loadings without actually going anywhere.

When FEAR Becomes Trauma

When a truly aversive event happens, something that induced a great deal of fear or pain, it may have lasting traumatic effects. Trauma happens when the memory of these events don't leave the system entirely. These can happen after one extreme experience, a few bad experiences, or a prolonged aversive situation. We call this emotional trauma **"pathological"** when the body/mind doesn't return to normal (homeostasis) after the event is over causing the FEAR system to remain active much longer than it should even in when the trauma is over. While a survivor of trauma may be able to function and appear normal, they may learn to cope with the level of FEAR-related hormones their body is continually pumping out – but this will remain a constant piece of a stimulus stack. This condition will result in a much quicker reaction to other stimuli. Those with histories of experiencing trauma can seem to explode over 'nothing' or seem to 'make things up to get upset over'. Triggers related to the trauma can be as subtle as a smell or sound initiating a flashback. Triggers may not even be rationally related to past trauma.

Any truly aversive event can become a traumatic experience:

• Abuse	• Fighting (bull fights/rodeo events)
• Neglect	• Racing
• Aversive confinement	• Forced work
• Multiple re-homing	• Service/military duty
• Hoarding	• Laboratory research/testing
• Natural disasters	• Physical trauma/injury
• Social deprivation	• Illness/disease

Unfortunately, we can't talk to our animals to determine their level of trauma (we may never know whether or not they have nightmares or flashbacks). We also don't always have complete histories on our animals, so it can be hard to differentiate trauma from a lack of socialization. To measure trauma related to these incidents we need to rely on the tangible behavioral responses. We consider this pathological trauma in animals when the individual begins reacting to harmless stimuli and when the fear responses interfere with normal behavior. We can measure their level of avoidance by observing what triggers reactions and what degree of generalization the avoidance has reached. We can measure their arousal and reactivity levels, an individual with Post Traumatic Stress (PTS) will have an extremely exaggerated startle response and exhibit hyper-vigilance. We can also measure changes in their disposition, mood and cognition, but only if we knew them before and after the trauma (which unfortunately rarely happens with animals). They may appear jumpy, irritable, and easily triggered. The fear may generalize to such an extreme such that the whole world becomes a threat. Some of the most extreme expressions of PTS in animals can include: screaming, self-injurious behavior, stereotypic behaviors, trance-like state, unpredictable aggression, instability, depression, trembling, pacing, withdrawal, timidity, avoidance of people or specific stimuli.

Trauma has been grouped into levels to help categorize and understand how to handle/treat it:

- **Level 0:** There are no long-term consequences.
- **Level 1:** Learned fear, only affecting life when the stimulus is present or anticipated, but the animal is totally fine otherwise.
- **Level 2:** Generalized Anxiety, learned fear is generalized to similar stimuli or antecedents, but the learner is still fine most of the time.
- **Level 3:** Phobic, it impairs normal function, reducing pleasurable activities whether the stimulus is present or anticipated.
- **Level 4:** Severe generalized fear. This impairs normal function when stimulus is present or not, the fear has been generalized to multiple aspects of life.

In human research it was shown that only about 25% of survivors of trauma suffer from a related emotional disorder. We most often think of Post-Traumatic Stress as the only emotional disorder as a result of a traumatic event. But trauma can lead to a spectrum of emotional disorders including Post Traumatic Stress, Phobias, Generalized Anxiety, and Depression.

Trauma is common in horses who come from a traditional background. Equine trauma is frequently overlooked and even justified. Ideally, we who choose to educate ourselves will be working our hardest to not only prevent this, but to heal it when and where we can. Most of us don't have horses from the time they are foaled (that would be a super lucky horse). Most of us are cleaning up damage other humans (and sometimes ourselves) have caused. But how can we help repair a horse who's been through trauma and has lasting effects?

One of the biggest advantages we can provide our horses is a sense of control in their lives. Having the perception that we can control, turn off, or prevent certain events in our life can reduce the lasting effects of trauma and help individuals be more tolerant to unpleasant situations. This is one of the biggest benefits of Positive Reinforcement training, when used ethically. With positive reinforcement horses can walk away, say no to training, or even initiate the next repetition, allowing our horses to have more choice and control in their training and ultimately their lives. A horse with a strong sense of control and choice will be more resilient to aversive situations (like vet emergencies) than a horse who is already feeling a lack of control.

Social companionship is a vital piece of the puzzle for preventing and reducing the effects of trauma. Social support has a buffering effect shown in every social species. It's important to remember that humans are rarely enough social support for a social species like horses. Having other, healthy horses can substantially speed their recovery and buffer the effects of future trauma.

Our goal should be to restore and maintain our horse's sense of security and trust in humans, other animals and the world in general. While we would love if we could write up a rehab program or provide a medicine to fix this problem, healing from trauma can be a slow process with frequent steps backward. Realistically our goal with any trauma survivor is to help them be able to function in regular life with the capacity to enjoy life and engage in positive social relationships. Luckily recent studies in dogs with PTS have discovered that most are able to nearly or completely re-adapt to regular life.

There are wounds

that never show

on the body that

www.EmpoweredEquines.com

are deeper and more hurtful than

anything that bleeds

~Laurell K. Hamilton

A World of Reinforcement

Food is by far the easiest and most consistent reinforcer to use in any planned training session. It works effectively as a training tool in sessions - but our whole life is not a training session. There is a whole world full of reinforcers we can benefit from learning about and utilizing. There are many times in our day to day life that where our horse may want something other than food. With this we can bring our training into the real world and open our conversation with our horses to an entirely two-way communication. But how do we know what our horses want and how do we use these effectively and ethically?

We want to be a well-trained human for our horses. We should be as good at listening as we are at teaching with our horses. But listening requires a great deal of observational skills and a solid understanding of equine behavior. An observant and knowledgeable handler will learn to see what their horses are asking of them and when they're uncomfortable with a situation. Many horses have learned throughout their life that their voices won't be heard and that attempts at communication and honesty will be punished. These horses can be extremely difficult to read, it requires a trained eye to see problems before they become serious. Other horses have learned that they'll only be heard if they scream (literally or figuratively) - subtle behavior like pinned ears aren't enough, they need to go right in for the bite. This lack of warning can be extremely dangerous, even as we try to allow them more honesty. We also have the scenario where the horse may work with humans who aren't as observant, aware, or caring as an educated trainer. So how do we help these horses learn appropriate ways to communicate? With positive reinforcement techniques we can teach our learners safe ways to ask for what they want as well as 'yes' and 'no' signals- with this we can improve their ability to communicate as well as our ability to listen!

It helps to first understand that all living creatures know how to ask for what they want. They can do so by any learned pattern. They learn that performing a specific behavior results in a specific consequence. If a horse kicking their door gets their well-trained human to toss them hay (to quiet them), they will kick the door to ask for hay. If pointing at an itchy spot gets their human with those wonderful fingers to scratch where they can't reach, they will learn to point to ask for a scratch. Being aware that these patterns happen can allow us to help prevent unwanted attempts at communication as well as teaching more desirable attempts. This can allow our horses to train us without force, violence, or yelling!

In the world of non-verbal humans, we call this type of behavior "**Manding**". *The individual is asking for something they want with their only means, gestures, sounds, and attempts at language.* Wow! Language! We really can have a two-way communication with our horses!

Our world is full of potential reinforcers; anything a horse wants in the moment is a reinforcer we can use. Knowing our horse's language and mands can help us learn what they want and what we can use as reinforcement. With this we can begin to bring our regular training into real life. If the horse wants to go out the gate, you can ask them to back away from the gate, reinforcing this behavior with the opening of the gate. This smooth communication can become our entire life. When a horse wants something, we can tell them what they need to do to get what they want. We can only do this after the initial behavior has been taught and is on cue.

Picture a child saying, "give me the salt" and their parent rephrases their request for them "could you please pass the salt?" - This is just like that! When they ask for something, simply teach them how you'd like their request rephrased, then reinforce it with what they're asking for (to be let out, fed, watered, and so on). If instead when the child said "give me the salt" their parents punished them, they may look for another way of obtaining the salt (reaching across the table to grab it) or they may go without the salt. That may not be a big deal in this scenario, but for horses they may find new, more dangerous ways of asking for what they need or go without something they need, for fear of being punished. If our horse has learned that kicking the door gets them hay, but we are worried they'll destroy our barn or hurt themselves, we can teach them new ways to communicate. We can start by fulfilling their needs before they need to ask so "loudly". But if we miss our opportunity, we can begin to retrain safer alternatives. If the horse begins kicking their door, simply cue a more appropriate behavior (going to a specific target could be good) and provide the desired reinforcer (hay in this case). We can also cue the behavior whenever we feed, ideally before the kicking begins.

What about a situation where the horse is already manding for something, but the way they're asking is potentially dangerous or otherwise unwanted? We can teach the horse a more appropriate behavior to use to communicate (we will go into further detail on how to handle unwanted behaviors soon). We'll reinforce the desired behavior with the reinforcer the horse is asking for with the inappropriate behavior. For example, if the horse is kicking a gate to go to the other side, this is unsafe for the horse and detrimental to your property. So, replace it - when you see the horse begin to mand, cue a more appropriate way for them to ask, maybe hang a bell on the gate? When they do the correct new behavior, reinforce it with what they want. Make sure to always offer to open the gate when they do this new behavior, to make it more effective than the previous kicking. This only works if we're able to give the horse what they want when they ask.

Inspired by the use of communication applications with pictures for non-verbal humans, we at the Empowered Equines Rescue designed a cork board with symbols to develop communication with some of our horses, just to see to what extent we could bring this. Really, it became unrealistic to use this. Unlike pets who live next to us 24/7, we aren't able to give horses the same level of freedom and control. I can't always bring my horse in or out when they ask because it would disrupt the whole herd. I can't always stop what I'm doing to scratch their itch for them (though I do try). It became clear that while we can add this level of communication to their life, they really can't really have that much control, which is a bit heartbreaking. Where possible, we can add ounces of control and choice, but realistically, we can only do so much.

We can, however, take this two-way communication actively into our training, adding a sort of "yes" and "no" in our horse's language. While observant and caring handlers can easily learn to listen to the horse's body language and subtle communications to see how the horse feels while they're training, there are times when we want to give our horses more clear, consistent, obvious, or safer ways of communicating with us. We can do this in two ways - with the use of consent signals as well as providing the horse with an alternative behavior that is always acceptable and reinforced. These two options allow horses to be more open and honest with their communication, especially in the case of horses who are more shut down and less honest in their communication. This doesn't replace the need to be observant and careful trainers, but can provide us some safe wiggle room. It can also empower our horses with more control and choice in their lives.

Importance of Choice

One of the most valuable aspects of positive reinforcement training is our horse's ability to participate freely. They have the option to partake in the fun or they can say *"no"* or *"I'm not ready for that yet"*. Better yet, we have the ability to listen. Negative reinforcement requires the handler to add something the learner finds aversive to remove it when the learner performs the right behavior. If when using negative reinforcement the horse says *"I'm not comfortable with this behavior yet"* and the handler accepts that answer, by relieving the aversive, the learner has learned a way to avoid the aversive without complying. While this is wonderfully empowering to the horse, they are learning to use their voice, learning that their voice will be heard, no longer so afraid that they push themselves beyond their comfort zone – but they've also learned now that they don't need to do anything. Negative reinforcement doesn't work if the horse is allowed to say "*no*" and walk away.

One aspect to consider is that in our modern world our horses are entitled to feeling safe and comfortable in their environment. Now that we do not depend on horses for our survival, their

Feeling safe should always comes before obedience
Safety should never have to be earned

blind obedience and compliance does not come before their sense of security. It's our choice whether to own a horse and it comes with responsibility to provide the best for our horses - even if it doesn't always match up with what we want for our horses. Remember safety always comes before obedience and safety should never have to be earned. As people who care about our horses and who want our horses to be free and comfortable in their choices and in themselves, we want our horses to have the right and ability to say "no". Especially if we can teach them to say it in a safe and easy way. I'd much rather my horse tell me *"I'm not ready for this"* by walking away than by running, bucking, bolting, or biting.

At the same time, we still want the horse to do what we're asking so what do we do if they say "*no*"? The first thing to keep in mind is that when we switch to positive reinforcement, there is now something in it for the horse. They're going to want to do what we ask, not because it will hurt if they don't but because something wonderful will happen if they do. *When working to avoid an aversive the horse will only work as much as needed to earn relief. When working for something they want they will continue to try harder, building on their own behavior in hopes of reward.* The horse still wants to perform the behavior, but for whatever reason they chose not to. We need to sort out what's causing them to say "*no*", what's outweighing their desire to play with us?

First, we need to check all potential medical concerns, be thorough, ask a vet or specialist depending on the situation. Be sure to discuss the specific situation, you are your horse's only means to health care, it's important you stand up for them. Next, check the environment. Is the living situation ideal for that individual horse? Some horses enjoy the privacy and safety of their own stall, while others prefer open environments and the safety of friends. Do they have appropriate turn out time with plenty of exercise? You also want to ensure the equine company is appropriate for your horse, unfortunately horses don't get to pick their friends and often end up with bullies and victims among the herd. This can really become apparent in their training situation, if they feel the need to defend their resources, even from you, the provider. It helps to keep the horse mentally and physically stimulated even when you're not around. There are many enrichment options and toys, most horses prefer the sort that provide food (good thing they're supposed to be eating 24/7!). I'd say most of the time if a horse says "no" without a physical reason it's because there's something wrong with their environment.

Finally, you want to check the training itself. Is your timing accurate? Treat delivery clear? Rate of reinforcement matching this stage of the skill? Does the value of the reward match the complexity of the skill? Does the horse really understand what you want? Are they being over-faced (the skill is too difficult or scary to do)? Remember training isn't just about the click and treat. Keep your horse's whole life in balance and the rest should sort itself out.

It's vital our horses have the ability to communicate with us, openly and honestly, like any healthy relationship. You can't fix what you don't know is broken. If your horse can't be open and honest with you about everything there may be a number of things that they are struggling with, many of them could be very easy to fix, that you may have never known about. The lovely thing about positive reinforcement is that they can safely and clearly communicate when things aren't going well for them. When a horse knows they can keep themselves safe by saying "no" when things get too much for them to handle – they're often much more willing to say "yes" when they can! They will feel safer, bolder, more curious, and playful if they know they can be safe by their own means.

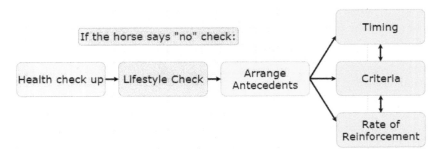

Empowerment

Now that we've opened our horses up to more complete conversations, how do we know if they're being honest? How do we know for sure that our horse isn't just tolerating us and what we ask of them just for the food? How do we know if they're enjoying this? How do we know all of this isn't just a matter of reinforcement history and conditioning? We know that Positive Reinforcement is the kinder option to behavior modification. The real question should be, do we need to modify behavior? If so, how much?

The truth is when an animal is living in domestication, even with the best of environments and husbandry set up, there will be times they need to be handled for care. Things like vet and farrier attention are unavoidable. Positive reinforcement offers us the kindest way to prepare our horses for these necessary life situations. We can offer our horses benefits to captivity, if done correctly, so behavior modification for husbandry is vital.

What about the rest? The stuff just for us? There are thousands of things we train horses to do every day that they just don't need to know. Which color corresponds with the human word "blue", they don't care. In fact, most of the things we ask of horses they already know how to do, and we are just putting it on cue for our own convenience. These are unnecessary but can be a great deal of fun for human and horse. In captivity horses can lack stimulation and enrichment, and these things can help fill that void (page: 19). It can help replace the uncertainty of nature, without real risk or harm and can keep horses emotionally and mentally active.

But what about behaviors we ask for just for us that may be to the detriment of the horse? There are some things we ask a horse to do that may not be for their own good, but rather our pleasure. These things include, but are not limited to, riding, driving, and tolerating the tools required for these things. If we can use positive reinforcement to overcome the pain and fear involved in vet procedures we certainly can overcome the pain of ill-fitting tack or the discomfort of carrying a rider. So where is the ethical line? That's for you to decide. In the meantime, we need to look at the whole picture and not settle with just using positive reinforcement, when there are kinder options available. Awesome we got them doing what we want, but is that really right? We need to ensure our tools fit, and are the most comfortable we can make them. We must also ensure the horse is comfortable and happy with this job.

Control reduces conflict, stress, fear, and anxiety. Because we can stop and start it. Our goal is to provide our horses with a sense of control to reduce conflict and stress. I think most of the time there is very little conflict or stress simply because we're using positive reinforcement and are good observers, and work at our learner's pace. But there will be times when conflict may be real, so we use measures to put them in control and allow them to communicate their control over our training in a safe way.

How do we know if our horse is really happy to do something and not just in it for the treat? Aside from using our common sense and observational skills - which are two of the most important things when handling an animal, we can also offer an alternative. Hay, a food toy, or a simple behavior you will always reinforce (even if it wasn't cued) can serve as that alternative. With an alternative the horse can tell us *"what you're asking is harder than just eating hay/ playing with my toy"*. The higher value the alternative the more honest the horse will be. Because they can get what they want elsewhere, we know they actually do like this (or not). This forces us to be better trainers and more careful observers, so we don't lose out over the alternative. However, we can also remove the alternative in "no choice" situations like the essential medical procedures.

We can utilize this by training an "**always reinforce-able behavior**" which is a safe behavior that is easy to do and is always reinforced when offered – and is never under stimulus control. This technique gives us a measure, if the horse prefers to use this behavior we know the value of the skill we're working on has fallen too low – or has become too difficult. Because there is another go-to option we can say *"doing this skill is still more salient than x"*. I strongly believe this behavior should be something like targeting so we can remove it in "no choice" situations.

We can give our horse a slightly louder voice by teaching them to give us a signal when they're ready for more, or a signal when what we're asking is getting too difficult. We can teach our horses a sort of consent, *"go ahead"*, or *"I'm ready"* signal, by allowing them to trigger when we begin the next repetition of our training. We'll use latency (a delay before the initiator behavior or reluctance to initiate the next repetition) as a measure of their choice. If they are slow or reluctant to initiate the next repetition, we know we are tipping towards conflict or stress. If they are quick to ask for the next repetition, we are not. This can help us gauge how comfortable our horse really is with what we're asking.

Initiator Signals

When we are training our horses anything we can teach them a simple way to tell us "I'm ready for more", "let's keep going". This doesn't seem like a big deal, they want to participate because we're giving them treats, right? But this can become an extremely useful tool when counter conditioning, working with anything the horse isn't sure about, or anything you're not confident with. This allows us to check in with our horses, asking if they're still OK with what we're doing and if they want to carry on. With this we can spot problems early on, before it becomes dangerous for either of us.

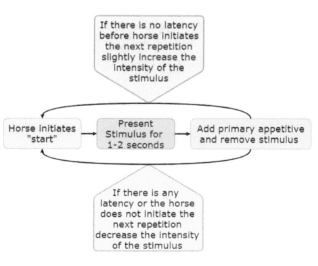

The concept of **initiator signals** have become quite popular in dog training, thanks especially to Emily Vegh and Eva Bertlisson and their book *Agility Right from the Start*. Peggy Hogan has been working with them to develop these techniques and adapt them for horses. These initiators are easy to teach but take careful observation to implement

158

correctly. Simply begin a basic training routine, but between each repetition wait for the horse to do a specific behavior before beginning the next cycle. I like to wait until my horse stands facing forward or looks at me as an initiator signal, but you can use anything - backing up a step or touching a specific target could also work.

To help the horse learn the process, we will cue the specific behavior we have decided we want to use as the initiator signal. Eventually we will not need to cue the behavior; the horse will perform the behavior without being cued as communication to us that they are ready to move on to the next behavior. When the horse has learned how to start each repetition of the training cycle they can start communicating, but how do we measure this? Each cycle the horse should promptly use their initiator signal to cue the next repetition. If there is latency before the initiator signal or if the horse doesn't provide the initiator signal you know the horse is becoming conflicted about what they're doing and it's time to slow down and reassess your training.

This communication allows us to clearly see if our horse is feeling safe and comfortable in their training - like a form of consent given with each repetition.

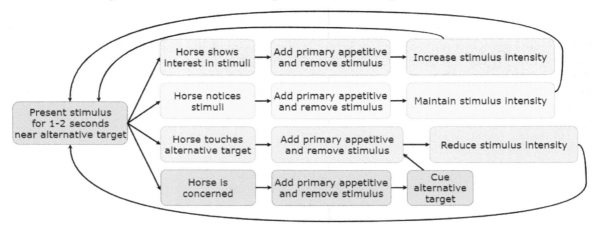

Always Reinforce-able Behavior

There are many situations where we may want to provide our horses more choice and control over their interactions with humans or training sessions. Some horses have anxiety around humans, aggression with minimal warning, stress related to fear or resource guarding. There are even scenarios where horses really enjoy human interaction and positive reinforcement, but push themselves over-threshold to earn reinforcement. Horses like these can all really benefit from empowerment tools like initiator signals and always reinforce-able behaviors.

We know that we can provide our horses some choice by having alternative resources available during our time with them. We can provide hay, grass, or food toys during our training and interactions with our horses - so we can measure how much our horses are enjoying what we're doing together. We know if they chose to go to the alternative the value of working with us is less than the hay, grass, or food toy. These alternatives are easy to provide in any regular training and can help reduce conflict or stress during our interactions. These options are usually sufficient for most horses. In the situation of a horse who really enjoys postiive reinforcement and human interaction, who often pushes themselves over-threshold, we need to find a stronger alternate to provide them. This is where an always reinforce-able behavior can be extremely valuable.

Always Reinforce-able alternative behaviors are all about empowering our horse with an added level of control and choice. This allows them to earn reinforcement even without complying to what we want from them. Providing a horse with a behavior that is always an reinforce-able option can be a safe default for our horses to offer us when they're not comfortable with what we're doing or need a break. It can help to use a behavior like a specific target as opposed to a behavior they do with their body, as you can remove it in situation when they must comply (veterinary procedures and such). This can be a great tool to use when working on introducing new or difficult behaviors (if you're questioning if the horse is physically comfortable with something) as well as riding or other skills you'd like to have as "optional" for your horse to participate in.

This should not overshadow your ability to read and listen to your horse, don't wait for your horse to tell you they'd prefer not to do this, try to notice the signals before they go to their always reinforce-able option. This is a back up and a safe option for your horse, it can allow them to have more choice and more honesty in your training, but it is not a replacement for good training. Our training should be engaging and fun enough that the horse chooses to enjoy partaking in the reinforce-able behaviors we are working on as opposed to the alternative, easy answer of the target.

Teaching an alternative reinforce-able behavior isn't something for everyone, but can be a valuable tool for those horses who need more control and choice in their lives. We'll use the example of a special target as an alternative behavior, but you can pick whatever you find appropriate for you and your horse. The goal is for this behavior to be reinforced whenever the horse offers this behavior, regardless of whether you've cued this. It provides the horse a strong alternative to whatever else we may be asking, allowing our horse to be honest about how they feel about the skills we're working on. This helps us assess our training plan and goals appropriately for this horse.

Of course, the horse may choose to stick with the easier of the two options; if one behavior requires a lot of work it's easier to just keep touching the ball. Luckily research has shown that this fades with time. At first when the horse learns that going to this behavior always results in a reward they may park themselves in front of it and only do that behavior hundreds of times in a row. It's important we remain consistent with it though, as this is always a reinforce-able behavior. Over time the horse will decide to start doing other behaviors again. It gets boring just clicking the "treat" button over and over again. Make sure the other behaviors you ask for are engaging and fun, and don't push it too early on. Over time this alternative behavior will fade to the background and the horse will begin to respond more honestly.

This gives our horse the ability to express their opinions in a complete and honest way. This gives them two reinforce-able options at all times (what we cue and the alternative behavior) so they can be totally honest.

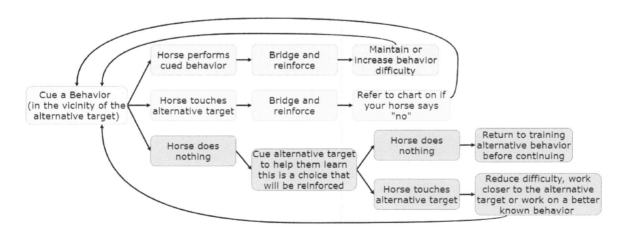

Initiator Signal:

Teaching the horse a way to let us know when they're ready for the next repetition in their training can be extremely empowering for our horses. It can also provide them a wonderful sense of control. This can be an extremely valuable tool when working on counter conditioning or veterinary procedures.

Antecedents:
- A quiet area
- A comfortable distance from friends
- A common object (a brush or feed bucket could work)

Shaping Process:

1. Choose a specific behavior you'd like to use. You could use something as simple as the horse looking at you, raising a hoof, taking a step back or forward or touching a specific target, any behavior you'd like.

2. Practice the behavior you want to use several times until the horse begins comfortably offering the behavior.

3. Hold up the object the horse is familiar with (a brush works) and reinforce. Cue the behavior you plan on using, if they don't immediately begin offering again.

4. When the horse does the desired behavior, immediately present the object again, reinforce and remove the object. Repeat this process until the horse readily offers the behavior after each repetition.

5. The horse will recognize that their behavior is bringing about the presentation of the brush and the reinforcement. At this point you can begin to use this horse to human cue for more complex training.

Counter Conditioning:

6. As the horse gets the hang of the signal you can begin to utilize it for counter conditioning, giving the horse a degree control and comfort over the situation.

7. When your horse gives you the signal, present the object you're aiming to counter condition at its smallest value (size, volume, proximity) for a moment, reinforce and remove.

8. Repeat this process, waiting for the horse to give you the signal they're ready for the next repetition. If the horse gives you the signal promptly then gradually increase the value of the stimulus. If they show any hesitation or latency decrease the value of the stimulus.

9. You can repeat this process allowing the horse to guide you with how comfortable they are with the stimulus at any given time. This gives them the power to say when they're ready to continue.

Initiator Signal:

Once you've taught the horse an initiator signal you can also use this signal in training behaviors. This can be very beneficial for horses that are a bit slow or cautious, allowing us to see when they're ready to move forward.

Antecedents:
- A quiet area
- A comfortable distance from friends
- A well known behavior

Shaping Process:

1. Start by practicing your initiator signal until the horse begins offering it.

2. Once the horse offers the initiator signal, cue the simple, well-known behavior; mark and reinforce when they perform the behavior. It's important to start with a behavior we're sure they're comfortable with to ensure we're getting an accurate measure of their usual training speed.

3. As they get the hang of initiating you to cue the next behavior you can begin to mix up which behavior you cue after the initiator. Use the same behavior several times to see if the horse continues offering the initiator at the same rate. If they begin to slow down, showing reluctance, you know that performing this behavior creates some conflict or stress in the horse. You'll want to break down this behavior some to find where things become uncomfortable or difficult for the horse.

4. If you're working on a new behavior, using the initiator signal can let you know when the horse is ready. If they become reluctant, you know you aren't providing enough clues or information to help them get started.

Always Reinforce-able Behavior:

We can start with teaching the horse a simple behavior, like touching a specific target (I used a hanging jolly ball). This simple behavior is one we will simply never put under stimulus control, it will always be reinforced if it's offered. This way, if we ask the horse to do something they're not comfortable with, they can offer this simple behavior instead reinforcing whenever the horse offers the correct answer to the cue or whenever the horse does this alternative behavior. By providing an alternative that still has all the components the horse may enjoy, the treats, problem solving, and human engagement, we are providing a higher value alternative so the horse can make a more balanced decision. They don't need to give up anything in order to say "no thanks". I like to use something physical like a target – so I can remove it the rare times when "no" is not an option (veterinary procedures we haven't been able to prepare for). It's not fair to give your horse choice if you aren't going to listen, so taking the option away physically and visually can help them understand this when a situation is not free choice. Whenever the horse uses their alternative behavior during training we should reinforce it. Once this alternative behavior is well conditioned around well known behaviors, we can begin to introduce more difficult skills, things you're not really sure how the horse feels about doing. After lots of practice keep a mental note of which behaviors they perform eagerly and which they prefer to utilize their alternative behavior with. Given this information we know what the horse is or isn't comfortable with.

Antecedents:
- A quiet, comfortable area
- A comfortable distance from friends
- A unique target

Shaping Process:

1. Practice targeting the special target again and again until the horse begins freely offering this behavior without the cue.

2. Ask for another well known, easy behavior in the vicinity of the target. If the horse goes and touches the target, reinforce the behavior. If the horse doesn't go to the target try adding long pauses between your reinforcement and cue, allowing the horse to try offering a behavior, like touching the target. As you practice doing well-known, comfortable behaviors with your horse always have the target available, if they ever go to it reinforce that behavior, even if they go to it hundreds of times in a row.

3. If your horse doesn't go to the target, practice cuing it between other behaviors until the horse starts offering it again and going to it when there's a long pause between cues.

4. Work on these fun, easy behaviors between when the horse is offering you the target touch, until the horse is engaged in training and not going to the target frequently. If the horse continues to go to the target and doesn't re-engage in training, up your rate of reinforcement and decrease the criteria of the skills you're working on. The horse should be enjoying the training, not just tolerating the situation to earn a reinforcement.

5. At the point when the horse is eagerly participating in training around the target, only going to the target rarely, you can begin to work on more behaviors you're less certain are fun for the horse.

What is RAGE?

Aggression in horses can lead to some of the most dangerous situations we're ever presented with when working with them. RAGE is a fairly complex emotional system - it can feel unpredictable and explosive. It helps to first understand what causes rage in order to understand how to best address it. There are two main situations aggression occurs, avoidance and seeking.

Avoidance type rage is what we are most used to seeing with horses, especially in a traditional stable environment. This type of aggression is in response to something the animal is trying to avoid, usually something they're afraid of, but are unable to easily escape from. When normal avoidance behaviors and flight responses do not provide the relief the horse is looking for, they will resort to aggression. We see this in nature, when running from a predator. If they're cornered or caught they'll resort to fighting to free themselves. If the aggression works in defending them, they may be quicker to turn to this option again in the future. Soon these aggressive behaviors can become their learned, go to response to any aversive situation.

There are thousands of scenarios horses are put in on a regular basis that can trigger avoidance aggression, especially in traditional training techniques. Negative Reinforcement training techniques require you to add an aversive - the horse needs to work out how to earn relief (page: 44). If they exhaust the choices they think will work they may progress to aggressive behaviors. Obviously this can be dangerous, but if we release the aversive at this time we risk reinforcing the aggressive behavior. However, if we don't relieve the aversive when the horse is becoming aggressive, the horse may sink into learned helplessness. Remember, Learned Helplessness occurs when the horse feels there is no escape - they shut down and stop trying (page: 124). Unfortunately, many humans take advantage of this, because a shut down horse can appear to be safer. However, Learned Helplessness can fade, causing a sudden recurrence to extreme aggressive outbursts. This is neither a dependable nor ethical approach to stifling aggression.

Seeking type RAGE can appear similar, but this occurs when the horse feels a need that they can't satisfy. Except in this case this is something the horse wants to obtain. We often describe this type of rage as frustration - picture a horse unsuccessfully trying to get the treats out of a toy - they get frustrated and stomp the toy. We can relate to this feeling when our car won't start when we turn the key. We have an expectation that turning the key will turn on the vehicle, but it doesn't work, so we get frustrated and try again and again until we're fed up! As positive reinforcement trainers we want to watch for this type of frustration appearing in our training. If we see this it can mean our rate of reinforcement is too low, our criteria is too high, or our timing is unclear. Another aspect to seeking type aggression is in the case of play. PLAY behaviors can mimic common RAGE behaviors, but true anger only occurs when the PLAY desire goes unsatiated. We see this a lot when young horses are trying to get their older herd members to play.

Horses dislike the RAGE system, if they can avoid it they will. The only time these seeking or avoiding situations turn to rage is when their perceived needs are not met. Which leads us to the logical conclusion, the best way to get rid of aggressive behaviors is to prevent them by fulfilling their perceived needs. This can be a lot harder than it sounds. Sometimes it can be difficult to find what the initial trigger of the aggression was, let alone how to fix it. The key to prevention is knowing our individual and being able to predict when and where the aggressive responses will come. We can not only avoid the common triggers, we can arrange the environment to block triggers or prevent the aggressive response (like using protected contact while we work through an issue). For those that we can't avoid we can replace the behavior with a safe alternative.

When a horse feels out of control of their safety or resources, the RAGE system comes to fix the problem. *A feeling of control is the antidote to aggression.* If the horse knows how to effectively avoid the bad things in their life and knows how to actively earn the things they want and need, then the RAGE system will not be needed. We can use this to help reduce aggressive responses by helping our horses find appropriate ways to get what they want. For a horse who is quick to resort to aggressive behaviors, teaching them safe and effective ways to control their lives can reduce their need to ever resort to aggression. We can teach the horses safe, appropriate behaviors to earn the reinforcement they want and avoid the situations they don't want to be in. With this we can replace the dangerous aggression behaviors with safe alternatives.

Another aspect to consider when dealing with aggression issues is our own personal relationship with the learner. If the horse is feeling defensive or anxious about an aversive history with us, it may reduce their ability or desire to try new things before resorting to aggressive type behaviors.

If we have a solid positive history developed with our horses they may be more comfortable exploring, trying new things, and being patient as they learn. This sense of control and safety in the relationship with us, helps ease and subside the need for aggressive behaviors.

Dealing with Unwanted Behaviors

Before we get started let's determine what unwanted behaviors are. It's important we recognize that horses don't have "good" or "bad" behaviors - but rather behaviors that work or don't work. While we frequently think of our horses are being "naughty", "fresh", "rude", "disrespectful" and so on, it's important we remove these terms from our vocabulary. Rather we should look at each behavior, "biting", "kicking", "invading space", and so on as just behaviors. When we use terms like those we add an emotional meaning behind the behaviors which can cause us to take it personally or encourage us to think of punishment. Rather let's focus on the behaviors themselves, they may be working for the horse, but that doesn't mean they're behaviors we want to see. Horses aren't out to get us, they're simply responding to their environment. What caused the unwanted behavior? What's reinforcing the behavior? Why do these behaviors work for our horse?

As ethical trainers we aim to use positive reinforcement and reduce the use of aversives in our training where we can. This can be difficult when thinking about behaviors we don't want - particularly ones that can be detrimental to the horse themselves or dangerous to the handler. Some behaviors need to be reduced and not just ignored, for their safety or for ours. *Remember, "positive" does not mean "permissive". Luckily we have options!*

- Ensure physical or emotional needs are met (call a vet and reassess their lifestyle)
- Change the antecedents (get rid of what triggers the behavior)
- Remove the reinforcement (find what is reinforcing the behavior and remove it)
- Train an incompatible behavior (teach them an acceptable alternative)

Before we begin approaching unwanted behaviors we need to understand them. Think back to when we were learning how to create behaviors and we learned our ABC's (Antecedent- Behavior - Consequence) (page: 36). Unwanted behaviors are no exception to the ABCs. First we want to look at which antecedents trigger the unwanted behavior. Do they do this behavior when they're stressed or tired, when a specific peer is around or at feed time? There are always specific antecedents that trigger these behaviors, but it may take some deduction to determine which.

Next determine which behavioral choices do they have in this scenario. Sometimes the horse really is responding the only logical way to the situation they're put in. If this is the case we need to change the situation. If possible arrange the antecedents to prevent the unwanted behavior or give them more options in the scenario. For example if you have horses fighting over food - providing more sources of food can prevent the fighting.

If there is another behavioral option the horse could perform in that situation but they are choosing not to let's look at why. What were the previous consequences for performing the unwanted behavior? Something must have reinforced it to encourage them to use this option. If the horse kicking their door got them fed earlier than usual (to quiet them down) the kicking behavior was reinforced. If chasing their herd member away from the food allowed them to keep all the food to themselves, the behavior was reinforced. Sometimes the behavior is self-reinforced, some behaviors feel good to do! So we can look at what is reinforcing the unwanted behavior, change it or provide an appropriate outlet for it. If the horse is chewing on objects around their stall because this is engaging and fun for them - providing them acceptable objects (toys and food) to mouth on can be a more appropriate outlet. While in the example of the horse kicking their door, ensuring everyone in the farm knows not to feed this horse while they're kicking will ensure this behavior doesn't get reinforced.

This being said, getting rid of the reinforcement of a behavior that was previously reinforced (even unintentionally) will often result in an extinction burst. So, while no longer feeding the horse who kicks the door will stop reinforcing it, it may be destructive or dangerous for this kicking behavior to go through an extinction burst. We can reinforce the absence of the behavior, when we catch them not pawing we can give them their food or drop them some treats. But this level of ambiguity can be difficult for some horses, who may begin to find other superstitious behaviors to fill in the blank. What we can do instead is provide the horse with another behavioral option that will be reinforced. For example, stationing on a target during feed time. We can even use a behavior that contradicts the unwanted behavior - like stationing two front feet on a mat. They can't both station on the mat and paw - if the stationing is reinforced but the pawing is not the pawing will quickly fade and be replaced by the stationing rather than having a true burst like it would without a known alternative behavior.

We can pull apart an unwanted behavior anywhere in its ABC chain. We can change the antecedents to prevent or discourage the unwanted behavior. We can provide other behavioral options that will be reinforced or reinforce a lack of behavior. We can also change the consequences, removing whatever reinforces the unwanted behavior and begin reinforcing the behaviors we do want instead. With these techniques we can pull apart and ultimately get rid of the behaviors our horses may do that are dangerous or destructive.

Change the Antecedents to prevent or discourage the unwanted behavior → Provide an acceptable alternative Behavior → Remove any reinforcing Consequence

Punishment

We talked about Punishment in reference to the learning quadrants. We know there are two types, Positive (adding an aversive) and Negative (subtracting an appetitive) (page: 37). But we haven't really gotten back to it much. Why? Simply because it's unnecessary!

Punishment works quickly to suppress unwanted behavior. *It stops a dangerous situation in the moment. This is extremely reinforcing to the punisher - which is where things get dangerous.* This is why people continue to use punishment even after all the proof of its risks and inefficiencies.

Unfortunately punishment only suppresses unwanted behaviors; if the cause of the behavior remains, the behavior will as well. This suppression may be extremely temporary or become dependent on your ability to punish it. The suppression can also fade with time as the horse becomes accustomed to the punishment, or as they learn or try new ways to avoid the punishment. The horse may learn easy ways to avoid the punishment which may turn into even more unwanted behaviors.

The fact that the behavior may recur, may cause us to increase our efforts to punish it. This escalation may be perpetual as the behavior continues and the punisher keeps being reinforced by the temporary relief from the unwanted behavior. It's a vicious cycle. *Remember, violence only inspires more violence.*

Without fixing the cause, without teaching the horse an appropriate alternative, without removing whatever reinforced the unwanted behavior - the behavior will never stop completely. What will happen with the use of continued or repeated punishment is the horse will become fearful. Punishment increases stress, anxiety, and avoidance behaviors. It reduces the horse's ability and desire to try. If they run the risk of being punished why would they try? As positive reinforcement trainers we rely on the horse's desire to participate with us, to escalate their own behaviors, to try new things. Which they won't do if they are in fear of being punished.

Remember how whenever a behavior is operantly conditioned (through the learning quadrants) the emotions are classically conditioned into the entire scenario as well. Meaning everything (and everyone) present during the punishment is also being aversively conditioned. Not only are you poisoning your cues and your antecedents - but also your relationship (page: 172).

This being said, we live in real life. Some horses are more sensitive than others. Punishment may happen, unintentionally sometimes, or in an emergency. Sometimes we are faced with a situation we weren't prepared for and must do what we need to in order to remain safe. Sometimes we do something that is punishing to our horse, without meaning to. Accidents happen, forgive yourself. Spend some time to re-balance your relationship and learn from this incident.

Reduce Pawing:

Pawing is potentially one of the most frustrating unwanted behaviors we may want to reduce. Pawing is a natural foraging behavior, digging for forage under snow, through substrate, or even breaking ice to get water. This can be displaced when the horse is frustrated, hungry or seeking reinforcement. It occurs commonly around feed time, when a horse is hungry and eager, which can cause it to be easily reinforced by accident. Once reinforced it can be a very hard behavior to get rid of.

Ensure needs are met:

1. Before we address reducing this unwanted behavior, we should recognize this is a natural foraging behavior, so we want to ensure this isn't happening because access to forage is too limited.

2. Having an appropriate outlet for this behavior can also help, for example, having toys they can paw or substrate to dig in.

Find the trigger:

3. If we know the usual context that triggers pawing we can try to rearrange the set up to relieve the symptom.

4. It may require catching the horse before the pawing begins in the normal situation it occurs, mark and reinforce the calm before the pawing.

Remove the reinforcer:

5. Along the lines of finding in what context pawing usually occurs, we can also find what naturally reinforces this behavior. Do they paw at feed time? Then feeding could be the reinforcer. If they paw out of boredom or attention seeking, any interaction may actually be reinforcing this, even if we think we're punishing them. If the behavior happens more frequently, then whatever follows it has been reinforcing it, intentionally or not.

6. After determining what has been reinforcing this behavior, eliminate it if possible. Try feeding or providing attention before the pawing begins, not after it starts. This alone can be frustrating and lead to an extinction burst, so don't stop here, teach an alternative behavior.

Teach an incompatible behavior:

7. Stationing front feet on a mat (page: 73) can contradict pawing behaviors, backing up (page: 69) or standing at a nose station could also work.

8. After teaching the behavior cue it in the normal situation when pawing occurs. Try to cue it before the pawing begins, not always after the pawing begins to prevent unwanted behavior chains.

Reduce Body Foraging:

Foraging for food is a common and natural behavior that horses do all the time. However when they forage for treats on our body, potentially nipping our skin or injuring us, it's not so good. This behavior can be risky for us and frustrating for the horse.

Ensure needs are met:

1. As this is a natural foraging behavior we want to ensure the horse has adequate access to forage.

2. We also want to make sure the horse has a healthy and appropriate outlet for this with slow nets and foraging toys.

Find the trigger:

3. The trigger here is usually fairly obvious, we have food on us and the horse wants it. They are simply doing the next logical step, find and take the food. Rather than removing the trigger, it can be more useful to teach the horse an appropriate way to act in this situation.

Remove the reinforcer:

4. Be careful never to reinforce body investigating behaviors. While I welcome gentle snuggles and investigation from my horses (which is a personal choice) we never want to reinforce this behavior or it could escalate dangerously.

5. If this behavior had been previously reinforced, removing the reinforcer alone won't do the job. When reinforcement for a behavior suddenly comes to a stop the behavior can escalate in an extinction burst, which can be dangerous.

Teach an incompatible behavior:

6. We absolutely need to teach the horse an appropriate alternative behavior for this situation. Standing calmly facing forward (page: 65) is the ideal default behavior to teach in this situation. Working in protected contact (page: 39) until the horse is proficient with this can also help.

7. In dramatic cases you may also want to teach the horse a solid back up (page: 69) and head down cue (page: 68) in protected contact to ensure the horse can give you comfortable space at any given time before attempting full contact.

Pulling on the Lead:

Pulling on the lead happens commonly, especially when there's something delicious to reach for or they're going somewhere really fun! Unfortunately the lead is on the horse for a reason and it's not a tool for our horses to drags us around with. It can be dangerous if a horse pulls, potentially hurting us or getting loose into a dangerous environment.

Ensure needs are met:

1. When a horse pulls on the lead it's always to get somewhere better than walking beside us. Whatever they're working to get, make sure they have an adequate amount of. If they're in a rush to be turned out, make sure they have enough time outside to play. If they're pulling for grass, ensure they have enough grazing time (if diet restrictions apply, enrichment can substitute this).

Find the trigger:

2. Finding the trigger is usually easy in this situation as they usually drag us right to it! A nice grazing spot, their friend, their stall, or their paddock are the usual culprits.

Remove the reinforcer:

3. Every time they rush and get to their goal they're being reinforced for rushing and pulling. That being said, pulling back or becoming more aversive is likely to get us in more trouble. Teaching an incompatible behavior is a much more complimentary approach.

Teach an incompatible behavior:

4. Teaching a horse solid leading cues (page: 70) as well as back up (page: 69) and standing calmly (page: 65). With these behaviors we can redirect our horse away from pulling, ask for a stop, turn or back up.

5. You may need to increase your rate of reinforcement when there are heavily competing resources. When a horse is eager to rush to their paddock, putting heavy reinforcement on stopping, waiting and walking quietly beside you while work near competing resources is a good tactic.

AVERSIVES IN TRAINING

Poisoned Cues

The idea of poisoned cues first requires a good understanding of what a cue is and isn't. Remember our ABCs? Antecedent-Behavior-Consequence (page: 36). A "cue" is an antecedent to a trained behavior that results in an attractive consequence. A cue eventually becomes a conditioned appetitive, just like a click. Remember Classical Conditioning (page: 33) when X=Y? When a neutral stimulus is paired repeatedly with an appetitive stimulus it becomes a classically conditioned appetitive. So when we have a 'cue, behavior, appetitive' repetition then the cue and behavior becomes conditioned as an appetitive, something they enjoy doing! As simple as that. We can also test this – the animal should be willing to work for the ability to earn the cue that results in positive reinforcement. Remember behavior chains? (page: 79) That is when we reinforce a new or difficult behavior with the ability to do a well conditioned and loved behavior.

What about negatively reinforced trained behaviors? These we call a "Command", so we can differentiate in common language. So we have a cycle of 'command (aversive or conditioned aversive), behavior, relief of aversive'. This also happens when the command itself is no longer aversive just a predictor of an aversive (remember the conditioned aversives from earlier?). For example when saying "walk on", giving a squeeze, kick, then spank until you get the behavior then remove the aversive. The verbal command may not be an aversive, but it predicts an aversive. Just like the cue became a conditioned appetitive, the command becomes a conditioned aversive. This lays out like a math equation as well with a command, behavior, aversive cycle. Causing the command to become a conditioned aversive.

The Poisoned Cue is the combination of a cue and a command. The aversive can appear in any part of the shaping process, as part of the antecedents or as part of the consequences. Keep in mind that both forms of punishment are aversive to the learner in the consequence; either an aversive is directly added (positive punishment) or an appetitive is removed (which feels aversive). Whether you use an aversive to punish or if you use it to coerce the desired behavior, if an aversive becomes any part of your ABC loop it can poison the entire scenario. So if an aversive enters an appetitively conditioned cycle or if an appetitive enters an aversively conditioned cycle, would the resulting conditioning be aversive? Appetitive? Both? They become conditioned as conflict, frustration, or stress. Poisoned cues have a major fallout - it creates reluctance, latency, conflict behaviors, behavioral breakdown preceding cue and/or behavioral breakdowns after the cue.

Remember when we say a cue is poisoned, we mean the cue and all other antecedents, not just the intentional cue we've chosen to put on the behavior. The smell in the room, the color of your hat, the lead rope, the halter, the way you're positioned, the tone of your voice – everything they see, smell, feel, taste, and hear can all be poisoned depending what the horse thinks predicts the aversive. We've taken an appetitive situation and counter conditioned it the wrong way to predict an aversive.

> *Cue* - A discriminative stimulus (SD) established through positive reinforcement
> *Command* - A discriminative stimulus (SD) established through negative reinforcement

| Antecedent (Poisoned Cue) | → | Behavior | → | Appetitive | + | Aversive anywhere in the process | ...... | Conflict, latency, and behavior breakdown |

It's important we take care not to poison our cues with the use of aversives. It can take time and a keen eye to see the real damages that occur. A poisoned cue can cause tension and conflict around the behavior, causing the behavior to become stiff or uncomfortable. Horses may become reluctant to perform behaviors when the cue has been poisoned or they can become hesitant about trying or offering the behavior. There is frequently behavioral breakdown with a poisoned cue - the horse may correlate a specific part of the behavior with the aversive, so they begin to fade out certain parts or over-exaggerate other parts. Ultimately we want the horse to feel confident and comfortable offering new behaviors, performing known behaviors and exploring new parts of their world. Fear of aversives/punishment will put a rapid stop to all a horse's effort and desire to try new things.

If this happens in your training, accidentally or from past experiences we can still right this wrong. Start by finding out what has become poisoned – find your baseline, then add in variables, find when latency, distraction or conflict behavior starts. Is it the presentation of an object? Wearing a particular tack piece? Or your verbal/visual cue? Even your food reward can be poisoned. Remember how we counter condition by turning an aversive stimulus into an appetitive with careful pairing; we often do this to help our learners overcome fearful stimuli (page: 136). Unfortunately if we aren't careful with our timing and arrangement we can actually counter condition the appetitive to predict an aversive. If you only pull out your treats when something aversive is going to happen, that food is going to predict something bad is going to happen - poisoning the food.

Once we've determined which stimuli are poisoned it's truly easiest to throw it out. There is some debate over whether or not you can "un-poison" a situation, but by rebuilding the behavior and putting a strong reinforcement history on it we can overshadow the poisoned history. When we reteach the behavior we need to approach it in a completely new way, if you used targeting to get it before, try free shaping. We want to change as many of the antecedents as we can to divide this from the previously poisoned experience. We can also change any tools used enough for the horse to learn this is different; change the color, shape, size, design, sound, feel, and visual cue. Ideally we should just get rid of it, but if this isn't possible for whatever reason change it as best as possible and rebuild the behavior. Treat this like an entirely new behavior, gradually bringing it back to the desired goal and necessary entities of the behavior, but leaving it as different as possible.

Necessary Aversives

So we're convinced, using aversives is unnecessary and dangerous in our training, right? Unfortunately, there are times in life that aversives can and will happen. Having a strong, positively conditioned relationship with our horses can help maintain our relationship through these situations. Think of it as an emergency love supply for when things get tough. We can also prepare in advance for those aversive situations we know our horses will need to endure. We all need to go to the doctor or have the dentist look at our teeth every now and then - so do our horses. These situations can be very aversive for horses who don't understand what's happening or that this will help them in the long run. It's important to prepare our horses as best as possible for potential veterinary experiences in their future. Unfortunately, we can't always prepare them for everything and sometimes scenarios pop up faster than our training can prepare them for. In circumstances like these we should refer to the Humane Hierarchy (page: 128) to determine how to best address the situation we're in.

Hoof Lifting:

Teaching a horse to lift their feet and allow you to hold and manipulate their leg is a vital skill for basic husbandry care. Horses need their hooves cleaned regularly and trimmed periodically, so it is imperative they're prepared for these events.

Antecedents:
* A quiet, comfortable area
* A comfortable distance from friends

Shaping Process:
* <u>Shaping</u>

1. While the horse is standing facing forward, turn to face their hip. Allow the horse to get used to their leg being touched, reinforce as you run your hands up and down their lower leg.

2. Mark and reinforce any muscle or weight shift off the leg you're working with.

3. Shape this until the horse begins to raise this leg up. Mark and reinforce each leg lift.

4. As the horse gets used to lifting their leg up for reinforcement, begin to just run your hand under their hoof. Catch and hold the hoof for a millisecond, mark this quick moment and immediately feed. When catching their hoof, just pause it where it is, don't try to move it to a new position yet.

5. Very gradually begin to hold the hoof for moments longer, keep a very high rate of reinforcement, allowing them to put their hoof down between each repetition.

6. If the horse begins to get concerned, struggle, pull their hoof away, paw or strike - immediately reduce your criteria. Do not increase the restraint, that's what's causing the stress. Increase your rate of reinforcement. It can help to have an additional person to feed more promptly to ensure your timing is perfect. Mark and reinforce the behavior exactly where it's going well, before it goes wrong.

7. As your horse gets comfortable with you holding their hoof build duration up to several seconds. From here you can begin slowly molding the leg towards a comfortable cleaning position. Mark and reinforce every tiny movement. Keep a high rate of reinforcement until the behavior is totally finished and fluid.

Hoof Lifting:

8. Gradually build up the horse's comfort with the restraint and manipulation of their hoof and lower leg.

9. Begin this process again with the next hoof until all hooves are taught - they tend to get easier as you go.

Stimulus Control:

*   At this point you'll want practice alternating standing facing forward with hoof behaviors. To help reduce the chance of pawing or striking becoming unwanted behaviors.

Hoof Cleaning:

Once a horse is comfortably lifting and allowing you to hold their hoof up, they'll need to get used to some tools being used on their feet. Hoof picks, files and nippers can cause pulling, vibration and scraping feelings the horse will need to get accustomed to.

Antecedents:
- A quiet, familiar area
- A comfortable distance from friends
- Tools, hoof pick, rasp, nippers

Shaping Process:
- <u>Shaping</u>

1. When the horse is calm and comfortable with you holding and gently manipulating their hooves and lower legs you can begin to add tools. Start just by gently tapping the pick against their hoof. Mark and reinforce the tapping sensation.

2. Begin picking the horse's hoof, start by marking and reinforcing each pick. If you have an additional person or can reach to feed you can do a couple picks and reinforcements between putting the hoof down. If you're on your own, put the foot down with each reinforcement.

3. Gradually add up how much time and the intensity at which you pick the hoof. At this point you can begin reducing your rate of reinforcement, by adding duration.

4. When the horse is comfortable with having all four hooves picked and brushed clean you can experiment with some various tools. Practice gently rasping the foot - if you're not sure how to do it, just do a gentle file, enough for them to get used to the feeling, without actually altering their hoof.

5. At this point you can practice holding their foot between your legs, like a farrier might, tug at the edge of their hoof, rasp the edges, and pick at the hoof with more intensity. Get your horse comfortable and calm with you playing at their hoof with a strength similar to farrier tools.

6. Remember the first few times with the real farrier to reduce your criteria and significantly increase your rate of reinforcement.

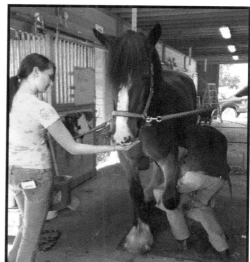

Hoof Care:

There will be times we ask the horse a bit more in relation to their hoof care. Some farriers hold the horse's hoof forward on a pedestal to file the edge. There may also be times you need to soak a horse's hoof in case of abscess or infection.

Antecedents:
- A quiet, familiar area
- A comfortable distance from friends
- Tools, hoof pick, bucket of water, hoof stand
-

Shaping Process:
- <u>Shaping</u>

1. As your horse is comfortable with you lifting, holding and manipulating their hoof and lower leg you can begin to take this exercise up a notch with added tools like buckets and pedestals.

2. You can reproduce the farrier's hoof stand with a bucket; practice moving the leg forward and resting the hoof on the object, mark and reinforce while they stand calmly with each hoof on the pedestal.

3. You can also practice placing the horse's hoof in an empty bucket. Mark and reinforce for standing calmly with the hoof down in the bucket.

4. From here you can practice putting water in the bucket, low enough to be just around the hoof, not reaching skin. Place the hoof in the water bucket, marking and reinforcing as they relax into it.

5. Keep practicing until the bucket can be fill around their coronary band and the horse is comfortable.

6. Practice both tools with each hoof.

WORKSHEET

Leg Wraps:

Preparing a horse for having their legs wrapped can be surprisingly important. Even if you don't participate in any sports or events that benefit from leg wrapping, an injury or infection could also lead to the need for leg wraps.

Antecedents:
- A quiet area
- A comfortable distance from friends
- Polo wraps or standing wraps

Shaping Process:
- <u>Shaping</u>

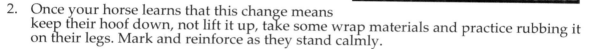

1. While your horse stands calmly facing forward, stand facing toward their leg, not toward their back hip like you would while hoof cleaning. Run your hands up and down their lower leg, mark and reinforce when they keep their hoof down. This can be confusing and frustrating if you've just taught picking the hoof up behaviors, so set the horse up for success by changing your posture and approach as much as possible.

2. Once your horse learns that this change means keep their hoof down, not lift it up, take some wrap materials and practice rubbing it on their legs. Mark and reinforce as they stand calmly.

3. Practice loosely draping the wrap around the horse's leg, continue reinforcing as they remain calm and comfortable.

4. At this point begin adding tension and duration on the wrap, so you can finish the wrap before reinforcement.

5. Practice this on each leg until they become comfortable with a variety of wrapping situations.

Stimulus Control:
- Once taught alternate this with hoof lifting behaviors. Help the horse differentiate when it's expected to lift the hoof and when it's expected to keep the hoof down.

Stethoscope:

Preparing a horse for a stethoscope listening to their heart and lungs might not sound like a big deal, but can be concerning for some horses. While most horses who are comfortable being groomed have no issue with this, some have an aversive history with vet examinations.

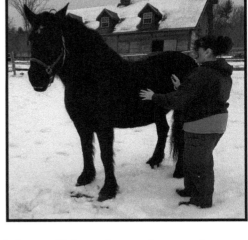

Antecedents:
- A quiet, comfortable area
- A comfortable distance from friends
- A small, cold metal object to practice with (a metal bottle cap works well)

Shaping Process:
- <u>Counter Conditioning</u>

1. Start with your horse standing calmly facing forward while doing something they're comfortable with, such as being brushed or fussed over. Allow them to target the strange new metal object. As this is a person and practice they're used to there shouldn't be much issue. If there is, go slow, at the horse's speed with a higher rate of reinforcement.

2. Practice pressing this funny object against the horse's side, neck, belly and behind their front leg. Mark and reinforce each time the object touches them. They may twitch like a bug, that's alright.

3. Add duration, as sometimes it's an odd duration that they need to have the stethoscope against them. In a colic or sickness situation you may not be able to feed, so build a solid duration.

WORKSHEET

Oral Syringe:

Preparing a horse to take medicine from an oral syringe is an extremely common necessity for horses

Antecedents:
- A quiet area
- A comfortable distance from friends
- A clean and empty syringe

Shaping Process:
- <u>Counter Conditioning</u>

1. Start with your horse standing calmly facing forward, practice reaching under their head and touching their opposite cheek with your hand. Mark and reinforce as you put your hand around their head, gently holding their head in your arm.

2. Work on this until the horse is completely comfortable having their head held, begin gently touching their mouth with your opposite finger. Mark and reinforce each touch. Never hold the horse firm, your hand is here for your stability not to restrain the horse in any way. If you struggle with keeping yourself soft and not restraining the horse - or if the horse isn't comfortable with this you can also practice having them take the syringe from the front without your arm around them.

3. Practice sliding treats, like baby carrots, into their mouth through the side where the syringe will go.

4. Work on this until the horse is comfortable with your touching the side of their lips and sliding treats in, whether with you standing in front of them or with your arm around their head. At this point begin adding an empty, clean syringe. Touch the syringe to their lip, mark and reinforce.

5. When the horse is comfortable with you placing the syringe in the corner of their mouth, practice filling the syringe with water and gently squeezing a little water out with each repetition.

6. Practice this with syringes of water many times between syringes of any bad tasting medicine. When you do need to use bad tasting medicine, seriously increase your rate of reinforcement.

Needle Preparation:

Most horses get vaccinations regularly and will need their blood drawn a few times in their lives. It's important we prepare our horses for this difficult situation. It's also important to go back and practice several times with a high rate of reinforcement between real needles.

Antecedents:
- A quiet, calm area
- A comfortable distance from friends
- An alcohol swab
- A paper clip/pen cap

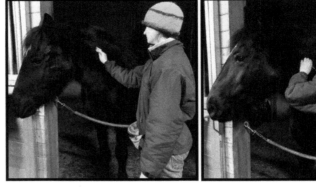

Shaping Process:
- <u>Counter Conditioning</u>

1. Start with your horse standing calmly facing forward. Open the alcohol swab and let them smell it from a distance. Reinforce as they remain calmly standing facing forward while you move the alcohol smell around them.

2. When they're comfortable with this step, gently rub the alcohol swab on a spot on their neck. Mark and reinforce the rubbing. If this bothers them reduce your criteria and increase your rate of reinforcement. Keep practicing until they're comfortable with this.

3. Breaking this into several small sessions is ideal for horses who have an aversive history and aren't quickly progressing.

4. When they're comfortable with the alcohol step, begin rubbing the area vigorously and gently pinch up the skin, like you might in a subcutaneous injection. Mark and reinforce each time you pinch up the skin.

5. Work on this until they're comfortable and relaxed while you clean and pinch the area just like you would when giving a real injection.

6. At this point, gently, very gently, touch the tip of the paper clip/pen cap to the skin as if it were a needle. Don't try to make it hurt like a needle might. Just a touch.

7. When they're accepting of this you can practice running the paper clip/pen cap gently, not pressing, just smoothly running down the jugular where an intravenous needle would be placed. Mark and reinforce each touch and movement with the paper clip.

8. Practice this a great deal before and after any real needle with a high rate of reinforcement, to maintain the appetitive history and reduce the poisoned effect.

Thermometer Preparation:

Unfortunately there will be at least a few times in your horse's life where you need to take their temperature. Rectal thermometers are not particularly comfortable and a cause for concern for many horses.

Antecedents:
- A quiet area
- A comfortable distance from friends
- Thermometer

Shaping Process:
- <u>Counter Conditioning</u>

1. Start with your horse standing calmly facing forward while doing something they're comfortable with, such as being brushed or fussed over. While standing beside their hip reach over and gently touch and manipulate their tail. Mark and reinforce as they allow you to wiggle their tail.

2. Gradually exaggerate this to the point of being able to lift and hold their tail to the side.

3. As you hold their tail out of the way use the thermometer to touch their anus, mark and reinforce. Practice this a few times.

4. With the thermometer lubricated practice sliding it in, mark, remove and reinforce.

5. Practice this several times.

6. At this point practice turning on the thermometer, mark and reinforce each time the thermometer beeps.

7. Practice taking their temperature for real! Keep a high rate of reinforcement to counter the natural aversiveness of this situation.

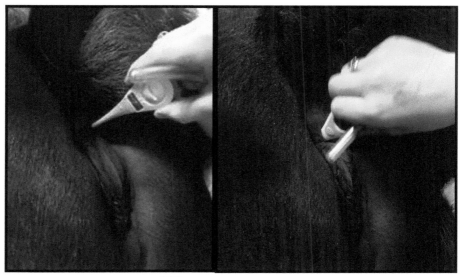

Eye/Ear Inspection:

Being able to look into a horse's eyes and ears is important for regular veterinary exams and in case of medical problems.

Antecedents:
- A quiet, calm area
- A comfortable distance from friends
- A small tube can make a good fake tool

Shaping Process:
- <u>Counter Conditioning</u>

1. Start with your horse standing calmly facing forward while doing something they're comfortable with, such as being brushed or fussed over. If they know cheek target you can cue a cheek target and hold the tube up beside their eye. Mark and reinforce as you hold the tool up beside their eye.

2. If they're not comfortable with this, break it down by first holding the tool away from their face several feet. Mark and reinforce as they relax with you holding the tube around their face, a good distance away.

3. Gradually bring the object closer. Reinforce any interest or curiosity.

4. Practice cupping your hand over their eye. Mark and reinforce. Many horses enjoy a nice gentle eye rub, this can help them get comfortable with this hand motion. Practice cupping your hand over their eye and bringing your face close. Mark and reinforce each time you practice.

5. Practice running your hands over their ears, mark and reinforce any touch.

6. As they get comfortable with you touching their ears begin gently manipulating the ears around, marking and reinforcing each gentle manipulation.

7. Practice this with a few different people working with your horse, so they can get used to new people like a vet.

8. Remember when it comes time for the real vet to increase your rate of reinforcement and decrease your criteria.

Smile:

Smiling is an adorable, sweet trick that can make all your pictures hilarious! It's an easy skill for horses of all abilities and a great way to prepare for dental inspection.

Antecedents:
- A comfortable area to work
- Some smelly things (essential oils work great)

Shaping Process:
- Capturing

1. A "smile" is really just a horse's natural "Flehmen Response" which they do when they're processing scent. So using some new and unusual smells can be a great way to inspire the behavior.

2. Capture the smiling behavior whenever they're smelling the essential oils (or other stinky things you're using) by marking and reinforcing as usual. Work on this until they begin offering the behavior, even without the scent triggering.

3. Once they begin offering it freely you can add a final cue.

Using familiar and easy tricks can be a great way to help your horse relax in a new environment. Punk and Marshmallow traveled to a local horse fair to teach people about positive reinforcement, so practicing their fun tricks when we arrived helped them settle in quickly!

Tongue:

Sticking their tongue out is a funny and adorable trick, but can take some seriously careful timing to capture! It can also be another great way to prepare for dental examination.

Antecedents:
- A comfortable area to work
- Applesauce or molasses

Shaping Process:
- Capturing

1. By smudging some molasses or applesauce (whichever the horse likes better) on their top lip you can encourage the horse to lick their lips. Very carefully mark the very moment their tongue pops out!

2. It takes super careful timing to catch this. Keep it up until the horse begin offering sticking their tongue out without anything encouraging it.

3. Once they begin offering it freely you can add a final cue. Don't use your own tongue sticking out as the cue or you may accidentally lick apple sauce off your horse's nose!

Dental Inspection:

Being able to look into a horse's mouth and examine their teeth can be helpful in assessing age, dental health, and capillary refill.

Antecedents:
- A quiet, calm area
- A comfortable distance from friends

Shaping Process:
- <u>Counter Conditioning</u>

1. Start with your horse standing calmly facing forward while doing a chin target or cheek target to your hand. Mark and reinforce as they stand calmly resting against your hand while you gently rub your hands over their nose.

2. Use your fingers to gently massage their top lip, mark and reinforce regularly. If they move away from the chin/cheek target stop and allow them to rest a moment before asking for the target and starting again. If they do this more than a couple times, recheck your rate of reinforcement and reduce your criteria.

3. Gradually begin manipulating the horse's lips, holding them open and massaging their top gums. Mark and reinforce as they relax into this, most horses really enjoy their top gums being rubbed when they relax into it.

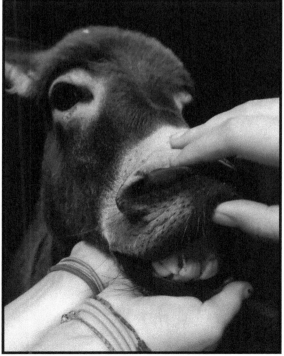
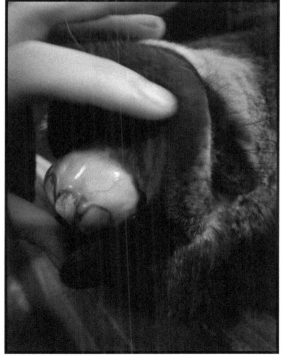

Getting Started with Positive Riding

Riding with our horses can be a ton of fun for both parties if we approach it with positive reinforcement. That being said, I debated heavily whether or not to add a section on riding. I believe the decision to ride a horse is not something to be taken lightly. It should be considered from all angles and with the horse's best interest in mind. Take into consideration, not just their physical ability (can they be ridden?) but also their emotional wellbeing (should they be ridden?). The answers to these questions are extremely personal and intimate, determined together by horse and rider. For horses who have had a lot of experience being ridden with no major fallout it can be tempting and easy to just begin adding treats to our old riding. Realistically though, as the threats of the aversives fade, the behaviors tend to fall apart. This leaves us to either back up the aversive conditioning or reshape the behavior with positive reinforcement. We have less fallout and behavioral breakdown if we shape the behaviors with a fresh new, positive history from the start. Whether or not your horse was very experienced with riding it's important to treat them like they have never carried a rider. A horse who has been ridden before, without much trauma involved, may require less desensitization and counter conditioning to prepare for our re-approach to riding positively. It's important to still go through the steps, to ensure there are no lingering aversive attachments to any of the tools or aspects of riding. This may be the first time their voice is being heard, so listen carefully, be observant and prepare thoroughly.

We need to think about our choice to ride in all of these ways and make some decisions on our personal ethical line for each of these topics:

- Age
- Horse/human weight ratio
- Horse + human health/fitness
- Emotional wellbeing
- Solid R+ foundation
- Desensitization + Counter conditioning
- Environment choices
- Tack/tool choices
- Appropriate ride duration

I implore you to do your own research to find which aspects and approaches are right for you and your horse in regards to riding. If you determined you could both enjoy it (the horse and rider) and want to begin to venture down this path, you can start by ensuring you have a solid foundation with positive reinforcement training and desensitization. You want to have developed a good relationship and a really clear, two way communication with your horse on the ground before attempting anything that puts either of you at risk. The horse also has to be confident in their self control and ability to handle the situations they're put in. You don't want to begin riding the horse if there is any lingering fear, confusion, or frustration around anything in your training environment. When preparing for riding we spend much more time helping the horse become comfortable in their environment and using their voice, than actually teaching behaviors. Teaching behaviors is actually quite simple, what's more difficult to prepare for is the emotional and physical impact of carrying a rider. We want to prepare for our training environment, the areas we plan to go to, the tack and tools we use, and the obstacles the horse may need to navigate. We also need to ensure our horses are physically ready. Take into consideration the horse's age, size, and fitness level when you determine when or if you begin riding. Not all horses want to be riding horses. There are so many alternatives to riding that can be just as fun for us that may be more enjoyable for horses who aren't physically or emotionally ready for this.

When getting started, we want to keep in mind where our horse would prefer to do their riding. Some horses really enjoy exploring the new and venturing into the great outdoors. Others only enjoy this with a trusted equine friend nearby, while the rest would prefer to play somewhere safe and familiar like a paddock or arena. You can spice up the familiar with obstacles and enrichment - even fun mounted games for you to do! While we can help adapt an outgoing horse to enjoy a more quiet arena and a homebody horse to learn to adventure, we want to remember to keep this fun for them, never pushing them beyond their comfort zone.

Determining which tools you choose to use can be another challenge. There is so much contradictory research out there. Do the best you can, learn the options, and choose what fits your riding goals. I find a well fit treed saddle can provide the most weight distribution for heavier rider to horse ratio pairs or for pairs who enjoy longer or more active rides. But it requires continual upkeep to maintain fit, as the horse's shape changes continually. This can be expensive, but is vital if you ride frequently or athletically. I personally love the treeless options out there, they are wonderful for lighter or less frequent riders, like myself. They require a better understanding of how they fit and how to pad them appropriately. They're easy to adapt to the horse's changing shape if you learn how to watch and adapt for problems. For very mild riding, bareback or bareback pads can be fabulous. There is so much that goes into these decisions; I've provided a long list of reading materials and further research for you to use to help make your decision.

Riding is a privilege, we must be ever grateful for it and never take it for granted. Appreciate this gift your horse is offering you and make your decisions on how much and what to ask for with their personal best interest in mind. There is no universal answer for what type, length, or tack choices make riding work. This needs to be adapted to each pair.

When I was early in my transition to positive reinforcement Revel came home with me. He already knew how to drive, so I thought it would be quick and easy to just begin riding by adding treats to his old training. I'd ride with his bitless bridle and leg aids with lots of treats on top. Revel is a very forward horse who really enjoyed the trail so this worked well enough for what I was looking for. Until...
One of my teen students wanted to learn about starting a horse for riding with clicker training. She wanted to practice with a safe horse, so Revel got the job. She reshaped all his basic riding behaviors. I was awe-struck with the change in Revel's attitude and demeanor. He began to enjoy riding so much more, he responded to his cues more promptly, and was so mentally engaged in his training! You can see in the photos above how his expression changed.

Tack Choices

The concept of poisoned cues brings up a big question in horse training. Which tools do we use? Some tack items were designed for the comfort and safety of our horses. Blankets can keep horses warm when their body isn't able to do the job - for health or physical reasons. Fly sheets and masks can make being outdoors much more comfortable for some sensitive or allergic horses, allowing them to live a more healthy lifestyle. Well-fit saddles can distribute the weight of a rider - easing the burden of the job. Bareback pads, saddle pads, and treeless saddles are all further options to provide comfort for horses who will carry a rider. These tools are all here for the benefit and well-being of our horse, but even still we should take care to introduce these items carefully, so the horse feels comfortable and safe with these objects.

There are other tools, however, that have been designed with the human in mind. Tools like halters (flat and rope), leads, bridles (bitted and bitless), whips, flags, spurs, and so on. These items were designed to give humans leverage and physical control over the horse. When used correctly and fit appropriately they were designed to put some sort of aversive pressure on the horse, to manipulate them into performing a specific behavior, then the aversive is relieved when they comply. Some of these are naturally aversive to most horses (remember it's the horse who decides

Used correctly tools like whips, bits, spurs, knotted rope halters and leverage devices work by creating threats, fear, discomfort, annoyance or pain to alter behavior. They learn through escape and avoidance how to earn relief from these tools. These tools were designed to be aversive to the learner and it can be extremely difficult (or impossible) to avoid the aversive nature of them. Using these tools can easily run the risk of poisoning your positively trained behaviors.

what they find aversive). But tools like rope halters, with knots landing on sensitive facial nerves, spurs which pinpoint the rider's heel, whips and flags (which most horses know are aversive even when they're swinging and haven't yet touched the horse), are extremely difficult (if not impossible) to remove their aversive value. It's easiest to just leave these tools behind or recycle them into new tools, like targets!

Bits are a more difficult topic, having been around for thousands of years they've changed rather little. They were an adaptation from the typical nose-ring used with livestock, put in the mouth instead for more physical control for the rider. They designed this tool this way, adding joints, pressure points, spikes and leverage in order to provide more extreme control during times of war. Since war has evolved to no longer include horses (happily!) we have designed modern sports to replicate the skills needed during war times. Sports like racing measured a horse's speed, jumping measured their athleticism, and Dressage measured the rider's level of control, as well as the horse's physical fitness for their job at war.

Used correctly smooth, soft tools like flat halters, bitless bridles (without strong leverage or pressure points), neck ropes and so on can serve as a back-up safety measure when trained appropriately.

Here Emerson is training positive cues with a neck rope, using a flat halter with reins as a back up for safety. She's also using a well-fit saddle to keep them both comfortable while riding, as well as several pouches full of treats.

189

Because of this we've stuck with the traditional tools, like bits and whips, to control our horses rather than investigate modern, more ethical options. There is ample research to prove that horses in general find bits aversive, even before contact with the reins is made. Often when people believe their horse prefers the bit, it's really because the horse understands this communication, until something else is equally understood. The gap the bit makes in their mouth can trigger the body to think it's eating, causing breathing, salivation, swallowing, and digestive problems. The bit controls the horse through aversive pressure on the bars, tongue, palate, and cheeks of the horse. While soft hands and gentler bits can make this less aversive, when mixed with positive reinforcement the use of bits runs a high risk of poisoning your riding cues.

While flat halters and bitless bridles (without strong leverage or pressure points) were also designed originally to be aversive, they tend to only be aversive when pressure/force is applied to them, at rest horses can be comfortable wearing them. These make better safety tools to use in conjunction with positive reinforcement as they allow the horses to be comfortable and feel safe, but they also give us a physical form of control in an emergency, especially when we take our horses outside of fenced areas or when we put ourselves on their backs. While we should train every behavior first and then add the tactile cue of the tool, the tool should not be aversive to the horse when used just as a tactile cue. However, if something happens that we weren't prepared for we have a backup plan. While this plan may cause the application of an aversive, hopefully our reinforcement history will outweigh this one aversive experience and not poison our cues entirely. Thus, the importance of our cues not being aversive except in a true emergency. We should also learn from our emergency experience and do what we can to prevent it from happening again, whether it means preparing our horse or changing the environment.

As you delve into the world of positive reinforcement you may find your tack room ends up getting a lot more colorful, filled with cones, hula hoops, mats, tarps, pool noodle, pin wheels, targets, and tutus! You'll have more toys than you can count - painting sets, basketball hoops, balls, and giant dice! All your riding tack will have treat pouches and fanny packs will definitely be making a come back!

Recommended Reading:

Gillian Higgins *Horse Anatomy for Performance*. (2012). David & Charles.

Gillian Higgins *How Your Horse Moves: A unique visual guide to improving performance*. (2012). David & Charles.

Gerd Heuschmann *Collection or Contortion?: Exposing the Misconceptions and Exploring the Truths of Horse Positioning and Bend*. (2017). Trafalgar Square Books.

Gerd Heuschmann *Balancing Act: The Horse in Sport an Irreconcilable Conflict?*. (2012). Trafalgar Square Books.

Deb Bennet *Principles of Conformation Analysis: Equus Reference Guide*. (2012). Active Interest Media.

McGreevy P, McLean A. *Equitation Science*. (2010) Wiley-Blackwell.

Mclean A, McGreevy PD. *Ethical equitation: Capping the price horses pay for human glory*. (2010) Journal of Veterinary Behavior: Clinical Applications and Research.

Bidda Jones, McGreevy P. *Ethical Equitation: Applying a Cost-Benefit Approach*. (2010). Journal of Veterinary Behavior.

Hilary M. Clayton *Effect of added weight on landing kinematics in jumping horses* (2010) Equine Veterinary Journal.

Tack:

Jochen Schleese *Suffering in Silence* (2013). Trafalgar Square Books.

P. DE COCQ, P. R. Van Weeren, W. Back *Effects of girth, saddle, and weight on movements of the horse* (2010). Equine Veterinary Journal.

W. R. Cook *Damage by the bit to the equine inter-dental space and second lower premolar* (2011) Equine Veterinary Education.

Manfredi, Jane & Clayton, Hilary & , Rosenstein. *Radiographic study of bit position within the horse's oral cavity*. (2005) Equine and Comparative Exercise Physiology.

Doherty O, Casey V, McGreevy P, Arkins S *Noseband Use in Equestrian Sports – An International Study*. (2017). PLoS ONE.

McGreevy P, Robert A. Corken, Hannah Salvin, Celeste M Black *Whip use by jockeys in a sample of Australian Thoroughbred Races – An Observational Study*. (2012). PloS ONE.

WORKSHEET

Halter:

While we can work with our horses and have all our behaviors on non-tactile cues, but for safety, we'll need to teach our horses to wear a halter and respond to halter cues.

Desensitization/Counter Conditioning:

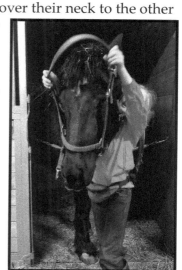

1. Start by holding the halter, folded up so it's rather small. Encourage the horse to target the halter, mark and reinforce as the horse shows interest. Gradually unfold the halter, encouraging the horse to keep targeting it.

2. Hold the halter open and upright, as the horse targets it begin to ask for a bit more, nuzzling around into it. Mark and reinforce anytime the halter slides around their nose or face.

3. Hold the halter so the crown piece and nose band are in your hand and the rest hangs loose, allowing the horse to stick their nose through the hole. Mark and reinforce any approach with their nose through the hole.

4. As you reinforce, it can help to sometimes feed with their nose through the hole, encouraging them to reach deeply into the halter. As the horse gets comfortable with this step, gradually loosen the crown piece apart from the nose band, so the crown piece reaches higher up their face, while the nose-band goes around their nose.

5. When the horse is ready slip the crown piece over their ears and heavily reinforce as you remove it again. Practice this several times until the horse is completely comfortable with this step.

6. If you're working with a donkey, mule or horse who prefers you halter by bringing the strap over their head, rather than slipping over their ears, you want to practice bringing your arm over their neck. Cue head lowering and reach over their neck, start low by the withers, and scratch the other side if they enjoy it. Mark and reinforce as you progress through this.

7. When the horse/equine is comfortable with you reaching over their neck to the other side, combine this with their nose through the nose-band. Bring the horse's nose through the nose-band and reach over their neck, mark and reinforce several times, and then remove the nose-band.

8. When they're ready, reach over, bring the strap over their neck, hold it in position while you reinforce a few times and remove the halter.

9. As you build duration on this skill practice buckling the halter with a heavy rate of reinforcement. After a few repetitions you can practice putting the halter on before a basic training session, unrelated to the halter. Keep the halter predicting the beginning of something great.

10. As the horse is comfortable wearing the halter, practice adding a lead rope hanging loose, or draped over their neck so they don't get tangled up.

WORKSHEET

Halter:

With positive reinforcement we can have all our behaviors on visual or verbal cues. That being said, there will likely be times we want our horses to recognize and respond appropriately to traditional looking and feeling cues.

Cue transferring:

1. When they're comfortable wearing the halter you can begin adding tactile cues on the halter with your leading behaviors. Remember tactile cues are simple, non-escalating stimuli. Before starting to add halter cues, practice jiggling the halter around on the horse's (or mule's) face, mark and reinforce as the halter wiggles.

2. Practice gently pulling on the halter in all directions. Mark and reinforce as you pull on the halter, you aren't looking for a behavior to happen with the gentle tugging, you just want to make sure the horse doesn't find the stimulus aversive.

3. If the horse is comfortable with you moving the halter around and with gentle tactile pressure all over their head you can safely use it as a cue. If they do find this sensation aversive you may want to find a softer halter or something with less of an aversive history, or take your time counter conditioning these sensations.

4. When your horse is ready you can begin to use the halter as a cue. Begin by starting your basic leading practice, like you would at liberty, walking, turning, and stopping. As the horse gets on a roll begin adding the tactile cue from the halter a moment before your regular leading cues.

5. As you prepare to step forward, gently lift up on the lead, then step forward. Mark and reinforce as they walk on.

6. When you're ready to stop, gently pull back on the lead and cue the halt. Mark and reinforce as they come to a halt.

7. When you want to turn, gently pull or push on the lead to turn left or right, promptly use your regular cue or target to get the turn you're looking for. Mark and reinforce as they turn correctly.

8. Practice this until fluent, gradually begin spacing the time between the tactile cue and your old cue, giving the horse time to respond to the tactile cue.

9. Work on this until the horse is calm and confident responding to their tactile cues. Remember to never prolong, repeat or escalate your tactile cues. If the horse is confused or doesn't respond correctly, return to your old cue or shaping process.

WORKSHEET

Saddle Pad:

Even if you never plan to ride or use a saddle, teaching your horse about saddle pads can be a beneficial exercise. It can help prepare a horse for being toweled or blanketed. So whether you use a towel or a saddle pad, this can be a good exercise.

Desensitization/Counter Conditioning:

1. Start with the horse standing calmly facing forward, while you hold the saddle pad. Mark and reinforce any interest in or curiosity toward the pad.

2. Fold the pad in half a few times and encourage the horse to target it. Mark and reinforce interest in the pad.

3. Gradually unfold the pad as the horse gets comfortable targeting it and allowing you to touch them on the neck and sides with it. Brush them with it as if it were a grooming tool. Mark and reinforce standing facing forward or targeting the pad.

4. Work on this until the horse is calm and comfortable with the pad fully unfolded. Begin rubbing the pad against their side, shoulders and top-line. Mark and reinforce any relaxation while they stand facing forward.

5. Begin picking up and placing the pad directly onto their back. Mark and reinforce as the pad is placed gently onto their back.

6. Gradually increase how quickly or swiftly you swing the pad up onto their back. You want to be sure the horse is entirely comfortable with the pad swinging all over them, not just having it gently placed on them.

WORKSHEET

Blanket:

Not all horses need blankets to keep warm, but there may be times during illness or injury they need to be blanketed. They may need fly sheets, fleece coolers, or therapeutic blankets.

Desensitization/Counter Conditioning:

1. Start with the horse standing calmly facing forward, fold the blanket up as small as you can; using a fleece or mesh blanket before a noisy nylon one can help. Allow your horse to sniff and investigate it. Mark and reinforce any interest or curiosity.

2. As the horse stands facing forward, begin rubbing the folded blanket gently on the horse's side. Reinforce as you do so.

3. Gradually unfold the blanket, step by step, moving the blanket around their body and draping it over their back. Reinforce regularly throughout the process.

4. As the horse gets comfortable you can practice swinging it up onto their back more quickly and less folded.

5. When the horse is comfortable having a blanket swung up on them begin to practice with new materials, like mesh and nylon, that make different sounds and feel different.

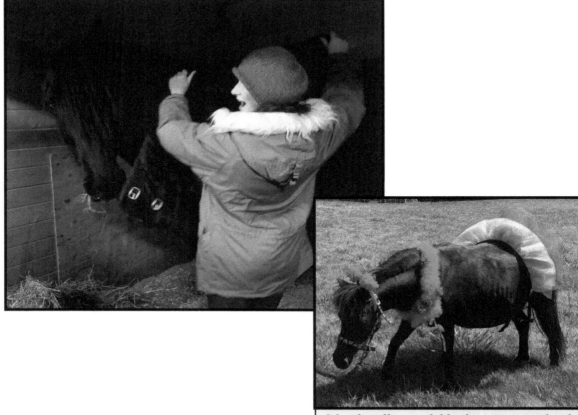

Marshmallow took blankets to a new level with her adorable tutu!

WORKSHEET

Saddle:

If you plan on riding with a saddle it's important we desensitize and counter condition all the aspects of the saddle.

Desensitization/Counter Conditioning:

1. Start with the horse standing calmly facing forward, hold the saddle out and allow your horse to sniff and investigate it. Mark and reinforce any interest or curiosity. Using a soft foam or light treeless saddle first can help introducing the new sensation without the weight.

2. Keep the stirrups rolled up or flipped over so they don't hang. Encourage the horse to target and touch the saddle as you hold it up for them. As the horse stands facing forward touch the saddle to their sides high and low. Mark and reinforce each time it touches them.

3. As they get comfortable with the saddle moving all around them practice placing it down gently on their back. Mark, remove, and reinforce.

4. Repeat the process until the horse is completely calm and comfortable with the saddle swinging up onto their back. At this point leave the saddle on top, mark and reinforce, and encourage the horse to take a step or two. Mark and reinforce any small movement with the saddle on. Remove the saddle before repeating the process.

5. If at any point the horse becomes concerned or shows signs of avoidance, go back a few steps and re-approach more slowly and with a higher rate of reinforcement.

6. As the horse gets comfortable with the saddle being put on their back, practice walking around with the saddle on board. Keep a high rate of reinforcement and keep an eye that the saddle doesn't fall.

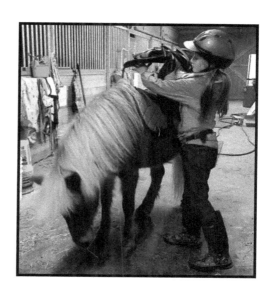

Girth:

The girth is a whole new story and should be taught separately from saddling, especially for horses who have an aversive history with girthing. If the girth is a known problem, please ensure there are no medical problems causing this trouble before attempting to counter conditioning this.

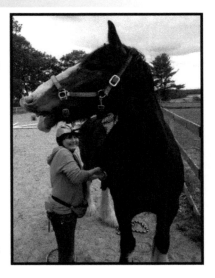

Desensitization/Counter Conditioning:

1. Rather than using a saddle, it can help to divide the situation entirely by using a surcingle or just a rope. With the horse standing calmly facing forward, rub the rope/surcingle against their body, mark and reinforce as you work its way onto their back. They should be comfortable with this with all the previous work you've done - if they're not, return to some of the basics before this.

2. Drape the rope/surcingle over the horse's back, reinforce. Then practice reaching under their belly to grab the strap on the other side. Mark and reinforce.

3. If they're comfortable with this step, pull the strap under their belly and touch it to the other side, not tight, still just touching their skin all the way around. Mark, let go and reinforce. Repeat this a few times until they're standing completely calm while your grab and line up the strap for "buckling".

4. At this point hook the strap on the loosest hole where it's still touching them all the way around, but not snug. If you're using a rope, just tie it loosely in a quick release knot. Mark and reinforce as you do this. Then practice walking a bit with this sensation wrapped around their body.

5. After some walking untie/unclip the girth and rub out the area, reinforce. Break this down into many sessions if your horse has an aversive history or is uncomfortable progressing through this.

6. If they're comfortable you can begin to add tension. Remember when girthing, always buckle it one hole at a time. Don't yank it to the tightest hole. It can help to do a hole, then go to the other side, do a hole, then walk a bit. Reinforce at each step.

7. Do this until the girth is snug, then reinforce and remove the girth. Practice this several times until you're certain there is no concern or avoidance related to this.

8. At this point you can put this together with your saddling. Place the saddle on the horses back, mark and reinforce each step. Reach under and grab the girth, mark and reinforce, buckling it on the loosest hole where it touches. Practice walking around like this. Remove everything before repeating.

9. Practice this again, if the horse is comfortable, tighten the girth just a bit more, so it's snug but not riding tight. Practice doing some of your basic leading obstacle skills with the saddle and girth like this.

10. Remember to practice this in a variety of situations, not just when riding. It will also help to maintain moderate to high value reinforcement with this situation to help maintain the appetitive correlation.

Stirrups:

Stirrups are yet another component to saddles that needs to be prepared for. It's not often when we have stirrups hanging loose and banging against our horse, that's rather impolite of us to do. But practicing with loose stirrups can help prepare the horse for movement and sensation down their sides when there is a rider aboard.

Desensitization/Counter Conditioning:

1. When the horse is comfortable having the saddle on and girthed up you can practice unrolling the stirrups and letting them fall gently to their sides. Mark and reinforce as the stirrups thump down. Using plastic or rubber stirrups for this is ideal, if you're using heavy metal, hold them so they don't thump hard.

2. When the horse is comfortable with the stirrups sliding down and bouncing gently against their body, practice leading the horse around the obstacles with the stirrups hanging loose. Mark and reinforce regularly and ensure the horse is comfortable.

Line Up at the Block:

Lining up at the mounting block is an important first skill to teach the horse as you prepare for mounting and riding. You want the horse confident and standing calmly before you hop on.

Antecedents:
- A quiet, comfortable, fenced, and safe area
- A mounting block or steps

Shaping Process:
- <u>Shaping</u>

1. With your target, lead the horse up to the mounting block, standing lined up beside it.

2. You can use either a mat or a stationary target to help the horse grasp this idea more directly if needed.

3. Practice having the horse stand calmly facing forward while next to the block, while you walk up and down the steps on the block.

4. Practice rubbing the horse's top-line and scratching where they like while on the block. Mark and reinforce as they remain stationed.

5. Use your target to reposition them or circle them back around, if they move or swing away.

6. Take your time with this and ensure the horse is completely comfortable with this level of physical intrusion. This needs to be done at your horse's speed.

First Sit:

The first sit has a lot built into it! Don't be anxious, take it slow, and make sure you pick a nice day. Break this into as many tiny sessions as needed. I find doing bits of these steps in all our agility games and other training can be a great way to introduce the horse to the idea of it, without letting it build up in our minds.

Antecedents:
* A quiet, comfortable, fenced, and safe area
* A mounting block or steps

Shaping Process:
* <u>Shaping</u>

1. While your horse is lined up at the mounting block, you can rub the horse's top-line, reach over, and rub their other side. Allow your weight to settle onto them, laying over their back on your belly, rubbing their other side. If the horse moves at all stand up and slide down to the ground.

2. As they get comfortable with you laying over their back you can send them to a target nearby or have a friend lead them a few steps with a target. If they show any signs of concern, just slide down to your feet.

3. Practice this for a while until the horse is comfortable and relaxed with you laid across the body and carrying your weight.

4. Now, while at the block, swing a leg over their back, then immediately swing around slide off the other side. Practice this several times with a high rate of reinforcement.

5. Finally, as the horse shows that they're very comfortable and doing well, sit on the back and pause, if they're relaxed you can try feeding from their back, if not just slide off again and build duration on this more slowly and carefully.

6. Take your time with this and ensure the horse is completely comfortable with this level of physical intrusion. This needs to be done at your horse's speed.

Desensitizing the Rider:

Work on the horse getting comfortable with the rider climbing on board and sitting on their back. At this point it helps to have an extra person on the ground to lead or guide the horse at a walk around simple agility obstacles, like weaving or ground poles. This helps the horse become comfortable with the rider and find their balance with the added weight of the rider.

Antecedents:
- A quiet, comfortable, fenced, and safe area
- A mounting block or steps
- Weaving markers
- Ground poles

Shaping Process:

1. When the horse is comfortable having a rider on board, you can begin to include the rider as a prop during your agility.

2. Just like when adding the tack, practice weaving, going over ground poles and doing other simple agility obstacles with a rider on board. The rider can gradually begin to move about as the horse gets comfortable.

3. The rider can practice basic balance exercises while on the horse and while the horse is being guided through the simple obstacles. These are great for the rider but also desensitizes the horse to the rider's movements. This can help develop balance and coordination for the horse and rider working as a pair:

- Hold the pommel of the saddle or a bit of mane with one hand, hold the other arm straight out and make small circles gradually getting larger. Practice this in both directions and with both hands.
- Practice making arm circles with both arms held straight out.
- Lift one leg up, tucking up your knee, then stretch it back out straight and long. Practice this several times with both legs individually.
- Hold your calf up off your horse's side and make larger circles with your toes, softening your ankles. Do this with both feet evenly.
- Reach forward as far as you can, scratching your way up your horse's neck.
- Reach behind you with one arm and scratch your way towards their tail, do this on both sides.

WORKSHEET

Walk/Stop:

As the horse gets comfortable with a rider on board you can begin to transition cues up to the rider and fade the need for an additional ground person. First, we'll want to inspire forward movement and secure a reliable stop.

Antecedents:
- A quiet, comfortable, fenced, and safe area
- Four stationary targets set in a large square, with a ground pole between each

Shaping Process:
- <u>Targeting</u>

1. While the rider is aboard, a second person can send the horse from one target to the next on this square. As they get rolling the rider can begin feeding the horse after the clicks, giving the horse the chance to start thinking about the rider. If you don't have a ground person to help, practice this a great deal on the ground before hopping on, so they don't have any confusion over what is expected.

2. Soon the rider can begin adding the desired cues. As you send to the next target the rider can cue "walk on" while sending to the target. As you approach the next target the rider can cue "whoa".

3. Fade the influence of the person on the ground, only using the ground person if the horse becomes confused or frustrated. Keep your rate of reinforcement high and your sessions short. If you only make it to one target that may be great for that session! Sometimes I like to hop on for a short minute then get off and do a few laps on the ground to keep them in the momentum of the lesson.

Steering:

While working on sending to targets can help get us walking forward and stopping on cue, we may also want to turn at some point, not always just following a path of targets. We'll use our hand-held target to accomplish this.

Antecedents:
- A quiet, comfortable, fenced, and safe area
- A hand-held target

Shaping Process:
- <u>Targeting</u>

1. While sitting on the horse, practice holding the target out to each side, where the horse can reach just by moving their head. Just get them recognizing that targeting can work the same from above. If the horse is concerned about the target moving around it can help to have the ground person introduce the target and transition it up to the rider.

2. Once they get the hang of targeting from above you can begin to shape steering. Hold the target out to one side and encourage your horse to step over to reach it. Mark and reinforce the step more so than actually reaching the target. Repeat this several times on one side.

3. As the horse gets the hang of stepping over to reach the target, you can fade the target and begin to add your final cue. I use holding my hand out to the side, holding a neck rope or rein. You can use any cue you like, but remember not to maintain or escalate a tactile cue or you run the risk of poisoning the cue.

4. Continue this until the behavior is solid on one side, then repeat the process with the other side.

5. Alternate the two directions until the horse is comfortably predicting the cue.

Back Up:

Having a solid "back up" cue is valuable in itself, but can be a further provision to keeping our stop cues solid.

Antecedents:
* A quiet, comfortable, fenced, and safe area

Shaping Process:
* <u>Cue transfer</u>

1. At this point we should have a solid "back up" behavior on the ground. Practice either on the ground or with a ground person cuing the horse to back up, the usual way repeatedly until the horse gets in the swing of it.

2. Begin using your new, mounted cue immediately before the previous cue, gradually add space between the two cues, allowing the horse to respond to the mounted cue without needing the old cue.

3. Practice this new mounted cue from their back, repeatedly in all scenarios to ensure its well known and has a solid history of reinforcement.

Cue Proofing:

From here you can return to your target square or any pattern of stationary targets, including steering.

Antecedents:
- A quiet, comfortable, fenced, and safe area
- Four stationary targets in a large square with a ground pole placed between each
- A hand-held target

Shaping Process:
- <u>Targeting</u>

1. While riding, use your send to/walk on cue to send the horse to the first target.

2. Use your steering cue to turn towards any other target in the series. Then send to that one.

3. Begin mixing up the order and direction of sending around to the targets.

4. Begin alternating in your "whoa" cue in novel locations, not always at a stationary target. Alternating in your "back up" cue can also help keep a more forward horse ready to stop and back up when needed. Keep a high rate of reinforcement and high value reinforcers on these behaviors for more active, forward thinking horses.

WORKSHEET

Expand your Ridden World:

At this point you can begin to generalize your targets to the whole world around you, not just your simple square. You can easily generalize to all your agility obstacles and then beyond to the trails, parks, and anything else you can imagine.

Antecedents:
- A quiet, comfortable, fenced, and safe area
- A full agility ring!

Shaping Process:
- <u>Targeting</u>

1. Begin sending to targets, adding obstacles between the targets.

2. Soon you can send directly to the obstacles themselves, mark and reinforce, keeping a heavy rate of reinforcement for negotiating obstacles.

3. Be sure to keep varying which behaviors you bridge and reinforce directly, sometimes just reinforcing when they start walking where you send them. If your horse is more forward keep a stronger focus on stopping, backing up, and careful negotiation of obstacles. If your horse is more relaxed and slow-going, keep a higher rate of reinforcement on walking, turning, and doing the more active obstacles.

Oh, the places You'll Go...

In the words of one of the most motivating motivators, "Oh, the places you'll go" (Dr. Seuss). Your dreams are becoming reality, as your relationship becomes mutual, built on communication and compassion. There is nothing that can't be done with a good friend by your side.

I hope at this point you've learned some new things and are better prepared for the ventures ahead of you. As we turn from farmers to scientists our empathy and compassion deepens, along with our ability to provide our horses with greater opportunities. Ethology and observational skills open our doors to a new understanding of our equine companions. We can read and translate what we're seeing in a more complete and accurate way than ever before. We're no longer romanticizing or justifying the past. We're looking forward to a kinder future. As we approach horses with an understanding of their natural behaviors as a species and as individuals, we can begin to modify and adapt their behavior to better adjust to life in domestication with special attention to their needs. This compromise comes with major perks for the horse; the ability to remain safe and happy for life. It also comes with some real benefits for us humans as well, gifted with the friendship, companionship, and partnership of these exceptional beings. With our knowledge of learning theory and ethical training techniques we can use our brains to help our horses adapt to this new lifestyle and stay healthy, having just as much fun as we are! They can enjoy adventures, agility, cognitive enrichment, and even become active participants in their own care. With this knowledge and power comes a moral responsibility. We owe it to our horses to ensure we use this to benefit them, first and foremost. Our horses owe us nothing, we brought them into this world to join with us as friends and we owe them the very best we can offer. This means we need to continue educating ourselves, continue growing more compassionate, and never settle for "good enough".

With the understanding that learning theory and neuroscience provides us we can further empower our horses with a voice and control over their own life as well as our partnership. Our communication and relationship as a whole is finally becoming mutual. While this opens many doors for our personal benefit, as people and potentially as riders, it also comes with great responsibility. At the beginning of this book I asked you, if you gave your horse the ability to say "no", would they? Many of us may have answered "yes" to that question. In the horse world as it was, "no", was not an option for horses. Compliance was a survival skill. I hope now you have the ability to see and the tools to change the world, so that more horses want to say "yes". Now that we know what our horses are saying, we must learn to listen. I hope this book has provided you with some tools to reach your dreams with your horses. We are beginning to approach horsemanship in a wonderful new way, with brains over brawn. With knowledge and with kindness we are shaping the new era.

GLOSSARY

Agonisitic: Of, relating to, or being aggressive or defensive social interaction (such as fighting, fleeing, or submitting) between individuals usually of the same species.

Antecedent: A preceding event, condition, or cause.

Appeasement: To make concessions to (someone, such as an aggressor or a critic) often at the sacrifice of principles; to cause to subside; to bring to a state of peace or quiet.

Appetitive: Any of the instinctive desires necessary to keep up organic life; especially: the desire to eat.

Aversive: Tending to avoid or causing avoidance of a noxious or punishing stimulus; having an active feeling of repugnance, dislike, or distaste.

Behavior Chain: Related behaviors in a series in which each response serves as a stimulus for the next response.

Biomechanics: The mechanics of biological and especially muscular activity (as in locomotion or exercise); also: the scientific study of this.

Bridge Signal: A stimulus that marks the desired behavior, it "bridges" the gap of time that occurs between the behavior and its reinforcement.

Capturing: An act of catching, winning, or gaining control by force, stratagem, or guile; reinforcing a behavior that happens naturally to put it on cue.

Causation: Something that brings about an effect or a result.

Classical Conditioning: When a stimulus (such as the sound of a bell) is paired with and precedes the unconditioned stimulus (such as the sight of food) until the stimulus alone is sufficient to elicit the response (such as salivation in a dog).

Cognitive: Of, relating to, being, or involving conscious intellectual activity (such as thinking, reasoning, or remembering).

Cognitive Bias: Refers to a systematic pattern of deviation from norm or rationality in judgment, whereby inferences about other people and situations may be drawn in an illogical fashion.

Command: A discriminative stimulus - a stimulus that provides information about which behavior will relieve an aversive.

Conditioned Appetitive: A stimulus repeatedly paired with and predicts an appetitive stimulus.

Conditioned Aversive: A stimulus repeatedly paired with and predicts an aversive stimulus.

Conditioned Reinforcer: A stimulus repeatedly paired with and predicts an appetitive stimulus that can now be used to positively reinforce another behavior.

Consent: To give assent or approval.

Continuous Ratio: Reinforcing every time the learner performs the correct behavior.

Continuous Interval: Reinforcing continuously as they do the behavior for the whole duration.

Counter Conditioning: Changing the conditioning of a stimulus to its opposite meaning through repeated pairing with an opposite stimulus.

Criteria: A standard on which a judgment or decision may be based; the standard behavior required to earn reinforcement.

Cue: A discriminative stimulus - a stimulus that provides information about what to do to earn reinforcement.

Development: To cause to evolve or unfold gradually: to lead or conduct (something) through a succession of states or changes each of which is preparatory for the next.

Desensitizing: To make emotionally insensitive or callous; specifically: to extinguish an emotional response (as of fear, anxiety, or guilt) to stimuli that formerly induced it.

Displaced Behavior: Occurs when an animal is torn between two conflicting drives, activities often consist of comfort movements, such as grooming, scratching, drinking, or eating.

Domestication: To adapt (an animal or plant) to life in intimate association with and to the advantage of humans.

Dominance: Commanding, controlling, or prevailing over all others; in our context, think of it as a temporary one-on-one relationship between two horses over who gets access over resources first. Access is usually acquired by the dominant horse though aggression.

Duration: The time during which something exists or lasts.

Enrichment: To enhance, to increase the desirable quality, attribute, or ingredient; in our context adding quality to our animal's habitat by adding desirable stimuli.

Ethogram: A comprehensive list, inventory, or description of the behavior of an organism.

Ethology: The scientific and objective study of animal behavior especially under natural conditions.

Ethics: A set of moral principles, a theory or system of moral values; a guiding philosophy.

Experimental Ethogram: Ethogram organized into categories to test a theory.

Fine Motor Skills: The use of precise coordinated movements.

Fixed Interval: The learner is reinforced at a set duration of time while doing the behavior.

Fixed Ratio: Every set number of times the learner performs the behavior they are reinforced.

Flooding: A behavior therapy technique where the patient is exposed directly to a maximum intensity anxiety-producing situation or stimulus, either in the imagination or in reality.

Function: The action for which a behavior is specially fitted or used or for which a thing exists.

Gross Motor Skills: Control over the large muscles of the body.

Habituation: Stimulus decreases in meaning towards neutral through self-determined gradual exposure.

Intermediate bridge: A series of continuous and instantaneous signals marking a progression of successful instants advancing toward a successfully completed behavior. A steady stream of articulated syllables issued as an animal begins to cooperate with a trainer, and continued until the animal begins to deviate from the requested behavior (at which point they are stopped, until the animal returns to compliance) or until the behavior is successfully completed, (at which time the string of behaviors is punctuated with a terminal bridge).

Keep Going Signal: A bridge signal that marks that the horse is doing the right behavior to lead to reinforcement, but not yet getting the reinforcer.

Learned Helplessness: A mental condition in which one becomes unable to help oneself due to previous failed attempts at controlling one's life.

LIMA: Least Invasive, Minimally Aversive

Luring: Attracting or enticing a specific behavior with a desired stimulus (usually food).

Molding: To physically shape, manipulate or form the body into the desired behavior.

Mimicking: To imitate or copy in action.

Morals: The principles or rules of right conduct or the distinction between right and wrong; founded on the fundamental principles of right conduct rather than on legalities, enactment, or custom.

Negative Punishment: Removal of a pleasant stimulus when an unwanted behavior occurs to reduce the likelihood of it occurring again in the future.

Negative Reinforcement: Removal of an unpleasant stimulus when a desired response occurs to make the behavior happen more.

No Reward Marker: A signal to mark the behavior the horse is doing is not going to lead to reinforcement for the horse.

Operant behavior: Occur when emitted behaviors are weakened or strengthened by the consequence. Shaped by the ABCs and learning quadrants.

Operant Conditioning: A learning process in which the likelihood of a specific behavior increases or decreases in response to reinforcement or punishment that occurs when the behavior is exhibited, so that the subject comes to associate the behavior with the pleasure from the reinforcement or the displeasure from the punishment.

Poisoned Cue: Occurs when the learner associates unpleasant things with a cue; can result in the learner either hesitating to perform the behavior or not do it at all.

Positive Reinforcement: The offering of desirable effects or consequences for a behavior with the intention of increasing the chance of that behavior being repeated in the future.

Positive Punishment: The addition of an unpleasant stimulus when an unwanted behavior occurs to reduce the likelihood of it occurring again in the future.

Primary Reinforcer: Anything that provides reinforcement without the need for learning, the reinforcer is naturally reinforcing to the organism.

Proprioception: The reception of stimuli produced within the organism; a sense or perception, usually at a subconscious level, of the movements and position of the body and especially its limbs, independent of vision.

Protected Contact: Working with a physical barrier between the trainer and the learner to keep both safe.

Rate of Reinforcement: Frequency of reinforcement for the behavior.

Reinforce: To strengthen or increase the frequency of the behavior.

Relief: Removal or lightening of something oppressive, painful, or distressing.

Respondent Behavior: A reflex that occurs in response to a specific external stimulus. All organisms have an inherited response elicited to environmental stimuli.

Reward: Something given or received in return or recompense for service.

Shaping: Is differential reinforcement of successive approximations.

Species Ethogram: A comprehensive list, inventory, or description of the behavior for an entire species.

Stereotypy: A repetitive or ritualistic movement, posture, or utterance.

Stimulus Control: The behavior occurs immediately when the cue is given. The behavior never occurs in the absence of the cue. The behavior never occurs in response to some other cue. No other behavior occurs in response to this cue.

Superstition: A behavior that was unintentionally reinforced or punished, when there is no real correlation between behavior and consequence, accidentally causing the behavior to increase or decrease in frequency.

Targeting: Touching a specified object with a specified body part, can be used to shape future behaviors.

Tactile Cue: A discriminative stimulus of, relating to, or being the sense of touch.

Terminal Bridge: A bridge signal that marks and ends the correct behavior and leads to prompt reinforcement.

Tonic Immobility: Muscular paralysis that occurs during significant stress or injury; apparently temporarily paralyzed and unresponsive to external stimuli. In most cases, this occurs in response to an extreme threat such as being captured by a (perceived) predator; despite appearances, the animal remains conscious throughout tonic immobility; animals in TI often taking advantage of escape opportunities.

Unconditioned Triggers: A stimulus the animal is born knowing how they feel about.

Variable Ratio: Reinforcing each behavior randomly.

Variable Interval: Reinforcing during the duration of the behavior as random quantities of time pass.

Welfare: The state of doing well especially in respect to good fortune, happiness, well-being, or prosperity.

CPSIA information can be obtained
at www.ICGtesting.com
Printed in the USA
BVHW021102030619
549991BV00018BA/355/P